THE ENCYCLOPEDIA OF
RUGBY UNION

THE ENCYCLOPEDIA OF
RUGBY UNION

DONALD SOMMERVILLE

AURUM PRESS

First published in Great Britain 1997
by Aurum Press Ltd, 25 Bedford Avenue, London WC1B 3AT
© 1997 Brown Packaging Books Ltd

A catalogue record for this book is available from the British Library.

ISBN 1 85410 481 0

2 4 6 8 10 9 7 5 3 1

1998 2000 2001 1999 1997

Conceived and produced by Brown Packaging Books Ltd
Bradley's Close, 74-77 White Lion Street, London N1 9PF
Editorial plus additional material: Chris Marshall
Design: wda

Printed and bound in the Czech Republic   60206

ACKNOWLEDGEMENTS
The author would like to thank the following people for their assistance during the research for this book: Allan Lochrie, the staff of the Museum of Rugby at Twickenham, Maureen Sharp of the Scottish Women's Rugby Union, Rosie Golby of the Rugby Football Union for Women, Michelle Tracy at the International Board in Dublin.

Title page: *Olivier Merle (left) and Damian Cronin battle in the line-out during France's 22-19 win over Scotland in the 1995 World Cup.*

PICTURE CREDITS
All pictures Colorsport except:
Alpha/S&G: 46, 118; Hulton Getty: 11, 14, 15tr, 16, 20, 28, 31, 39, 54, 63tr, 63b, 64, 76, 77, 79, 96, 117, 131, 132, 133tl, 153tr, 163b, 164, 172; The Illustrated London News Picture Library: 52, 68, 71, 84, 85, 87t; INPHO (Billy Stickland): 57; International Rugby Football Board: 27, 35tl, 43, 51, 60, 67, 75, 83; Mark Leech/Photosport: 30, 136bl, 146, 147t; Mark Leech/Presse-Sports: 136t; Mary Evans Picture

· CONTENTS ·

· PROFESSIONALISM ·
· AND THE FUTURE ·

English rugby union club Bath (right) take on rugby league's Wigan in the union leg of the 'cross-code challenge', a one-off pair of games played in 1996. Such a match would once have been unthinkable. Bath won this game; Wigan triumphed under league laws.

Rugby is the finest game in the world, with a long, proud and incident-packed history. The world's oldest club (Guy's Hospital in London) has already celebrated its 150th anniversary, and the first international match (Scotland *v* England) took place as long ago as 1871. Since then rugby has thrived and spread so that the game is now played in at least 100 countries worldwide. And new competitions and developments continue to take place. In the international arena, 1996 saw the first Tri-Nations competition between South Africa, Australia and New Zealand result in an All Black triumph, while at the other end of the spectrum Mexico played their first international,

drawing 10-10 away to Colombia. Unfortunately, however, all too few recent headlines have been concerned with the playing of the game. It is perhaps appropriate that a sport whose chief attraction is its fierce on-field confrontations should inspire equally divergent off-field views.

Rugby fans have good reason to be happy with the state of the modern game. At every level of play, from the very highest down through the lowly ranks of junior club rugby, playing standards are rising and games are faster, more skilful and more exciting. There is a great deal of money in rugby, helping the top players spend time developing the fitness and skills that the rest of us can enjoy watching in safer and more comfortable stadiums. There is more television coverage of the sport, which can only bring more people into the game to everyone's benefit. The newly introduced Super 12 competition (which features provincial and state sides from South Africa, Australia and New Zealand) and the Tri-Nations series proved that recent changes in the laws of the game have encouraged a fresh and dynamic style of play and will reward the teams that play this style well. And a new, non-racist South Africa has returned to the international rugby world.

RUGBY'S CHARACTER IN DANGER?

But rugby fans also have good reason to be worried about the future of the game. Clubs, provinces and unions in virtually every major playing nation have been wrapped in seemingly endless violent disputes that threaten to tear rugby union apart. Many of the traditions that have been rugby's strength and at the heart of the sport's appeal seem to have been sold off in return for dubious short-term gains. This has put rugby at the mercy of television moguls, rich club proprietors and greedy players, who, many believe, are involved only for the money they expect to take out of the game. Former trends that saw the likes of Western Samoa and Canada leading the challenge of the 'minor' nations to the established powers of the sport are being reversed. Money has brought many of the strongest players from the

Below: *Queensland's Barry Lea scores despite the attentions of Natal full-back André Joubert in the final of the 1994 Super 10 competition, which Queensland won 21-10.*

Pacific islands to play for Australia or New Zealand, and money has also brought an equally unhealthy concentration of leading northern hemisphere players in England, to the detriment of the game in their various native lands. And even after the changes in South Africa, how many black faces are there in the Springbok team?

The upheaval in rugby union followed the announcement in 1995, shortly after the conclusion of the third World Cup, that open professionalism was to become a permissible part of the game. It was quite a shock since only a few weeks earlier almost every senior rugby union administrator in the northern hemisphere at least was seemingly saying 'over my dead body'. But suddenly heads popped up out of the sand, and it was recognised that this time there was probably more than just talk to reports of a planned breakaway by top players. It was also acknowledged that in any case every leading player was already making some and perhaps most of his income out of his connection with the game. Professionalism, it was finally realised, was an inevitable and indeed a necessary part of top-class modern rugby union.

The new era has inevitably led to discussions on the future of the game between traditional rugby administrators and the television and commercial interests coming into the sport. The main problem faced by the administrators is the difficulty of defining precisely what it is they wish to protect and develop. And if enthusiasts cannot decide what is for the good of the game, there is little chance of television executives or the sponsors' marketing departments worrying about it. It may be that the money men will pay

some attention to the vague idea of the 'good of the game' because they do not wish to kill the goose that will lay their hoped-for golden egg, but this can never be their priority. Any shareholder – rugby fan or not – who found that his or her company's executives were more concerned with the good of rugby than with the profits of their corporations would have every right to complain of being swindled.

It is not in any way a criticism of those newly involved in the game to say that assurances about preserving rugby union's traditional values are likely to last about as long as New Year's resolutions when they are seen to conflict with the bottom line of profit and loss. The businessmen are simply doing their jobs or protecting their investments. Rugby will certainly change under their influence but then it has never stood still. If in a year or two, when the dust settles a bit, the game is still being run by rugby people, then all should be fine, but if instead rugby union becomes some second-rate imitation of world soccer or the top American sports, with their billionaire club owners and millionaire players, then the game will be the poorer.

POSITIVE LAW CHANGES

If the response of rugby's bosses to the new world of professionalism has been very uncertain, then almost everyone actively involved in the game and most commentators and spectators agree that they have done rather better with their most recent revamp of the laws. Two provisions have been especially important: the instruction that back rows must remain bound to the scrummage until it ends, and the toleration extended to 'supporting' in the line-out. The former change has had several effects. For instance, it has reinstated some of the traditional emphasis on powerful and intelligent scrummaging, both to keep opposition back rows tied into the scrum for a few vital moments longer and, on occasion, to wheel them away from the point of attack. The upshot is that the ball carriers are given room to show off their pace and skills. Supporting in the line-out has also produced a variety of benefits. Teams now usually win most of the ball on their own throw, and clean, quick ball tapped off the top can give backs 20 metres of space to operate in, far more than in any other situation. Additionally, there is less kicking for touch because sides do not want to give their opponents this sort of possession.

It is one thing to make the laws, but they also have to be interpreted sympathetically if they are to achieve the desired effect. Inconsistent application of the laws, unfortunately, is one of the game's current problems at the top level. Interpretation often varies depending on whether you are north or south of the equator, with northern hemisphere referees tending to be tighter and southern hemisphere referees more tolerant.

One of the 'grey' areas of the laws is playing the ball on the ground. Southern hemisphere referees have been encouraged to be lenient in this area where such a policy is seen to enhance continuity. Northern hemisphere referees tend to think that this is opting out of refereeing the game

Below: *The professional set-up enables clubs to attract the best players. Michael Lynagh, François Pienaar and Philippe Sella (from left to right) joined London's Saracens in 1996.*

properly. Southern hemisphere referees think their colleagues in the north are too strict. Such inconsistency is not good enough. With money at stake, top players are rightly going to demand higher and more uniform standards of refereeing. The top nations, clubs and provinces are going to play each other more often in the future, and they and their fans are going to want to know where they stand. Modern, professional rugby requires uniform interpretation of the laws, and it is up to the game's rulers to provide it.

POOR RELATIONS

The mix of new and old competitions that has been evolving since the 1995 World Cup has generally worked out very well for the major countries in both hemispheres and for many of the less powerful rugby nations. Not everyone has benefited, however. The Pacific islands, for example, have been left out on a limb. Their proposed competition did not get off the ground, and their best players are still being lured to Australian state and New Zealand provincial sides. The latter tendency is fair enough if it is the best way the players concerned can earn their living, but when they also become qualified for their adopted country it may become damaging to rugby in their home countries. In 1997, the International Board began steps to remove the anomaly of players switching countries willy-nilly, and it should be a dead letter by the year 2000. Strong Western Samoan or Fijian national teams will strengthen rugby's appeal within the islands and enhance the game internationally.

On-field developments have thankfully overshadowed problems with the game's organisation in the southern hemisphere since the 1995 World Cup. Sadly the same has not been the case in Europe. Clubs have threatened to resign from unions, players have boycotted national squad sessions, touring teams have been insulted by having to play against provincial selections made up of second or third division players and England have nearly been thrown out of the Five Nations Championship because of a dispute over television rights. Fans have been shocked and amazed at the level of bitterness shown by almost everyone involved. Agreements now seem to have been patched up on most of the contentious issues, and it is to be hoped that they will last. But so much ill will has been created that further disputes, perhaps seriously damaging ones, are sure to arise.

A 'SIX NATIONS' CHAMPIONSHIP?

Partly because of off-field squabbles, new club and provincial competitions introduced north of the equator since 1995 have had a slightly mixed start. For example, the European club championship – the Heineken European Cup

Above: *Emile N'Tamack, captain of French club Toulouse, hoists the Heineken European Cup after his side had beaten Welsh hopefuls Cardiff in the inaugural final in January 1996.*

– was a rather low-key affair in its first season and was not well televised in its early stages in 1996-97. Nonetheless, it seems set to go from strength to strength and will help raise playing standards for those who play in it.

One innovation increasingly discussed in Europe is the possibility of expanding the Five Nations tournament by admitting Italy. The Italians are probably not strong enough at the moment to win many matches against the original five, but on their day they are certainly good enough to worry any opponent. Playing in a 'Six Nations' would be the best possible way to develop the game in what has not traditionally been a rugby hotbed, and the presence of a sixth team would enrich the championship in general.

To stand still in the modern world is to be rapidly overtaken, and there are plenty of other sports to challenge rugby's image of itself as a world game. With more money than ever in the sport, there is a special opportunity to put rugby unquestionably in that category. It would be a tragedy if such a chance were to go begging.

CREATION OF THE GAME

A nineteenth century football match at Rugby School. What would the players of that era have thought of today's professional game?

In the past 170 or so years, rugby has changed from the pastime of a few English schoolboys to a sophisticated international sport played and followed by millions. Rugby quickly spread from Britain throughout the English-speaking world and into Europe. Just as quickly, the game began to change to make it faster, more skilful and more fun for players and spectators. The boys who chased footballs about at Rugby School all those years ago could hardly have guessed what they were beginning.

CHAPTER ONE

· ORIGINS OF RUGBY ·

THIS STONE
COMMEMORATES THE EXPLOIT OF
WILLIAM WEBB ELLIS
WHO WITH A FINE DISREGARD FOR THE RULES OF FOOTBALL
AS PLAYED IN HIS TIME
FIRST TOOK THE BALL IN HIS ARMS AND RAN WITH IT
THUS ORIGINATING THE DISTINCTIVE FEATURE OF
THE RUGBY GAME.
A.D. 1823.

The plaque outside Rugby School, England, which commemorates William Webb Ellis's far-reaching breach of the rules of football.

Games with some similarities to both modern soccer and rugby have existed for over 2000 years. Most of these games seem to have involved great crowds of players wrestling, shoving and kicking to propel or carry a stuffed animal stomach or some similar object from one end of a town to the other. There were usually few rules, and any number could play. Games often took place on some annual holiday to settle a local rivalry.

The authorities usually did not approve. Kings and princes commanded their subjects not to waste time with football but spend it more profitably in military training. Football matches were also regarded as a public nuisance, with violence, vandalism and disorder of every kind often accompanying the heaving mass of players. England, Scotland and France all had laws banning football in the fourteenth and fifteenth centuries.

Football survived nonetheless. Indeed, a few of the traditional village-against-village matches still take place in various places in the British Isles, with members of local rugby clubs frequently among the enthusiastic participants. Football survived because people, usually men, enjoyed it and because some in authority thought it had good qualities. Richard Mulcaster, headmaster of a school in London, published a book in 1581 that decried the violence of the game but argued that it might promote fitness and well-being if more carefully regulated. Around the same time, a book originally published in Italy described the game of *calcio*, which was played in Florence, as 'very good to breed up youth to run, leap and wrastle [*sic*]'.

There is no doubt that the changes that transformed these various types of free-for-all into a regulated sport began in the English public schools of the 1800s. School matches in those days were always internal affairs, with different groupings of boys from within the school making up the teams. In many schools, every boy on the roll was expected to attend and play in some way, whatever his age or size. Any organisation required was created by the boys themselves, entirely unsupervised by the masters, and each school developed its own method of how the game should be played. There were no written rules, and any necessary procedures would follow from established custom, as enforced, and on occasion modified, by the oldest and biggest boys at the particular time.

At Rugby School in 1823 there were only a few boys in the senior class. One seemingly rather unpopular senior boy took advantage of this situation to put his own mark on the game. Quite simply, he cheated and was big enough to get away with it, although his official memorial at the school puts things rather differently (see facing page).

No one actually knows if the traditional story of how rugby began is true. It came to be told in the 1880s and 1890s, after rugby had become formally established, when former pupils of Rugby School tried to research how the game had developed. Of course, by then, few of Webb Ellis's contemporaries were still alive and Webb Ellis himself had died in France in 1872. What is certainly true is that running with the ball in hand was accepted in the first written set of laws produced by the Rugby boys in 1845.

■ THOMAS HUGHES ■

Probably the most famous description of an early rugby-style match is found in Thomas Hughes's book *Tom Brown's School Days*. The book was published in 1857 and is set in the Rugby School of the 1830s. In his first match, young Tom saves the day for his team when he bravely falls on a loose ball under the feet of a group of older and bigger opponents and prevents a touchdown.

Hughes knew what he was talking about, since he was captain of football at the school in 1841-42. In his time, running with the ball was permitted, provided the ball had been caught from a kick or while bouncing – it was illegal to pick up a rolling or stationary ball. By the time of his death, in the 1890s, Hughes thought that too much handling had been introduced into the game.

By that time, former pupils and teachers of Rugby School had helped begin the spread of their game elsewhere. One former pupil, Arthur Pell, tried to establish a football club at Cambridge University in 1839 but did not get very far at first because the Cambridge men came from such a variety of schools that they could not agree on which playing rules to adopt. A club was successfully formed

Below: *The birth of rugby is re-enacted at Rugby School in 1991 as part of the build-up to that year's World Cup competition, hosted by the British Isles and France.*

Above: *Rugby and similar games spread through British territories in the 1800s. Here British soldiers play rugby in Afghanistan in 1879 during the Second Afghan War.*

among the students at Guy's Hospital in London in 1843, making it the world's oldest. Matches using the Rugby School rules also began to take place regularly elsewhere, including Oxford University.

Some Rugby old boys found their way to university in Ireland. The world's second rugby club, at Trinity College, was formed in Dublin in 1854. The first matches were again internal ones, contested by teams from among the club's membership. Towns in the Scottish borders also had a long tradition of football-type games, and similar games to those held in the English public schools were also being played in some Edinburgh schools in the early 1800s. The first adult club in Scotland, Edinburgh Academicals, was founded in 1858. The longest-running fixture in the history of the game, which was first played in 1858 and still takes place, is between two of the Edinburgh area schools, Edinburgh Academy and Merchiston Castle. The Merchiston captain in the first game against Edinburgh Academy also featured in the first recorded match in the British territory of South Africa, which took place in 1862. The player's name was A. van der Bijl, and the teams involved were Civilians *v* Military. During the second half of the nineteenth century, the British Empire was at its height, and old boys of Rugby School and others who knew the game soon spread it throughout the empire and elsewhere as they took up careers in business, public service or the military.

RUGBY GOES TO AUSTRALIA

Football of various sorts had been played in Australia at least as early as 1829, and a Rugby old boy called Thomas Wills tried to introduce his school's version of the game to Melbourne in 1857. He was unsuccessful, and in 1859, a group of Melbourne men drew up the first laws of what was to become Victorian (or Australian Rules) football. Sydney and New South Wales, however, did adopt the Rugby game. The details of the story are uncertain, but the first inter-club match in Australia took place in 1865 between Sydney Football Club and Sydney University.

Across the Tasman Sea in New Zealand, Christ's College in Christchurch had staff recruited from the English public schools and in 1862 is known to have had a set of football rules with similarities to those used at Rugby School. A football club was founded in Christchurch the next year. The first match definitely under Rugby School rules did not take place until 1870, however, when the Nelson football club (founded 1868) was introduced to the Rugby game. The players liked the rules, tried them out among themselves, and then played a match against the local Nelson College, New Zealand's first game. In North America, meanwhile, a football club had been formed in Toronto in 1864, and in 1869 two college teams, Rutgers and Princeton, played a 25-a-side match to Rugby-like rules. Harvard and McGill Universities played a genuine rugby match in 1874, but, as in Victoria, football teams in North America soon mainly opted for a different game.

THE GROWTH OF RUGBY IN BRITAIN

Wales, like the other parts of the British Isles, had various traditional football-type games, and the oldest rugby club in Wales, Neath, was not founded until 1871. Other clubs sprang up very quickly, however. Although they were often begun by men from the public schools, the Welsh rugby clubs soon began to attract numbers of working class players from the mines and factories. In much of England, the developing clubs were exclusively the province of the better-off public school and university type of player, but in some

▪ EARLY LAWS ▪

The boys of Rugby School produced a revised edition of their laws of the game in 1862. Some of its provisions have survived virtually intact since then:

'5. OFF SIDE. A player is off his side when the ball has been kicked, or thrown, or knocked on, or is being run with by any one of his own side behind him.
6. A player entering a scrummage on the wrong side is off his side.'

There was equally good sense, too, in a later clause:

'20. Though it is lawful to hold any player in a maul, this holding does not include attempts to throttle, or strangle, which are totally opposed to all the principles of the game.'

areas, notably the northern counties of Yorkshire and Lancashire, working men also took to rugby in numbers. In years to come this would have important consequences.

RUGBY AND SOCCER SPLIT

In the late 1850s and 1860s, numerous football clubs had formed in England, but they faced the problem of developing a standard set of rules for their matches. Club representatives met in 1863 for a series of fiercely argued meetings. In December of that year, they drew up a set of rules and formed the Football Association (FA), now the parent body of English soccer. The Blackheath club, founded in 1858 and England's third-oldest rugby club, objected and declined to join the FA because running with the ball and hacking were forbidden in the organisation's proposed set of rules. Blackheath and a number of other clubs, including Richmond, continued to play a game based on the Rugby School rules, and the two styles of football began to diverge.

Rugby rules clubs came to realise that they needed their own equivalent of the FA. On 26 January 1871, at a meeting in London, representatives of 21 clubs formed the Rugby Football Union (RFU) and delegated three of their number to draw up a code of laws. The story goes that it would have been 22 clubs, but the representative of Wasps went to the wrong place for the meeting, stopped for a drink, had a few more, and never did get there – a very familiar rugby experience! Ironically, hacking – that is kicking the shins or tripping an opponent playing or carrying the ball – one of the causes of the split with soccer, was already on its way out in rugby by 1871, largely because it was clearly very dangerous.

THE FIRST INTERNATIONALS

The first rugby international, between Scotland and England, took place in March 1871. The other home nations soon made their debuts, and the first complete series of home international games was played in 1882-83. The first overseas tour had already taken place, when New South Wales played seven games in New Zealand in 1882. In 1886, Scotland, Ireland and Wales formed an International Board to regulate international matches. England refused to join at first but did so in 1890. With this series of developments, the bare bones at least of rugby's structure were in place.

One development of the 1890s was less positive, however. In 1893, an RFU meeting rejected a proposal from the Yorkshire county that clubs should be allowed to compensate players who lost wages from their ordinary jobs through playing rugby. The dispute rumbled on for a time, with the RFU remaining staunchly opposed to any form of

Above: *The English team that played Scotland in the first international rugby match. The 20-a-side game took place in Edinburgh in 1871. Scotland won by a try and a goal to a try.*

professionalism. Finally, at the start of the 1895-96 season, 20 clubs from Yorkshire and Lancashire decided to form their own Northern Union (the future Rugby Football League) and permit 'payment for bona-fide broken time'. It was to take almost exactly 100 years to the day from that decisive August 1895 meeting for the much larger rugby union game to embrace professionalism and allow its players to be paid.

Above: *The Calcutta Cup, for which England and Scotland play each season. Closing down, the Calcutta Football Club converted its funds into silver to produce the trophy in 1878.*

▪ THE PLAYING POSITIONS ▪

The players are lined up as for a set scrum on the left of the field.

Forwards
1. Loose-head prop
2. Hooker
3. Tight-head prop
4. Lock or second row
5. Lock or second row
6. Blind-side flanker or wing forward
7. Open-side flanker or wing forward
8. Number eight

Backs
9. Scrum-half or (NZ) half-back
10. Fly-half, stand-off half, outside half or (NZ) first five-eighth
11. Left-wing
12. Inside centre or (NZ) second five-eighth
13. Outside centre or (NZ) centre
14. Right-wing
15. Full-back

Above: *The England front row of (from left) Jeff Probyn, Brian Moore and Jason Leonard against France in 1992. Leonard is at loose-head and will scrum down with his head outside that of the French No 3 opposite.*

In early rugby games, forwards slotted themselves into scrummages in the order in which they happened to arrive at the mark, 'first up, first down'. The Guy's Hospital team in London in 1905 are usually credited with being the first side to extend the idea of specialisation into the forwards and to allot specific scrummaging positions to individuals. Guy's traditionally had many South Africans in its student body, and naturally also in its rugby teams, and perhaps it may even be through that connection that scrummaging came to have such central importance in the South African game. Giant Springbok props and locks have been a fact of life from the earliest times to the present day.

SCRUMMAGE FORMATIONS

With specific positions came precise scrummage formations. Initially the standard one in British rugby was 3-2-3, which gave a reasonably powerful shove and was well suited to back rows who wanted to wheel and break away, dribbling the ball at their feet. In the 1920s, South Africa began using the 3-4-1 set up, which, with minor variations, is now standard all round the world. This is still more powerful and at the same time helps the two flankers to break more quickly when that is required. It was clearly superior to the old style but took some time to catch on entirely in Europe – especially in Scotland, where the wheel followed by a foot rush was a cherished tactic as late as the 1950s.

Hookers and then back rows were the first forwards to become true specialists, with back-row duties in general play being substantially developed by Wavell Wakefield,

New Zealand in particular among the southern hemisphere countries evolved its names for positions by a slightly different route. New Zealand had a single half-back (or scrum-half), and as players were withdrawn from the forwards to link him with the speedy three-quarters, they were given the designation of first and second five-eighth.

Backs also began to use rehearsed moves. Wales scored a try from one in the Test against the First All Blacks in 1905, but probably the most influential British back in this respect was the England player Adrian Stoop a few years later.

England captain in the 1920s. Front-row play soon became more and more technically demanding, with size and strength not being the whole story. Players caught on to this quicker than some selectors, however. As late as the end of the 1960s, even some national selectors in Britain and New Zealand had little understanding of the differences between loose-head and tight-head play. Several very effective Scottish and Irish props and Scotland coach Bill Dickinson did much to develop scrummaging technique around this time, but probably most influential of all in showing that this mattered far more than size was Ian 'Mighty Mouse' McLauchlan of Scotland and the Lions. McLauchlan was a relatively small man but was never bettered in the tight in his two Lions tours. England's most-capped prop, Jason Leonard, is a rare example of a man able to play on both sides of the scrum at the highest level in the modern game.

In the early scrummaging days, New Zealand were the real odd men out. Up to the British Lions tour of 1930, they used a two-man front row, both of whom were described as hookers, a middle row of three and a back row of two, making seven in all. This was reputedly a well-balanced unit when it came to scrummaging and seemingly also well adapted to provide a quick and tidy heel, which was obviously conducive to open back play. The eighth forward, known as a wing forward in New Zealand and a rover in Britain, helped provide this quick possession by putting the ball into the scrum, while the half-back was ready behind the rear feet to whip a pass away as soon as the ball arrived. This was all very well, but the rover was very neatly placed to obstruct opponents on his own put in and, from his advanced position, to stifle the opposing side's attempts to run the ball on theirs.

NEW FRONT-ROW LAWS

Dave Gallaher, captain of the First All Blacks, was a wing forward and was often described as a cheat by British critics, who thought his role was entirely destructive. Matters came to a head when James 'Bim' Baxter was manager of the 1930 Lions. Baxter became increasingly outraged at what he thought were illegal New Zealand methods. Baxter had clout, for he was also one of the English members of the IB, and when he got home he set about making changes. In 1932 new laws laid down that front rows had to be composed of three players. New Zealanders claimed that this set their scrummaging back for years and blamed this law change in part for their series defeat against the Springboks in 1937.

One of the reasons why the rover was able to operate so effectively was that up to comparatively recent times the offside line at scrummages was defined by the position of

the ball and not, as now, by the back feet. This meant that the rover, other flankers and the backs could follow the ball round or through a scrummage. Equally, the modern ten-metre gap between a line-out and the two sets of backs was not instituted until 1964. This naturally meant that backs

Above: *Fly-half Guy Camberabero kicks a goal in France's 1967 20-14 win over Australia. He is using the traditional style, whereby the ball is struck head on with the toe.*

often had little room to move in and this situation put a premium on the elusive dodging type of runner, particularly in the fly-half position, who could make space for himself and for his colleagues. The archetypes of this sort of player were Jack Kyle and Cliff Morgan, respectively Irish and Welsh stars of the 1950s, but inevitably they were often subdued by predatory flankers. Another important change to create a more open game, in addition to the alterations in the offside laws, was the removal in 1958 of the stipulation that players had to play the ball with a foot after a tackle. This helped back rows play a more constructive linking role.

In the modern game the position has in some respects come full circle. Players do have specific specialist roles in set plays and, of course, are more intensively coached and rehearsed in these than ever before. But, with the emphasis on continuity through many phases of possession, every player, forward and back, must also ruck and maul and tackle, as well as handle and carry the ball competently and

intelligently. Sean Fitzpatrick is probably the world's best hooker and somehow manages to pop up on the wing to score outrageous tries every now and again; Rob Andrew was a deadly goal and tactical kicker and usually made more tackles in a match than an old-fashioned 'non-tackling' fly-half made in a season; and John Eales – well he simply does a bit of everything, even goal-kicking, from his spot in the second row.

Goal-kicking forwards are a rarity in the modern game, although there have been a few good ones over the years, like 'Okey' Geffin, Springbok prop from 1949 to 1951, or Peter Brown, Scotland number eight from 1964 to 1973, but they were the rule rather than the exception in rugby's early days. Scores in those times could only be made by kicks. A touchdown did not count towards the final score but merely allowed the attacking team to 'try' a kick afterwards, and if this were successful, the valueless touchdown would be converted into a valuable goal. There were other types of goal also – a rolling ball could be fly-hacked for a field goal, or a player who made a fair catch or who was carrying the ball could drop-kick a goal. All these various types of goal were of equal worth.

THE INTRODUCTION OF POINTS

The first step towards making tries more important came in 1875, when the English and Scottish unions ruled that tries could be used as the 'tie-breaker' in matches in which the number of goals was equal. Over the next dozen years, the various countries each evolved systems to give points values to the different types of score. Some of these systems even gave the attacking team a point or perhaps half a point when they forced the defenders to touch down behind their own line. Bringing uniformity to this was one of the tasks of the fledgling IB when England joined the other three home unions in this body in 1890. There have been six changes in the scoring values since the first general version was laid down. Tries were upgraded from one to three points in the first 15 years, to four in 1972 and to five in 1992.

Penalty kicks did not exist in the earliest games. Players were expected to play with a sporting spirit, and if the game were stopped because of an illegality, it would resume with a scrummage. No doubt, then as now, players could expect a hack or similar 'warning' from an opponent whenever they were inclined to bend the rules. The first penalties were introduced in 1882, but rather like modern free kicks, goals could not be kicked from them – it was not until the formation of the IB that penalty goals were introduced. Even then they were a rarity. Scotland and England got one penalty goal each in their game in 1895, but the next time one appeared on the Calcutta Cup score sheet was 30 years later in 1925. Plenty of modern fans would like to see goal-kicking at that level of rarity once again.

STOPPING THE KICKING GAME

The most striking changes of all in rugby's history in recent years have been in the laws relating to tactical kicking. In the early years of the century and into the 1920s, Australia and New Zealand had experimented with laws forbidding kicking directly into touch from outside what was then the 25-yard area. This had never applied to international rugby or in Europe, and a breed of fly-halves evolved who were expert at working the touchline to keep the ball in front of their forwards. Perhaps the first, and certainly one of the best, was the South African Bennie Osler in the 1930s.

Right: Springbok André Joubert kicks for goal against New Zealand in 1994. Left-footed Joubert demonstrates the modern 'round-the-corner' method, striking the ball with the instep. He has used a tee, instead of a piling up sand or digging a hole.

■ THE INTERNATIONAL ■ ■ RUGBY FOOTBALL BOARD ■

Hardly an international match went by in the first dozen or so years after the first game in 1871, without a major dispute between the countries involved about one or other aspect of the laws. Matters came to a head after England beat Scotland by a fiercely contested try in 1884, and the subsequent arguments meant that the two refused to play each other the next season. Ireland then proposed the creation of a body to rule on such problems, and Scotland and Wales joined the Irish in setting up the International Board (IB) in 1886. But England were determined to be the leading voice and refused to join until 1890, when they were offered six votes to the other countries' two each. Originally the IB's authority applied only to international games, but it was gradually extended to cover all matches. Member unions now often have local variations in laws, and experiment with possible new ones, but only with the IB's consent.

The four home unions were the only ones represented on the IB until 1948, when Australia, New Zealand and South Africa were each given a single representative, with the four home unions all having two. The southern hemisphere countries got second votes in 1958, and France was finally admitted, with two votes also, in 1978. Old ideas of exclusiveness were finally abandoned in 1987, when a raft of other countries were granted formal membership. The original eight countries, who have kept their two seats each on the executive council, still dominate, but they have now also been joined by a single member from each of Argentina, Canada, Italy and Japan.

For most of its existence, the IB was based in England, although the major annual meetings have been held in other countries on some occasions since 1959. The IB has now moved its offices to Dublin to take advantage of tax advantages available in Ireland.

One match above all showed just how grim a game could result from such concentration on tactical kicking. When Wales beat Scotland 6-0, by a penalty and a dropped goal, at Murrayfield in 1963, there were reckoned to have been 111 line-outs in the match (or perhaps 112, no wonder they lost count). Welsh scrum-half Clive Rowlands, cruelly nicknamed 'Clive the Kick' afterwards, relentlessly worked the touchline to help his superior forwards and shut out the Scotland backs.

The old Australian and New Zealand experiment was turned into law in 1970, and nothing was ever quite that dreary again. It particularly changed the role of the full-back, who was required to counterattack more and more, since he could not merely thump the ball back down field into touch. The full-back was also increasingly available as an extra man in attack, for with less opposition kicking, he was not so tied to his traditional deep position. Half-backs like Gareth Edwards very quickly mastered the art of judging the flight of kicks so that they bounced into touch, but even so the amount of kicking clearly decreased and the ball was actually in play for significantly longer.

This has been the desired effect of most of the changes that have been made in the last dozen years. Teams are now well used to the idea of 'use it, or lose it' and the imperative to recycle possession, not least because defences are so well drilled that decisive breaks from set-piece play are now comparatively unusual. Perhaps because referees are too lax on squint feeds, strikes against the head in the scrum are now virtually unheard of in internationals, so a failure in handling skills or ball-retention will give away possession. And with supporting techniques in the line-out increasingly well developed, any touch-kicking other than from deep defence or right into an attacking corner looks more and more like a poor option to take.

Below: *A line-out from the 1973 Wales v Ireland Five Nations game. In those days before spacing requirements and legal lifting, own-throw possession was far from certain.*

▪ SCORING VALUES ▪

Generally agreed scoring values were first established in 1890 when England joined the other three home unions in the International Board. These values and later changes are given below. Changes have come into effect each time at the start of the Northern Hemisphere season shown.

Season	Try	Conv	Pen	DG	From Mark
1890-91	1	2	2	3	3
1891-92	2	3	3	4	4
1893-94	3	2	3	4	4
1905-06	3	2	3	4	3
1948-49	3	2	3	3	3
1971-72	4	2	3	3	3
1992-93	5	2	3	3	abolished

With the ball in play for longer and longer and the increase in the value of the try, matches have certainly become livelier and higher scoring. Competition rules, such as those of the Super 12, that reward try-scoring teams and those that keep in touch with superior opponents are clearly a good idea, but equally clearly no real rugby fan wants the game to turn into basketball where teams almost routinely score every time they get the ball. The best rugby matches are the ones in which you don't want to look away because

you might miss the decisive score; in basketball if you miss a score, there will usually be a couple just as good in the next minute or so.

Rugby has been described as a contact sport, but it is really a collision and confrontation sport. Pierre Danos, a French scrum-half of the 1950s, once said that rugby players came in two varieties – those who played pianos and those who were good only at moving them. Robert Paperemborde, the great French prop, once also said that in his view it was just as valid an example of attacking play when he drove a scrum forward a few centimetres as when a back made a dazzling run. Rugby will continue to prosper, despite the changes that the professional era will bring, if it maintains the element of physical confrontation combined with the variety of shapes and sizes of player and styles of play that Danos and Paperemborde clearly knew and loved.

Left: *France's Olivier Roumat soars into the air with a little help from his friends. With an accurate throw, a good team will rarely lose a line-out on its own put-in.*

Below: *Wales players face up to the Western Samoans before their 1991 World Cup clash at Cardiff Arms Park. Such challenge and confrontation is part and parcel of rugby.*

· COUNTRIES ·

South Africa's James Small, held by Ben Tune, finds Pieter Hendriks at his elbow, but Australia went on to win this 1996 Tri-Nations clash 21-16.

At the forefront of rugby union are the big eight nations, each with its own distinctive playing style. For example, there is the spoiling and harrying of the Irish, the brilliant and instinctive handling of the French, the fast rucking of the All Blacks, and the power and might of the Springbok forwards. Each of the eight has had its great days of triumph and a few disasters as well. And increasingly, they are having to fight off ever fiercer challenges from new contenders such as Canada, Italy and Argentina.

CHAPTER THREE

· AUSTRALIA ·

Australia celebrate as referee Derek Bevan signals Tony Daly's match-winning try in the 1991 World Cup final against England.

Australians claim that theirs was the first country outside Britain to play rugby. They may well be right for a Sydney newspaper reported a rough-and-ready football match played by soldiers in 1829. The first inter-school football match was in 1858 in Melbourne between Melbourne Grammar and St Kilda Grammar, and other games were reported in the years between these two events. That school game may have been played in a style based on the versions of the game known in the English public schools, but it would probably be stretching a point to claim it as a rugby match, although an old boy of Rugby School was active in trying to organise matches under Rugby School rules in Melbourne at that time.

In 1859, however, other sportsmen in Melbourne and the colony of Victoria began the process that would establish Australian Rules football, which remains the dominant winter sport in Victoria to this day. The first true rugby match in Victoria did not take place until 1888, and by then rugby was firmly established over the border in New South Wales (NSW). Historians of the game argue whether the first Australian rugby club was Sydney University (possibly founded in 1863 or 1864) or the Sydney (town) club (certainly founded in 1865).

One problem that the Sydney club faced in their first match, an internal game in 1865, was to prove to be an enduring one for the sport in Australia – that of finding suitable grounds. A newspaper report explained the consequences for that game: 'To play with full opportunity for exhibiting the tactics of the game, it will be necessary to choose ground where the contending parties are less liable to the intrusion of strangers between the bounds and among the players.'

The first inter-club encounter was between the Sydney club and the University a little later the same year. Rugby caught on quickly and within ten years or so there were various clubs in existence in and around Sydney. Many of the early clubs were cricket clubs first and rugby clubs second, with the rugby intended to keep the cricketers fit during the winter. The Wallaroo club, formed in 1870 and one of the parent clubs of the modern Northern Suburbs team, claimed to be the first club established principally to play rugby. By 1880 there were about 100 clubs in Sydney and the surrounding districts of NSW.

NEW ORGANISATIONS AND NEW CHALLENGES

Nine Sydney area clubs met in 1874 and agreed to form a governing body, calling it the Southern Union. The union changed its name to the New South Wales Rugby Union in 1892. Two of the founding clubs were actually schools, and schools soon proved to be fertile ground for the game. Clubs and schools commonly played matches against each other. This arrangement was less dangerous than it sounds since many of the schools concerned were boarding schools, and the rugby-playing pupils were virtually grown men who had been raised on prosperous country farms and sent to the city for the final stages of their education.

The other traditional powerhouse of Australian rugby is Queensland. A Brisbane rugby club was formed in 1867 but was on its own in the colony for 11 years until the Excelsior Club was founded in 1878. Several more clubs in Brisbane and other towns quickly followed, and in 1882 a group of enthusiasts met in Brisbane to discuss sending a team to play in Sydney and to consider forming a rugby union in Queensland. The governing body, officially known as the Northern Union, was not formally established until the next year, but organising a team proved an easier matter.

The first NSW *v* Queensland match was held on 12 August 1882 on the ground later to be called the Sydney Cricket Ground. New South Wales won comfortably. The score usually given is 28-4, but this may not be correct since these figures do not square with the reported number of tries and goals, whichever of the different NSW or Queensland scoring systems of the time is used. NSW also won a second game a few days later, but a return series in Queensland in 1883 was drawn, with one win each. One of rugby's greatest rivalries was off and running.

RUGBY ELSEWHERE IN AUSTRALIA

An early problem for rugby in Queensland was competition from the Australian Rules game, but with the prospect of inter-colonial competition with NSW (and soon regular

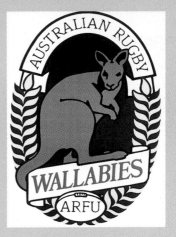

■ AUSTRALIAN RUGBY ■
■ FOOTBALL UNION ■

National colours:
  gold and green
Year founded: **1949**
No. of clubs: **723**
No. of provinces: **8**
Oldest provincial union:
  New South Wales,
  founded as the
  Southern Union in 1874.
No. of players: **33,000**
  adults/ 80,000 juniors
World Cup record:
  1987 fourth; 1991 winners;
1995 quarter-finals

international contact with New Zealand) rugby soon became the favoured winter sport. In 1892, the Northern Union changed its name to Queensland Rugby Union.

In other parts of Australia, rugby union has always tended to be a minority sport because of competition from other games. A Melbourne rugby union was established in 1888 and after various reformations settled down in 1926 as the Victoria Rugby Union. Victorian rugby has had a rather up-and-down history, struggling to compete with Australian Rules. It was probably strongest in the 1930s, when quite a number of players came through to selection for the national side. Victorians have since continued to figure in Australian representative sides but have usually had to move away from their home state to develop their rugby careers. Rugby has also been played in what is now the Australian Capital Territory since the 1870s, in Western Australia since the 1880s and in South Australia and Tasmania since the 1920s and 1930s. But only in comparatively recent years has the game reached the Northern Territory.

THE THREAT FROM RUGBY LEAGUE

The greatest upheaval in the history of rugby in NSW and Queensland was brought about by the challenge of professionalism. As in other countries, rugby matches in Australia soon attracted many paying spectators, while Australian players became aware of the split in the game in England and of the early growth of a professional league there. Players were also unhappy about Australian rugby union's attitude to helping with medical bills and other expenses. Local entrepreneurs and politicians became involved, and matters came to a head from 1907. That year, a professional New Zealand team arrived on its way to a tour against Britain's rugby league clubs and played three matches against top Sydney union players. These players were immediately expelled from the union, and they and others set about establishing a separate game.

Then, in the northern hemisphere winter of 1908-09, an Australian rugby union team successfully toured the British Isles. The tour itself is discussed below, but on their return home in 1909, most of the squad played in a series of matches against the best Australian league players, who had themselves just returned from a British tour, but one that had been financially disastrous. As had happened two years earlier, the union players involved were expelled from the game and turned to league, giving a further boost to the code in Australia. In its first couple of years, therefore, the union game lost the services of most of the top Australian rugby union players of the day, and the crowds and revenue naturally followed them to rugby league. The league organisers proved to be more astute and enterprising than the union committee men and further developed their advantage when they decided to keep league running

Below: *The 1908-09 Wallabies (light-coloured shirts) on tour in the British Isles. Most of the squad later played in cross-code matches in Australia and were barred from rugby union.*

during World War I, while union closed down. The result of all this is that rugby league has generally been more popular than union in Australia right up to the present day, and up to the 1980s, league continued to recruit many union players into the professional ranks.

STATE RUGBY

Rugby in New South Wales was none too well off in the years immediately following World War I. Only six clubs restarted in Sydney in 1919, and the 1920s saw many financial and other problems off the field. However, NSW did play New Zealand regularly both home and away, with income from these big matches being essential in keeping the game afloat in the state. There were also matches against South Africa in 1921 and the 'Waratah' tour in 1927-28, which is discussed later in the chapter. A number of Victorians and Queenslanders played for NSW in those years, and the Australian rugby authorities now recognise games played by NSW against international sides in that period as full internationals.

The reason that Queenslanders played for NSW during the 1920s was that having shut down for the war, rugby union in Queensland failed to resume when the conflict ended. Apart from a few games in 1919, no further union

matches seem to have been played in Queensland until 1928, when a number of schools converted back to union from league. The Queensland RU itself was reformed in 1929, and club competitions also resumed that year.

Queensland rugby took a long time after its revival to catch up with the game in New South Wales. About a third as many Queenslanders as NSW men won selection for Wallaby teams from 1930 up to the 1970s, and results of the inter-state series roughly reflected this ratio. Since the late 1960s, though, standards have rocketed in Queensland, and the results of the inter-state game have gone consistently their way. It would be wrong to say that standards have fallen in NSW for they have recorded many useful results since 1970, including wins over the national sides of each of the four northern hemisphere home unions. But developments in Queensland have been astonishing. Queensland were arguably the strongest provincial side in the world for much of the 1970s, and in Super 10 and Super 12 competitions in the 1990s they have often looked like the team to beat.

With the various upheavals in the history of their game, it took Australians a considerable time to form a national governing body for rugby union. In fact the Australian RFU was formed only in 1949 in response to a

Above: *The victorious Queensland side with the Super 10 trophy after their 21-10 defeat of South Africa's Natal in the 1994 final. Queensland hoisted the trophy the next year, too.*

proposal from the British-dominated International Board the previous year to give formal representation to the major southern hemisphere countries.

AUSTRALIA AND INTERNATIONAL RUGBY

The first British and New Zealand rugby tourists to visit Australia did not meet an Australian national team. Australia's first Test match was in 1899 against the second British Isles team to visit (the fourth 'Lions' team in all). Most Lions teams before and since have visited both Australia and New Zealand on tour, but the 1899 team (and the 1989 one) toured only Australia. The British team played attractive rugby by all accounts and were highly popular. The captain, the Reverend Matthew Mullineux, was even praised in verse by 'Banjo' Paterson, who had written 'Waltzing Matilda' a few years before:

Makes no row when the game gets tough,
None of your 'Strike me blue!
You's want smacking across the snout.'
Plays like a gentleman out and out,

Same as he ought to do,
The Reverend Mullineux

Although Mullineux's men won the Test series 3-1, Australia recorded a fine 13-3 victory in the first match. Queensland and a Sydney select team also beat the visitors , who were routinely described as the 'English team' in Australian reports, even though they were the first British touring side to include players from all four home countries.

▪ BALLYMORE ▪

Access to suitable grounds has been a long-standing problem for Australian rugby union, and Tests have accordingly been played at a variety of locations in both Sydney and Brisbane, and very occasionally in Melbourne. The famous Sydney Cricket Ground was used for many matches up to the 1980s, but the Ballymore ground in Brisbane was the first major venue to be created especially for rugby union matches.

Ballymore was acquired by the Queensland Rugby Union in 1966. At first a grandstand was built along only one side of the ground, but facilities were soon upgraded. The first inter-state game there against New South Wales took place in 1967 and the first Test, against New Zealand, in 1968. The game was far from being a classic but was certainly controversial, with New Zealand snatching a 19-18 win with a late and much-disputed penalty try – given by an Australian referee.

There was a major setback to development in 1974 when the whole playing surface was flooded under about two metres of water and silt, but the damage was made good and the nearby river rerouted to prevent a repeat performance. Ballymore now has all the facilities expected of a top-class international ground and is the home of the Queensland Rugby Union offices and museum.

Three of the four Tests were played in Sydney, but the Second took place in Brisbane, where, as an economy measure, mainly local players were selected to save on travelling expenses.

RIVALRY WITH THE ALL BLACKS BEGINS

The next international played by Australia was in 1903, and this one set the long rivalry with the All Blacks rolling. Unfortunately for Australia, the game set things off on the wrong foot, for the touring New Zealanders were far too strong for any Australian side throughout their ten-match visit. New Zealand won the only Test 22-3 in Sydney. Not until the seventh international between the two, in 1910, did Australia record their first win. The full story of this epic rivalry, as well as that between Australia and South Africa, is retold in Chapter 14.

In 1904, a British Isles team in Australia won all 14 games, including three Tests, and in 1908, an Anglo-Welsh 'Lions' team played nine games but no Tests on their way to New Zealand. Later that year, Australia embarked on their first northern hemisphere tour – to England and Wales. The touring party trained en route by shovelling coal in their ship's engine room but also took time on the voyage to think up an appropriate team name, finally deciding on the Wallabies. One other curiosity is that those First Wallabies also performed a supposedly Aboriginal ritual challenge before their games. The players found this rather embarrassing and, while the team name has lasted, this custom, unlike New Zealand's *haka*, has not.

THE FIRST WALLABIES

There were many variations of team colours in the first years of Australian international rugby, but the First Wallabies wore the light blue kit that had been adopted by the NSW team a year or so before their tour. For some home games thereafter Australian teams wore NSW blue in Sydney and the maroon of Queensland in Brisbane, but green and gold soon became standard. Until the 1960s, however, the shorts were gold and the jerseys green, but the colours have since been reversed to avoid a clash with the traditional Springbok green.

The First Wallabies played 31 games, winning 25, drawing one and losing five. The drawn match and four of the defeats were in Wales and included the international. Several of the games were very rough. Three Australians were sent off during the tour, and criticism of their disciplinary record and their tactics made the Wallabies especially determined when they faced England late in the tour. The Wallabies duly claimed a 9-3 Test win.

Another notable success came earlier in the trip, when Australia played Britain, represented by the English county champions Cornwall, in the only match of the 1908 Olympic Games rugby tournament. Australia won 32-3 to collect the gold medals. One player in the Australian side was Daniel Carroll, who went on to win a second Olympic rugby gold playing for the USA in 1920.

THE 'WARATAHS'

After World War I, with Queensland rugby dormant, New South Wales were effectively the Australian national side. The exploits of the 1927-28 NSW 'Waratahs' on their tour of the British Isles and France have become especially famous. The Waratahs played enterprising rugby, attacking from any area of the pitch. They played a full programme of five internationals, winning three but losing to England and Scotland. Stars of the team included fly-half Tommy Lawton (a Queenslander) and the captain, Johnnie Wallace, who had been a Scottish international from 1923 to 1926.

The only contact between a true Australian national side and northern hemisphere rugby between the wars was in 1930, when the Lions again passed through Australia.

Doug Prentice's British team were supposedly on the way to more serious business in New Zealand, but Australia won the only Test 6-5.

If Daniel Carroll's Olympic exploits supply one rugby trivia question then a good second one might be: how many matches did the Second Wallabies play? The answer is none, for the team arrived in Britain in 1939 just as World War II began and within a couple of weeks they were on the boat home again. The Third Wallabies did better than their predecessors – at least they got to play – and in fact had quite a successful tour. This visit, in 1947-48, was a marathon affair of 35 matches in Europe plus six more in Canada and the USA. Australia did not concede a try to any of the home nations. They beat Scotland, England and Ireland, but lost the Wales game as well as two further matches in Cardiff. One of these was against the Cardiff club, and the second was against the Barbarians. The latter game was a hastily arranged affair to raise funds to make sure the tourists could

Below: *The Third Wallabies scored 500 points and 115 tries on their 1947-48 tour of the British Isles and France. Both totals remain records for Australian overseas touring sides.*

pay their fares home. Yet it was such a success that a Barbarians match has since become an essential part of every major southern hemisphere tour to the British Isles.

From the 1950s through to the mid-1980s Australian sides enjoyed only modest success. There were eight Australian tours to various combinations of the major northern hemisphere countries, but Australia won only five out of 26 Tests. In addition, Australia lost many non-Test games, because their touring parties lacked strength in depth.

But there were still some Australian highlights. The 1967 Wallabies won three of their Tests against the home unions, their victories including Australia's first win over Wales and a comprehensive 23-11 success at Twickenham. The tour captain, John Thornett, a prop, played in only one international on the tour, the 14-20 defeat in a very dirty game against France. Instead the stars in most of the major matches were the scrum-half and replacement captain, Ken Catchpole, and the fly-half Phil Hawthorne, who prospered at the end of Catchpole's speedy service.

At home in Australia the Lions visits in 1950, 1959 and 1966 saw six straight Australian Test defeats, while the 1971 Lions did not even bother with a Test on their brief stopover

Above: David Campese on the burst, supported by Roger Gould and Mark Ella, during the Wallabies' victory over Wales on the 1984 Grand Slam tour.

on their way to New Zealand (although Queensland beat them in one of the two games they did play). In the era of air travel visits by the Lions were augmented by short tours by all the individual Five Nations. France were first in 1961, followed by England on their way home from New Zealand in 1963, Ireland in 1967, Wales in 1969 and Scotland in 1970, with further visits from each in subsequent years. Results for home matches from the 1950s into the 1980s were rather better from the Australian point of view than on their visits north of the equator but still far from impressive: 15 tours, 24 Tests, nine Australian wins.

THE EIGHTH WALLABIES

Australia were most consistent in this period against England, winning 19-8 in the single game played in 1963 and winning both the Tests in 1975. Australia also won their two Tests against Wales in 1978, but both were very rough games indeed, with Australia the principal culprits.

This mixed record changed decisively with the tour by the Eighth Wallabies in 1984. Former Argentinian Puma Enrique Rodriguez was a rock in the front row, flanker Simon Poidevin was everywhere on the field, and in the backs Nick Farr-Jones, Mark Ella and David Campese were the brightest but not the only stars. Ella scored a try in each international, and he and the team rounded off their Test programme with a superb 37-12 win in Scotland to complete their Grand Slam.

CONTINUED TEST SUCCESS

Since then Australia have, of course, been major contenders in all three World Cups, winning the 1991 competition and reaching at least the quarter-finals in the other two tournaments. They have also continued to have many Test successes, in particular against northern hemisphere sides. The Lions won the 1989 series 2-1, but individual home unions have come off badly whether they were playing at home or away. Wales were thrashed 63-6 in Brisbane in 1991 (with five-point tries this would have been 75); England went down 40-15 the same year; Scotland were comfortably beaten twice down under in 1992; and Ireland were on the wrong end of a 42-17 scoreline in Dublin a few months later.

Australia have been said to be rebuilding their side after the 1995 World Cup, but that did not stop them notching up almost 100 points in two home Tests against Wales in 1996 and going on to comfortable wins in Wales, Scotland and Ireland in the last months of the year.

EXCITING YOUNG TALENT

Everything is not perfect in Australian rugby in the late 1990s. The transition to full professionalism has raised much bitterness between the top players and the game's administrators, who tend to think that the players have cornered just too much of the cash that might have been spent to benefit the game more widely. The Australian team has also changed, with stars like Michael Lynagh and David Campese now retired from international rugby. However, plenty of established world-class players remain, such as John Eales and Tim Horan, along with exciting younger talents like Matt Burke and Joe Roff, to ensure that the Wallabies remain right at the top in world rugby.

Below: *Matt Burke evades Gary Armstrong as Australia beat Scotland 29-19 at Murrayfield in 1996. Burke, a classy full-back and goal-kicker, is one of Australia's fast-rising stars.*

CHAPTER FOUR

· ENGLAND ·

A demonstration of English forward power during their defeat of France in 1995. Here most-capped hooker Brian Moore has the ball,
supported by most-capped number eight Dean Richards, most-capped prop Jason Leonard (left) and flanker Tim Rodber (rear).

Forms of football that allowed handling and carrying of the ball originated in the first half of the nineteenth century at Rugby and other English public schools, including Winchester. When they moved on to university or other walks of life, old boys of these schools wanted to keep playing. One of the sporting periodicals catering for the leisured upper and middle classes of the time explained part of the reason why, 'Surely nothing could be better than football in October, an otherwise dull time of year for all except hunting men.'

When confronted with something new, as the old stereotype would have it, an American calls his lawyer and sues, but Englishmen form clubs and establish committees.

And this is exactly how rugby developed in England. The world's oldest club was formed at a London teaching hospital, Guy's Hospital, in 1843. Other clubs playing various versions of football soon followed in the London area. The oldest of those that have remained true to the rugby game are Blackheath (founded 1858) and Richmond (founded 1861). About 20 more London clubs came into existence in the 1860s, often looking to Blackheath and Richmond for guidance as to the playing rules they should use. A number of clubs founded in those days are now defunct, but Harlequins (founded 1866) and Wasps (founded 1867) are among those that are still at the forefront of English rugby.

■ RUGBY FOOTBALL UNION ■

National colours: white
Year founded: 1871
No. of clubs: 2049
Oldest club: Guy's
    Hospital, 1843
No. of players: 250,000
    adults/240,000 juniors
World Cup record: 1987
    quarter-finals; 1991
    runners-up; 1995
    fourth.

Blackheath representatives attended the meetings in 1863 that led to the foundation of the Football Association (FA) and eventually to the birth of soccer. Blackheath refused to join the FA because they disliked the playing rules that the organisation adopted. Instead, Blackheath developed fixtures with like-minded clubs such as Richmond. The two may first have played in 1863 but have certainly played regularly since 1867.

The game was not confined to the London area, though. Rugby football had been played at Oxford University as early as the 1840s and probably at Cambridge University (the only other English university at the time) in the same decade. The two universities first played each other in 1872, and their annual fixture – the 'Varsity' match – is the world's third-oldest. Schools in York and Durham played a rugby-like game in the 1850s, and England's second rugby club was formed at Liverpool in 1857, after members of Liverpool Cricket Club played an internal match, with Old Rugbeians making up one side against the Rest. There were clubs in almost every part of the country by 1870, the year in which the first county match took place, between Yorkshire and Lancashire.

THE RFU IS BORN

The Rugby Football Union (RFU) was formed at a meeting in January 1871. The meeting was called largely because of a challenge to play an international that had been issued by Scottish rugby enthusiasts. Representatives of 21 clubs attended the meeting, and the RFU was duly set up. Three old boys of Rugby School were delegated to draw up a code of laws for the game in England. Two months later, a team of 20, 10 of them Old Rugbeians, travelled to Edinburgh for the first international, only to lose to a better-organised and fitter Scottish team. Perhaps for the first time, but certainly not the last, there was a dispute over the first (Scottish) try.

The founders of the RFU were based mainly in London, and of those first 20 international players, most were from London clubs, with two or three each from Liverpool and Manchester. Many clubs from the north of England soon joined the RFU, however. During the 1870s and 1880s, as in the case of soccer, large crowds flocked to watch the most talented players throughout the industrial areas of the north, and the best became sought-after local heroes. By the time the English County Championship was first officially recognised in 1889, it was clear that Yorkshire, the first champion county, was the strongest rugby-playing area.

TO PAY OR NOT TO PAY

The RFU founders were all men of the gentleman amateur type who believed that rugby was a worthwhile activity only if it contributed to the player's physical and moral well-being. They believed that these values would be lost if the game was not kept separate from the world of work and money. But the competitive spirit and an influx of money into the game brought pressures. Top club matches in Yorkshire were regularly attended by 5000 or more paying spectators in the 1870s, and although the RFU did not encourage the creation of club competitions, the Yorkshire Cup was established in 1877. A league of top Yorkshire and Lancashire clubs – at this point still playing rugby union – began to operate in 1892-93, with attendances at matches sometimes exceeding 20,000. Players were undoubtedly lured from club to club through being found jobs or through other forms of financial assistance.

Below: *Moseley's Jan Webster passes during the 1972 club cup final. Moseley could not hold Gloucester, who won 17-6.*

Above: Leicester won the inaugural Courage club league trophy in 1987-88. Here Leicester fly-half Les Cusworth feeds his backs during the win over Waterloo that clinched the title.

Soon allegations of professionalism were being brought to county committees and the RFU. Matters came to a head with the defeat of the move to legalise 'broken time' payments in 1893 and the formation of the Northern Union in 1895. Even at this stage, both sides in the dispute still claimed to oppose professionalism but differed in what they saw as the best way to prevent it.

THE TAINT OF PROFESSIONALISM

The RFU responded to the northern breakaway by making increasingly strict rules on amateurism. It was not even necessary for an individual to take money for playing in a game to become a professional. Amateurs who knowingly played in the same match as someone who had once been a professional 'professionalised' themselves and hence were disqualified from playing any part in rugby union. The creation of local competitions was also seen as being detrimental to the amateur ideal, and the RFU in fact refused to allow club leagues to be introduced in England until the 1987-88 season. Only Ireland of the major rugby-playing countries held out longer against such an innovation.

For more than 80 years the only all-England competition was the County Championship. Yorkshire were the team to beat for the first half-dozen years, but after the secession of the strongest clubs to rugby league in 1895 (when the number of Yorkshire rugby union clubs went from 150 down to 14), it took 30 years for them to record another success. By the 1980s, though, the competition's importance and popularity had diminished. It had become apparent that standards in the County Championship had been overtaken by those in the top clubs, and players with those clubs made themselves available for their counties less and less often. In 1994, players from clubs in the top league divisions were specifically excluded from their county teams. The County Championship is still enthusiastically followed in certain areas of England, however. Half of Cornwall seemed to make their way to Twickenham for the 1991 final, which their heroes won. The conclusion of the 1996 championship found Gloucestershire and Lancashire joint leaders of the winners list with 16 championships each, followed by Yorkshire and Warwickshire.

Because of the RFU's stance on inter-club competition, for most of English rugby's history almost all club matches have been friendlies. Clubs preserved fixture lists against the same group of opponents, year in, year out, and it was very difficult for an improving or previously unfashionable club to get games with the acknowledged aristocrats of the system. The first great change to the friendly system was the creation of the national cup competition in 1971-72. Another sign of changing times was that the competition was sponsored – from its inception until 1989 by John Player, and since then by Pilkington.

The first winners were West Country giants Gloucester, who beat Moseley in the 1972 final at Twickenham. Coventry and Gosforth (the parent club of the current Newcastle team) both won twice in the 1970s. At the start of the 1980s Leicester were the top dogs, coached by Chalky White and basing their game around lively backs led from fly-half by Les Cusworth.

WEST COUNTRY GIANTS

When the cup began in the early 1970s, one contemporary rugby encyclopedia described West Country side Bath as being not quite in the top rank of English clubs. By the mid-1980s, Bath's position as the nation's number one club was no longer in doubt. Between 1984 and 1996, they reached ten finals, winning them all. Some of their wins have been almost exhibition matches, such as their 48-6 demolition of Gloucester in the 1990 final. Others have been tense and dramatic. The 1992 final was won by a dropped goal late in extra time when both the Bath and the Harlequins players were virtually out on their feet. In 1996, a controversial late penalty try gave Bath their victory over Leicester.

In an attempt to provide a stepping stone between club and international rugby, a competition was introduced in 1985 between the four divisional areas into which English rugby is divided – North, Midlands, Southwest and London. In theory this competition was to have the top 60 or so English players contesting places in the national team over a series of games. Such a competition would increase the players' big-match experience and give the selectors a better means of evaluation than the old system of national trial matches that everyone agreed was ineffective. It has done nothing of the sort, and most Divisional Championship matches have been dull. At the time of writing the RFU still seemed keen for the competition to continue, but the truth is that in the professional age clubs are set to dominate English rugby whether the RFU wishes it or not.

It was not until 1987 that England's rugby authorities finally made a genuinely positive response to the need to develop playing standards through increased competition. That year, the RFU set up national and local club leagues throughout England, a move that was made to seem even more overdue by England's disappointing showing in the World Cup earlier in 1987.

As in the cup competition since the mid-1980s, Bath have been the team to beat in the league in most seasons since it began. Coached for most of those great years by Jack Rowell, until he moved on to be England team manager and coach in 1994, Bath had an almost unbeatable team spirit to go with a host of international players. John Hall, Gareth Chilcott, Stuart Barnes, Jeremy Guscott and many more were all capable of brilliant rugby in their very different ways.

At the start of the professional era, however, Bath's dominance began to waver. Leicester, famed for their running rugby in the 1980s, created England's most powerful pack in the mid-1990s. Some even tipped Leicester to win a treble of league, cup and European Cup in 1996-97,

Above: *Bath skipper Phil de Glanville holds the Pilkington Cup aloft after his side's extraordinary 1996 final victory over Leicester, which was settled by a last-minute penalty try.*

but the French club Brive proved too powerful in the European final. Other clubs, like Harlequins and Saracens, strengthened their challenges using the power of their cheque books, and Richmond and Newcastle used their new proprietors' wealth to begin what they hoped would be a return to former eminence.

All this activity was accompanied by a most acrimonious and long-drawn-out series of negotiations on the structure and management of the game. The clubs'

▪ TWICKENHAM ▪

In the early years of international rugby, the England team played their matches at various locations, including the Oval cricket ground in London and in towns in northern and western England. At the start of the twentieth century, the RFU decided that this arrangement was unsatisfactory and began looking for a permanent home. Committee member Billy Williams led the search and eventually found a market-garden site in the London suburb of Twickenham. The RFU bought the ten-acre ground in 1907, and the first match was played there in October 1909.

Over the years, Twickenham has developed a great atmosphere of tradition. Some people even refer to the ground simply as 'headquarters' – a more respectful nickname than its original alternative description as 'Billy Williams's Cabbage Patch'. Besides being the venue for England's home international games, this great ground also hosts the annual Middlesex Sevens competition and the Oxford University *v* Cambridge University 'Varsity' match, both of which are high points in English rugby's social calendar.

Twickenham has changed dramatically in recent years, having undergone a total rebuilding programme. Some of the developments were in place for the 1991 World Cup final, but since then there has been a final transformation into a state-of-the-art 72,000-capacity stadium. The pitch is as immaculate as ever and, in addition to all the facilities you would expect in a modern ground, there is a fascinating Museum of Rugby beneath the West Stand. And of course, visiting teams still find it as hard as ever to win at Twickenham.

representatives and the RFU leaders seemed unable to agree on anything from the distribution of television money to the scheduling of matches or the provision of players to national squads and internationals. Time and again agreements have seemed imminent only for some further cause of dissent to be found or seemingly to be manufactured. Some on the clubs' side seemed determined to create a total split in the game, while some on the RFU side seemed likely to provoke one through their obstinacy. Fortunately, at the time of writing, enough good sense remained to prevent such a step into the unknown, despite all the bitterness and ill will that had been generated.

ENGLAND AND INTERNATIONAL RUGBY

England has always had the largest number of rugby players in the world, and the English authorities played the dominant role in the organisation of the game until very recent years. England has also had its share of innovators in the field of tactics, especially in the game's earlier days. Guy's Hospital are described as the first team to allot players specific positions in the scrummage, which they did in 1905. Previously players packed down to scrummage in the order in which they arrived at the mark – 'first up, first down', as the system was known. Wavell Wakefield, great England flanker and captain in the 1920s, is credited with developing forward tactics even further by allocating specific roles to the various pack members in every aspect of tight and loose play. Yet despite all this, England's national team have rarely managed to be the dominant force that one might expect. But fortunately for English fans there have been a good few glory years.

England avenged their 1871 defeat by Scotland in the first international match by winning the return match the next year in London. But it was 1883 before England first triumphed on Scottish soil. That 1882-83 season was the first in which the home international championship between England, Scotland, Ireland and Wales was played. England beat all three of their opponents that year to win their first title (and first 'Triple Crown', although the term was not invented until 1899). One of England's stars was Gregory Wade, who scored three tries against Wales. Wade, an Oxford student, was actually an Australian and later became prime minister of New South Wales.

England repeated their 1883 title triumph the following season and had notched up three more championships by 1892, two of which they shared with Scotland. Success then eluded England for a time, and in 1898-99 they suffered their first home international whitewash. There was better news from the first match against France, held in Paris in 1906.

England won 35-8, according to the scoring values in use then. Using the modern scoring system, the result would have been 53-12!

A major development in English rugby history was the building of a new national ground at Twickenham. The ground was opened in October 1909 with a match between Harlequins and Richmond, and the first Twickenham international was the England v Wales game in January 1910. Right from the start, Twickenham proved to be a hard place for visiting teams to claim a win. In that very first international at the ground, Wales kicked off and the ball was fielded by Adrian Stoop, one of the most influential of English backs in those days, who ran it straight back at them. A passing movement and what would now be called a quick ruck followed, before the winger F.E. Chapman was put clear to score with less than a minute played. England went on to win 11-6 and take the championship that year.

ENGLAND'S GOLDEN ERA

The first visitors to win at Twickenham were the Springboks in 1913. New Zealand won there in 1925 in a notoriously rough match in which All Black Cyril Brownlie was sent off, although he was evidently far from being the only sinner. It took until 1926 for England to lose a Five Nations match at their headquarters, Scotland winning 17-9 that year. Despite

Above: England players take a breather at half-time in the England v Wales match of 1923. England won the Grand Slam that year. Third from the right is Wavell Wakefield.

these defeats, the 1920s are often described as England's first golden era, with four Grand Slams won. Wavell Wakefield marshalled the forwards, half-backs Cyril Kershaw and Dave Davies created opportunities and wing Cyril Lowe, one of the smallest-ever international players, racked up a total of 18 tries – a career record for an England player that stood until Rory Underwood passed it in the modern era.

During the 1930s, England's fortunes were mixed. In January 1936, England notched up a historic 13-0 win over the All Blacks. England winger Prince Alexander Obolensky, who was of Russian descent, scored two tries. The second of these, a long diagonal run from his right wing position across the face of the New Zealand defence to score wide out on the left, was captured on film, and even in jerky black and white it is easy to see why the game became known as 'Obolensky's match'. England also registered three outright home titles during the decade, but just as characteristic of English rugby at the time was the 7-0 defeat by the Springboks in 1931-32. The England selectors – it would be a long time before there was anything so vulgar as a manager or a coach – picked three hookers as their front row, and South Africa unsurprisingly scrummaged them off the park.

From the end of World War II into the 1980s England had many fine players but consistently failed to realise their potential, as a result of poor organisation and chopping and changing in selection. The 1957 championship was the one true high point of the period, as England recorded their first Grand Slam since the 1920s, under the captaincy of hooker Eric Evans. The 1970s were perhaps England's worst decade of all with five 'wooden spoons' (bottom-of-table finishes) and their only 'championship' the five-way tie in 1973.

But English rugby was still strong when the preparation was right. In the early part of the 1979-80 season the North of England showed just what could be done, recording a stunning 21-9 win over the All Blacks. But the next week England picked a running fly-half, Les Cusworth, and sent him out with instructions to kick; the result – England 9, New Zealand 10.

BEAUMONT'S GRAND SLAM

That defeat, however, turned out to be almost the only blemish on that season. England went on to record their first Grand Slam for 33 years, under the popular and effective leadership of lock Bill Beaumont. The campaign included a comfortable victory over Ireland and the first English win in Paris for 16 years. The Wales match at Twickenham was rough and won narrowly 9-8 – three penalties to two tries – but the final game in Edinburgh finished England's season

Above: *Maurice Colclough (centre) comes to the aid of his captain Bill Beaumont (on ground) against France in 1980.*

off in style. Right-wing John Carleton scored three tries in the 30-18 win, and his fellow backs Paul Dodge and Clive Woodward in the centre and Mike Slemen on the opposite wing all contributed to an exciting English display.

THE CARLING ERA

The 1980 success proved to be a false dawn. England did not win another championship in the 1980s, and the 1987 World Cup was a disappointment, with England going out to Wales in the quarter-finals. However, by then a group of players had begun to assemble who would be at the heart of England's successes in the following years. Men like lock Wade Dooley, hooker Brian Moore and number eight Dean Richards were starting to make their very considerable marks, and in October 1988 England appointed as captain a young centre named Will Carling. Behind the scenes much was improved also. Far too little credit has been given to the contribution of Geoff Cooke, who was appointed England team manager in 1987. The 1989 Lions tour to Australia was perhaps the turning point in England's fortunes. The mainly English forwards provided that side with its competitive edge and they came home from the tour better and more determined players.

England should have won a Grand Slam in 1990 after a stunning 26-7 success in Paris but lost their way against a canny Scots team in the decider. They made no mistake in 1991. They began against Wales in Cardiff, where they had not won for 28 years, and cruised to a comfortable if dull 25-6 win. Fittingly, the closest match, with the Grand Slam at stake, was the final game against France at Twickenham. England just shaded it 21-19.

UPS AND DOWNS

The disappointment of the World Cup final defeat in the first part of the 1991-92 season was partly reduced by a second Grand Slam later that year after a horribly fierce England win in Paris. The next two seasons were rather quieter for England, although they did feature good home wins over the Springboks and the All Blacks and a shared Test series in South Africa.

By 1995, the Five Nations tournament, once seen as the international pinnacle, was coming to be regarded partly as a preparation for the World Cup, and England once again got it right with four wins. But then there was Jonah Lomu

in the World Cup semi-final and it was back to the drawing board. Will Carling stayed on to captain England to another Five Nations championship in 1996. He was one of the few early 1990s stalwarts to keep his place in the team.

Throughout these glory years England proved that when they played well they were a match for anyone, but on the biggest occasions their technique, commitment and confidence sometimes let them down. The triumphs had whetted the appetites of the English fans for success, however. The England team manager – since 1994, former Bath supremo Jack Rowell – is now under almost as much pressure as England's soccer manager to live up to public expectations. It would be astonishing if England ever reverted to the underachieving days of the 1970s, but the new professional era has seen so many organisational problems in the English domestic game that the national team will have to work hard to keep up with the drive and pace being developed in the southern hemisphere.

Below: *Jubilation on the face of England fly-half Rob Andrew at no-side in the 1995 Grand Slam decider against Scotland.*

CHAPTER FIVE

· FRANCE ·

France captain Abdelatif Benazzi on the charge against Scotland during the 1997 Five Nations clash in Paris, the final match to be played at the Parc des Princes. Benazzi, playing at flanker, had a storming game as France won 47-20 to complete the Grand Slam.

It is generally agreed that rugby in France began in 1872, when a group of British students formed a club and began to play in Le Havre. But the French have never been slow to assert their nation's historic importance, and their historians draw attention to the ancient game of *soule*, which was still being played in Normandy and Brittany in the nineteenth century. *Soule* is very old, perhaps even derived from games that the Roman soldiers played, and French writers have suggested, rather tongue in cheek, that all the 'British' forms of football are in fact descended from *soule*, the game having been brought north across the Channel by the Norman Conquest.

Such far-fetched theories are one thing, but the facts of rugby's development after those first games in Le Havre are rather simpler. By about 1877, British expatriates and some

Anglophile Frenchmen had begun playing casual games at weekends in Paris in the Bois de Boulogne, one of the city's foremost parks. During the 1880s, the game was also taken up by several colleges in and around Paris and caught the imagination of various athletics enthusiasts as well. The Racing Club de France was formed in Paris in 1882 as a multi-sport association and had a rugby section almost from the start. Stade Français had similar beginnings in 1883. Those two clubs contested the final of what was billed as the first French national club championship in 1892, although the only entries at that time came from teams in the Paris area. Racing took the title.

France was going through something of a fitness craze around that time, with sport being seen as having a vital part to play in creating a healthy and powerful nation. An official multi-sport governing body, the *Union des Sociétés Françaises des Sports Athletiques*, was formed in 1887 and would take rugby under its wing until the formation of the separate *Fédération Française de Rugby* (FFR) in 1920.

Direct contact with the game in Britain began in 1885, when a Paris Football Club team played against Civil Service in London. That Paris team was mainly made up of British players, but there was a greater French representation in the Stade Français team that became the first French side to host foreign visitors when the London club Rosslyn Park arrived to play them in 1892. Rosslyn Park won very easily, but a joint Stade Français and Racing team enjoyed a return trip to London the next year. An Edinburgh XV that included several Scottish international players came to Paris in 1896, with a Parisian side reciprocating in 1898.

RUGBY SPREADS TO THE PROVINCES

French rugby also began to spread from Paris in the 1890s. Various provincial colleges and universities took up the game in that decade, and it also began to make inroads in the southwest and south of the country. Besides the capital, these were the areas that had the strongest British connections, usually through the wine trade. And, of course, it is these areas that soon took over as the real centre of French rugby and have remained its heartland to the present day. By around 1910 there were probably about 100 clubs in existence in France, most of them forming part of municipal sports associations.

France played their first international on 1 January 1906, starting right at the top of the tree with a game against the First All Blacks. The venue was the Parc des Princes, and there was what was then a good crowd of 3000 to see the New Zealanders give an effective exhibition of running rugby, despite the heavy rain and muddy conditions, to win 38-8. The French team and spectators, however, were delighted with their two tries, one converted, since that equalled the highest score that any of the British teams had recorded against the All Blacks earlier in their tour.

France's first international against a home union country followed less than three months later, France going down 35-8 to England in Paris. The England match became an annual fixture, being joined on the French rugby calendar by a match against Wales in 1908, against Ireland in 1909, and against Scotland in 1910. The French lost all their early internationals by comfortable margins for those low-scoring days, and it was not until 1911 that France got their first win in what we now know as the Five Nations, when they beat Scotland in Paris. It was reportedly a fast and exciting game, with Scotland overhauling a substantial French lead early in

▪ FÉDÉRATION FRANÇAISE DE RUGBY ▪

National colours: **blue**
Year founded: **1919**
No. of clubs: **1757**
Oldest club: **Le Havre Athletic Club, 1872**
No. of players: **95,000 adults/142,000 juniors**
World Cup record:
1987 runners-up;
1991 quarter-finals;
1995 third

the second half, only for the French to pull ahead once more. A final, late Scottish try went unconverted, and France held out to win 16-15.

The Scotland match in 1913 was a less happy occasion, however. Scotland won 21-3, but the English referee so incensed the Paris crowd that he and some of the Scottish players were jeered and jostled off the pitch at the end. Scotland refused to play France in 1914 but forgot their grievances during World War I, so that the France v Scotland game in Paris in 1920 was the first to be played when the championship resumed after the conflict. Scotland won 5-0 in what was the last international to be played at the Parc des Princes until the 1970s. One curiosity of that game was that M.F. Lubin-Lubrère and Jock Wemyss in the respective forward packs had both lost an eye in the war.

FRANCE ON THE UP

Better times were clearly coming for French rugby. They beat Ireland in 1920, their first win outside France, and in 1921 they registered two victories in a season for the first time, beating Ireland at home in Paris and Scotland in Edinburgh. Then, in 1922, France nearly claimed their first win at Twickenham. They led 11-6 late in the second half, having scored three tries to none at that stage, when England were awarded a penalty and decided to kick for goal. If the kick had gone over, France would have won the game, but it fell short, the French failed to gather the loose ball, and the English followed up for a try, which was converted for an 11-11 draw. It would be a long time yet before France managed to beat England or Wales on their own grounds, but the first French win in Paris against England came in 1927 and the first at home against Wales was recorded in 1928.

Above: *France attack during their win over Romania at the 1924 Olympics. France and Romania were among the founder members of FIRA in 1934 and have a long-standing rivalry.*

For most French fans and players, who were based in the south or southwest of the country, international victories were all very well but rather remote from their real concerns. France had little travelling support in those days, and for the players a trip from, say, Perpignan or even a major city like Toulouse to Dublin or Edinburgh for a match would involve a journey lasting three or four days. What really caught the imagination and enthusiasm of French rugby fans of the time was the club championship. There were over 400 clubs in France shortly after World War I; ten years later there were almost 800. Clubs were dotted all over west and southwest France, with even very small towns and large villages having a strong team. However, the city-based Toulouse were easily the strongest club of the period, with five championship wins in the 1920s and a host of leading international players in their side. Philippe Struxiano, Toulouse and France scrum-half and captain in 1920, was an early advocate of good combined forward play, and leading backs Adolphe Jaureguy and François Borde were also with Toulouse for part of their careers.

Rugby teams were the local pride and joy, and rivalries were fierce. One of the best-known teams of the period were Quillan, from a town of about 3000 people in the Aude department. In 1929 the team they beat in the championship final were Lézignan, a locality – population 6000 – only about 40km (25 miles) away. With so much pride at stake in matches like this, it is no surprise that on-field brutality was commonplace, with crowd violence and intimidation of referees virtually routine. One of the Lézignan players even tried to kill himself after that 1929 defeat. There were other problems, too. Quillan were known as the 'hatmaker's club' because of the financial assistance they received from a local worthy in that business. Many players in the championship were effectively professional, and player-poaching was rife.

EXPELLED FROM THE FIVE NATIONS

The British unions had had their suspicions about the amateur status of French rugby for years. The Scottish RU had kicked up such a fuss after Stade Bordelais placed advertisements in Scotland in 1912, offering to find a well-paid job for a good fly-half, that the French authorities were forced to ban the members of the club committee for life. Matters came to a head in 1930, when a group of 12 French clubs became so upset by the various problems in their game that they broke away from the FFR to set up what they called the French Amateur Rugby Union. The four home unions, increasingly alarmed at developments in France, sent the FFR a remarkably pompous letter at the end of the 1930-31 season, cancelling all matches with France or French clubs 'until we are satisfied that the control and conduct of the game [in France] has been placed on a satisfactory basis in all essentials'. France did not play again in the international championship until 1946-47.

This did not seem to make much difference to French rugby at first. Certainly some of the most troublesome local competitions were suppressed, but the championship went on pretty much as before, and the rebel clubs quickly rejoined the FFR. France helped to set up a new international body, FIRA (*Fédération Internationale de Rugby Amateur*), in 1934 and played regular internationals against Germany, with games against Italy and Romania on a less frequent basis. However, it gradually became clear that standards were falling in the absence of top international competition, and in 1939 the French assured the International Board that their clubs had cleaned up their act and that they would suspend their championship. France would have been re-admitted to regular play but for the intrusion of World War II, although a British XV did play against a French select in wartime Paris in 1940.

French rugby league had begun operations at the end of 1933 and had started to prosper in the years up to World War II. Whatever else the war did to France, it helped French rugby union, for the puppet French government set up by the Germans after they conquered France actually banned league but allowed union matches and competitions to continue. There was no club championship for two seasons, but it went ahead as usual in 1942-43 and thereafter.

POST-WAR SUCCESS

France resumed playing a full international programme in 1946-47. There were regular wins for the first few seasons, with one highlight being the first success in Wales, at Swansea in 1948. The major step forward was in 1951 when France won three out of four games and were only pipped to the championship by Ireland, who beat them by a single point in Dublin. The high point of the season, however, was the first-ever French win at Twickenham. Scrum-half Gérard Dufau made decisive breaks leading to two tries, and flanker Jean Prat, one of the try-scorers, also dropped a goal as France notched up a comfortable 11-3 margin.

France shared the championship title for the first time in 1954. Just as welcome that year was France's first win over the All Blacks. The New Zealanders arrived in Paris

■ PARC DES PRINCES ■

France's first-ever international, against New Zealand in 1906, was played at the Parc des Princes in Paris, and the stadium continued to be used on and off for major matches until just after World War I. France's main ground then became the Stade Colombes, also in Paris, but in 1972 a return was made to a refurbished Parc.

For the next 25 years, the Parc was the venue for all of France's home matches in the Five Nations and most games against major touring teams, as well as for the French club championship finals. Visiting teams always found it a formidably difficult place to win at, with the high, tiered stands reflecting a thunderous barrage of support onto the playing area. Scotland won only one match at the Parc, and Ireland never won there at all.

It was entirely appropriate that the last Five Nations match played at the Parc was the Scotland match in 1997, victory in which clinched France their fifth Grand Slam. Even better, the triumph was sealed in the best expansive French style and by an emphatic 47-20 scoreline. Better still, it was the first time that France had completed a 'Grand Chelem' in front of a home crowd.

The Parc des Princes will be replaced as France's national stadium by the new Stade de France, which is being built for the 1998 soccer World Cup.

with four Test wins on tour already and went to work on what they hoped would be a fifth. The All Blacks totally dominated the match, monopolising possession from scrum and line-out and varying their attacks at will – but every move met a determined French tackle. France had a single scoring chance, and Jean Prat went over for the try with three tacklers round his legs. It was enough for a 3-0 win. The following year, France looked set to claim their first Five Nations outright. They came to the final match, against Wales in Paris, with three wins in hand and the chance to finish with a fourth for a perfect record. It was not to be. Wales won 16-11, and the two teams shared the title.

Above: *French fly-half A. Labazuy lands a penalty to register his side's only points in the 3-3 draw with England in 1959. France were outright champions that year for the first time.*

France had a mid-table finish in 1958, although this did include an impressive 16-6 win against Wales, France's first in Cardiff. France then went off on tour to South Africa, their first visit to a major southern hemisphere nation. The omens did not look good, since several leading players were unavailable for the six-week trip, and there were many injuries once the party began its games in South Africa. In all, three of the eight provincial matches were lost and one drawn, but the Tests were another story. The First Test was dull, with too much kicking by both sides, and finished 3-3, but the French realised they had nothing to be afraid of. They also decided that, big as the Springbok forwards were, they lacked stamina. A French commentator memorably described the South Africans as 'heavy, right down to their feet', and in the Second Test this proved to be an accurate appraisal as the faster French pack took command in the second half. France scored two dropped goals and a penalty to win 9-5 and achieve the unthinkable – a series win over the Springboks on their own turf.

TACTICAL PIONEERS

Throughout these post-war years, rugby in France had steadily become more sophisticated. The emphasis was increasingly put on ball-playing forwards making ground with inter-passing moves before releasing their speedy and inventive backs. The French were also pioneers in varying line-out play, with players switching positions and different types of throw being used. Mazamet's Lucien Mias was influential in developing these tactics with the national team, especially once he became stand-in captain on the 1958 tour. The French club of the 1950s were Lourdes, with five title wins. They had reached their first championship final as recently as 1945, losing on that occasion to Agen.

Although the French had been readmitted to the international championship after the war, this had not ended British worries about the domestic game in France.

There were repeated threats of expulsion in 1950-52 but the British quietly backed down after yet more promises of change had been made by the French rugby leaders. The French did make improvements to some aspects of their game, especially in tightening up on the more blatant abuses of player transfers and registration changes between clubs. And the French also asked, with some justice, how was it that they had leading players struggling to take six weeks off to tour South Africa, when the Lions, All Blacks and Springboks regularly went on three-month trips without anyone saying they were professionals.

French rugby historians describe the 1958 South Africa tour as a great turning point. From the moment the team returned, France changed into a leading, and at times dominant, force in European and world rugby. France won their first outright Five Nations title in 1959 and claimed three more outright wins and one shared title in the 1960s. There is no doubt that the greatest of these successes in French eyes was their first-ever Grand Slam, in 1968. It was not the most spectacular French side, with the half-back partnership of the brothers Lilian and Guy Camberabero both inclined to overdo the tactical kicking, but forwards like Benoit Dauga and Walter Spanghero ensured that France did not lack power up front.

FORWARD POWER

French rugby lost some of its sparkle for a time in the 1970s and early 1980s, following the example of the Béziers club, who made the French championship virtually their private property with ten wins between 1971 and 1984. Their triumphs were based unashamedly on powerful, aggressive, dominating forwards, and this style was generally taken up, although less successfully to start with, by the national team. Eventually, the formula worked, and the classic image of the French Grand Slam side of 1977 was of their captain, the tiny scrum-half Jacques Fouroux, berating the huge figure of

Below: *Jean-Pierre Rives acts as scrum-half, while back-row partner Jean-Pierre Bastiat holds back Fran Cotton (left) and Bill Beaumont at Twickenham in 1977. France won 4-3.*

number 8 Jean-Pierre Bastiat, while hard men like front-row forwards Gérard Cholley and Robert Paperemborde stood by just as willing to do what the 'little general' told them to.

FOUROUX IN CHARGE

Fouroux retired from playing after that season but was soon back as coach of the national team. Two more Grand Slams came France's way in 1981 and 1987, but there was much criticism of Fouroux's forward-based strategies when sparkling and talented backs like Serge Blanco and Philippe Sella were crying out for opportunities. Foreign observers could not understand, for example, why centre Didier Codorniou did not win more French caps. And of course the whole debate became entangled in the convoluted and fiercely contested internal politics that have always been a part of French rugby.

France were finally admitted as full members of the International Board in 1978 but still often had a feeling that the rest of the rugby world was somehow against them. French referees, for example, had not been appointed for

Below: *The French team celebrate a series victory in New Zealand after beating the All Blacks 23-20 in the Second Test at Auckland in 1994. France had won the First Test 22-8.*

Five Nations games or other major internationals until 1969. For France's own internationals, the match officials and the opposing players were almost always English-speaking – the Afrikaners being an exception – and all too often in the French view conspiring to do France down. This perception and the fragile on-field discipline of some French teams combined to prevent even more French successes. France should have completed another Grand Slam by beating Scotland in 1984, but lost their way in a flurry of arguments with the referee. It was much the same story in the 1991 World Cup game with England, and again in Paris in 1992 against the same opponents, when the French team completely lost their self-control.

VICTORY IN NEW ZEALAND

Even when French discipline held, England generally had the edge in confidence over the French throughout the early 1990s, and there were occasional inexplicably weak French performances against Scotland as well. This was all the more surprising, and disappointing for French fans, because when attitudes were right their team were truly formidable. The fine performances in the 1987 and 1995 World Cups were tokens of this, and there were also impressive wins over the All Blacks and the other southern hemisphere nations.

France and the All Blacks shared two Test series in France in 1986 and 1995, both of which featured matches of awesome commitment on both sides. But the really remarkable French success came on the 1994 tour to New Zealand. This began very badly for France. They lost an international 18-16 against Canada on the way, with Philippe Sella getting himself sent off. Sella was back in the frame by the time of the First Test in New Zealand, however, and celebrated his 100th French cap in the best style by being part of a 22-8 French win. The All Blacks had slightly more of the possession, but France had all the ideas and were far sharper when it came to taking their chances.

New Zealand fought back in the Second Test, but France led at half-time through a rather lucky interception try by Emile N'Tamack. New Zealand took control of the second half, however, and with a couple of minutes to go were well in charge, holding a 20-16 lead. Then France scored the sort of try that only they can. Winger and captain Philippe Saint-André picked up a loose ball deep in his own 22 and set off on a desperate counter-attack. Eight or nine French players joined in the brilliant high-speed passing movement that followed and ended with Jean-Luc Sadourny getting what Saint-André called the try 'from the end of the world'. France had won a Test series in New Zealand.

At the opening of the professional era, French rugby seemed very strong. France celebrated another Grand Slam in 1997 – seemingly with half their first-choice team on the injured list. At club level, Toulouse and Brive won the first two Heineken European club championships in 1996 and 1997. There was impressive strength in depth on the club scene, too. Three out of the four French clubs that entered reached the quarter-finals in the 1997 Heineken Cup, and all seven that participated in the European Conference tournament – the junior European competition – got to the last eight, with Bourgoin emerging as winners. There are some problems, however. The traditional structure of the game in France, the *rugby des villages*, based around teams in small towns and villages, is under threat, with clubs based in smaller places certain to struggle to raise sufficient revenue to keep their best players. And the French league first division is also still ridiculously large, with top players playing far too many matches. Even so, there is no doubt of the great potential in the French game. No one will take their challenge for the 1999 World Cup lightly.

Below: *Sébastien Viars about to set up right-wing Gerald Fabré (left) for Brive's second try against Leicester in the 1997 Heineken European Cup final. The French side won 28-9.*

CHAPTER SIX

· IRELAND ·

Emotion at Cardiff Arms Park as the whistle goes at the end of the 1997 Wales v Ireland Five Nations international. Ireland scored three tries for a ten-point lead at half-time, but then had to withstand a determined Welsh fightback to scrape home 26-25.

The Irish, of course, will tell you that they invented rugby, because William Webb Ellis was really born in Ireland and learned the handling game from his Irish cousins before exporting it to Rugby School. Or so the story goes. Unfortunately there is no concrete evidence to support this, and one major snag is that although Ellis's soldier father was stationed in Ireland at the time of his son's birth, in later life Ellis himself gave his birthplace as Manchester.

Types of football do indeed have a long history in Ireland. References to games go back at least to the mid-fourteenth century, and it is interesting to note that the authorities tended to take a dimmer view of hurling than of football in the various restrictive laws that were passed.

Local laws from Galway in 1527 said that men should not play at 'hurlinge of the litill balle with the hookie stickies or staves, nor use no hande balle to play without the walls, but only the great foot balle'. A game called *cad* was popular in Munster and especially County Kerry (home of the supposed Ellis cousins) in the seventeenth and eighteenth centuries. *Cad* existed in two forms – one was a cross-country, village-against-village free-for-all, and the other was played in a defined small area by limited numbers on each side. Written accounts clearly record that handling and carrying featured in both types, as they also definitely did in the somewhat different football games played in the Dublin area, notably by students at Trinity College.

Ireland's first rugby club was formed at Trinity College in 1854, and the first recorded game in Ireland was an internal one at Trinity in December 1855 between original and new members of the club. Several Trinity founder members are known to have had their earlier education in England at Rugby School or at Cheltenham College, which also played a game similar to that developed at Rugby School. Trinity's first outside game was in 1860, when they played Wanderers, a group of former Trinity students not to be confused with the present Wanderers club, which formed in Dublin in 1869. Trinity also drew up a written set of rules, which were widely published by a Dublin sports equipment supplier when they were adopted in 1868, and these helped spread the game even further.

THE GAME IN THE NORTH

By the mid-1860s, the Trinity club was big enough to field a second team, which played matches against other colleges and some senior schools in the Dublin area and as far north as Dungannon in Ulster. Ulster's first adult club began in 1868, when members of the North of Ireland Cricket Club formed the North of Ireland Football Club (NIFC, usually known as North) to play the winter game. Their first fixture was in January 1870 against Queen's University, Belfast, whose club was founded in 1869. That game included periods of play on three different days, and since Queen's fielded a team of 18 players against 13 from North, it is no surprise that Queen's won.

In 1871 North played, and lost to, Trinity for the first time. North widened their horizons a little further the next week when they played a visiting West of Scotland side, although they lost once again. Both North and Trinity themselves toured overseas, to Scotland and England respectively, in 1873-74, by which time a number of other clubs had also come into existence in Dublin and the Leinster area and in Ulster.

On their 1873-74 visit to England, Trinity tried to arrange an international but had to settle for a match against the Dingle club in Liverpool. The next step was clearly to form a national governing body to go one better. In the autumn of 1874, Trinity therefore called a meeting of clubs to form a union, and on 14 December 1874 representatives of seven clubs set the Irish Football Union going. It was not Ireland's only governing body for long, however, for on 13 January 1875 the Ulster clubs formed the Northern Football Union. The Ulstermen did not wish to go it alone but just make sure that Dublin did not take too much control. The two bodies negotiated a quota system to ensure that each was well represented in the first Irish national team and

continued to co-operate on selection and other matters until they eventually amalgamated in 1880 as the Irish Rugby Football Union (IRFU). A third body, the Irish Provincial Towns Rugby Union, also existed in the early 1880s, but this too was brought under the umbrella of the IRFU in 1885.

Since then, rugby has been almost the only Irish activity that has been consistently run on an All-Ireland basis, with little intrusion from political and sectarian problems. There have been minor squabbles over the years regarding which flag should be displayed at internationals and which, if any, anthem should be played, but almost the only time political troubles did have a definite effect was in 1972, when Scotland and Wales did not fulfil their fixtures in Dublin because of a supposed terrorist threat. Fortunately this proved to be an isolated incident. It was doubly sad for Irish fans because they had already won their two away games that season and had a good chance of claiming at least a championship and perhaps even a Grand Slam. In 1973 England received their best-ever welcome from the Lansdowne Road crowd when they resumed the regular schedule, which has not been interrupted since. Ireland won that match 18-9, with England captain John Pullin commenting afterwards, 'We may not be much good, but at least we turn up.'

EARLY INTERNATIONALS AND PROVINCIAL GAMES

All that was a long way ahead when Ireland played their first international at the Oval cricket ground in London on 15 February 1875. England won comfortably by two goals and a try to nil, and one Irish correspondent slated his team as being 'immaculately innocent of training'. That day Ireland played in green and white hooped tops, but for the return match the next season, also an England win, both teams played in white! Ireland did not finally settle on

■ IRISH RUGBY FOOTBALL UNION ■

National colours:
emerald green
Year founded: **1874**
No. of clubs: **250**
Oldest club: **Trinity College, Dublin, 1854**
No. of players: **14,000 adults/36,000 juniors**
World Cup record:
1987 quarter-finals;
1991 quarter-finals;
1995 quarter-finals

IRISH RUGBY
FOOTBALL UNION

Above: England v Ireland at Blackheath in 1894. Ireland beat the home side 7-5 that day and followed up with wins against Scotland and Wales to claim their first Triple Crown.

emerald green jerseys with the shamrock badge until the 1885-86 season. However, despite the defeat in London, the 1874-75 season can be counted a successful one for Ireland, since two new clubs joined the union late on and the bank account ended up with the healthy balance of £2.06.

Besides gaining a return fixture with England, other Irish rugby milestones were reached in 1875-76. Ulster beat Leinster one goal to nil in Belfast in their first meeting, and Ireland's first rugby cup competition, the Ulster Schools Cup, got under way. Munster became the third Irish province on the scene when they played Leinster in Dublin in 1877, losing by one goal to nil. This was fairly rapid progress, since the first Munster club to affiliate to the union had been Rathkeale as recently as 1875, although there is evidence that Queen's College (now University College), Cork, had been playing since 1872.

Leinster, Ulster and Munster all followed the Ulster schools' example by setting up cup competitions for their adult clubs in the 1880s. Unsurprisingly Trinity won the first Leinster trophy in 1882, and NIFC took the initial Ulster title

in 1885; Bandon were the first winners in Munster, in 1886. Rugby came slowest to Connacht, with only four clubs in existence by the mid-1880s. The cup competition there did not get going until 1896, when Galway Town won it.

IRELAND STRUGGLE AT NATIONAL LEVEL

Despite progress in the domestic game the national side took some time to record its first success. England more or less dictated to Ireland that the 1877 game would be played 15-a-side, the first such international. In one of the more unusual pieces of rugby selection, Thomas Gordon, one of the Irish three-quarters, was picked for the match even though he had only one hand. It was 1880 before Ireland even scored against England, let alone won or drew. John Cuppaidge scored a try under the posts that year, but goal-kicker R.B. Walkington was so nervous with the conversion that he missed. The first Ireland *v* Scotland game was in 1877, and it was against Scotland in 1881 that Ireland got their first win. But there was a sting in the tail for the team – they were each subsequently sent a bill for the after-match dinner because funds were so low.

Wales were added to the fixture list in 1882, but only became regular opponents from 1887. Ireland did not take the 1882 game or the 1884 match very seriously. Both were lost and Ireland even had to borrow a couple of Welshmen to make up a full side in Cardiff in the latter game. Ireland did not beat Wales until 1888, but by then they had at long last got their first win against England, a two goals to nil success in Dublin in 1887.

Irish rugby has never been short of lively characters but two in particular stand out from the 1887 team that beat England. One player called John Macauley realised after he was selected that the only way he could be available to play was if he got married. This unusual situation arose because he had used all his annual leave but knew that his employer gave an additional allowance for special occasions. Macauley brought his new wife to the game. One of his team-mates was D.B. Walkington, brother of the 1880 goal-kicker, who compensated for his poor eyesight by wearing a monocle – which he would carefully remove whenever he had to make a tackle!

TRIPLE CROWN SUCCESSES

By the start of the 1893-94 season, Ireland had played 43 internationals and won only five of them, but this was about to change. That season they beat England 7-5 at Blackheath, Scotland 5-0 in Dublin and finished with a 3-0 victory over Wales on a virtually flooded Belfast pitch to claim their first Triple Crown. One indication of how things have changed is that Ireland's heaviest forward was John O'Conor of Bective Rangers, whose weight is recorded as 13½ stone (86kg), scarcely big enough for a top-class centre these days.

Ireland reverted to type the next year, losing all three games but were champions again in 1896. Nine Irishmen went off to South Africa that summer with the British Isles team, and all played in at least one of the Tests, the Lions winning the series 3-1. Two of the same Irishmen would return to South Africa three years later to win Victoria Crosses during the Boer War. The championships of 1897 and 1898 were incomplete because of a squabble about professionalism in Wales, but Ireland took the Triple Crown again in 1899. This time the decider was in Wales and was continually disrupted by an over-enthusiastic crowd that kept spilling onto the pitch. Ireland managed to make the decisive score just before half-time and then held out against strong Welsh pressure for most of the second period.

IRELAND TOUR CANADA

A second milestone in 1899 was Ireland's first overseas tour. A squad of 17 players played 11 games in various parts of eastern Canada, winning ten of them. In the match they lost, the tourists could field only 14 fit men. The All Blacks and Springboks both came to Ireland for the first time during the

next decade, and unfortunately for Ireland they won the Tests and all their other games. Even worse was to come on the second Springbok visit in 1912, the South Africans beating Ireland 38-0 at Lansdowne Road.

Little rugby was played in Ireland during World War I, but the game quickly got going again afterwards, even though the country was divided first by rebellion against the British and then by civil war. In the 1920s and 1930s, Ireland won the championship outright once and had a share in the title four more times – better than in some recent decades but hardly glory years. In 1923 the IRFU bought the Ravenhill ground in Belfast and built a stand there in time

▪ LANSDOWNE ROAD ▪

Lansdowne Road is the home of Irish rugby. A sports ground already existed there when Ireland were planning their first home international in 1875-76, but it was turned down by the authorities as being 'quite inadequate'. Nonetheless it was first used for a major rugby match in December 1876, when Leinster played Ulster, and for an international in 1878, when England beat Ireland by two goals and a try to nil.

The lessee in those years was Henry Dunlop, who was secretary of an athletics club and one of the early figures in the Lansdowne rugby club. Lansdowne and Wanderers, two of Ireland's oldest and strongest clubs, still have their grounds adjacent to the national stadium and are very hospitable, which is just as well since there have generally been no public bars in the main ground. Some years after the first game, Harry Shepperd, treasurer of the IRFU, personally bought the lease from Dunlop, and after Shepperd died in 1906, the IRFU bought the lease from his estate. The union then negotiated a long lease with the owners and, having secured the ground's future, set about development. Just as Wales are now doing with Cardiff Arms Park, Ireland swung the pitch through 90 degrees. This work plus the construction of new stands on each side was completed for the Scotland game in February 1908, and many other updates and refurbishments have taken place since. Some have been more successful than others, however. Another new stand was opened for the Scotland game in 1927 before its roof had been put on. Naturally it poured with rain, but there was some compensation in the result – a 6-0 Ireland win.

Most of Ireland's home games since 1878 have been played at Lansdowne Road, but until 1954 internationals were also staged regularly in Belfast. In addition there have been three in Cork and one in Limerick.

Above: *Irish prop Chris Daly emerges from a maul during the Ireland v Wales Five Nations match at Belfast in 1948. Daly scored the winning try that day as Ireland defeated Wales 6-3 and claimed their only Grand Slam to date.*

for the 1924 England game – the only time England have played in Ulster. This ground was the venue for many of Ireland's internationals up to 1954 and has been used since then for other important games.

There was also considerable progress on the domestic rugby front. A national cup competition, the Bateman Cup, was set up in 1922 to be contested by the four winners of the provincial trophies. Lansdowne were the first champions, but unfortunately the competition was comparatively short-lived, coming to an end with the outbreak of World War II in 1939. Meanwhile, rugby in Connacht also developed substantially with more clubs coming into existence and the Connacht provincial team beginning to play the other provinces regularly from the 1936-37 season. Connacht did

not join the inter-provincial championship officially until 1946-47, however, and two shared titles in the 1950s are unfortunately their only successes to date.

Although internationals were discontinued during World War II, domestic rugby in neutral Ireland carried on, and Irish XVs played five matches against British Army selects. Ireland won only one of these games, the last, which was played in 1945. Karl Mullen and Jack Kyle were two youngsters making their top-class debuts in that match, and they would soon make a mark in the wider rugby world.

IRELAND'S GRAND SLAM

The immediate post-war years were the finest in Irish rugby history. The first championship after the war was played in the 1946-47 season, and Ireland gave little hint of what was soon to come, with two wins and two defeats, one of each home and away, for a mid-table position. The purple patch began in Paris on New Year's Day 1948 with a comfortable 13-6 victory over France. England were next at Twickenham,

Ireland scoring three tries to scrape home 11-10. Ireland then beat Scotland 6-0 in Dublin to go into the finale against Wales with the championship already secure and the Triple Crown and Grand Slam beckoning.

The match was played in Belfast before a fervent capacity crowd. The half-time score was one try each, but early in the second half, prop Chris Daly crashed over to give Ireland a 6-3 lead that they held to the end. Daly, who was shortly to go over to league, had his shirt ripped off by the celebrating crowd at the final whistle, but in fact the success was based on a fine combined forward effort. Hooker Karl Mullen captained the side in the Triple Crown games, although not against France, and his shrewd leadership, both in the preparation for matches and in the tactical decisions he made on the field, was highly influential in those pre-coaching days, Although the strength of the backs was mainly in defence, Jack Kyle was magical at fly-half. He scored tries against England and Scotland, and in the final stages of the Wales game his tactical kicking was crucial in enabling Ireland to hang on for glory.

Mullen led his men to a repeat Triple Crown the next season, and although the Irish were toppled from their perch by Wales in 1950, Mullen and eight other Irishmen were chosen to travel to New Zealand with the Lions that summer. Mullen was the skipper, and he, Kyle and back-row forward Bill McKay played in all four Tests. Irishman Sam Walker had led the Lions in 1938, and the run of Irish skippers continued with Robin Thompson in 1955 and Ronnie Dawson in 1959, then, with interruptions, through Tom Kiernan and Willie-John McBride to Ciaran Fitzgerald in 1983. The skippers were not the only Irishmen who made great contributions to these tours. Tony O'Reilly's six Test tries for the Lions is the best total to date, and his 22 tries in 24 matches on his second tour in 1959 owed much to startling pace and power that he never quite displayed in an Ireland shirt. But even these records do not compare with those of Mike Gibson and Bill McBride (as he was known in his early playing days). Both went on five tours to play 12 and 17 Tests respectively and were key members of the two finest Lions sides ever – the 1971 and 1974 teams.

Success largely eluded Ireland in the home championship throughout the careers of Gibson and McBride, although there were some good results on Irish tours and against major touring teams at home. Ireland's

Below: *Twickenham, 1982: John O'Driscoll (No 7), held by England's Peter Winterbottom, releases the ball into the path of Donal Lenihan, as Ireland beat England 16-15.*

first win over a major touring side was a narrow 9-6 success against the Wallabies in 1958. The Wallabies also lost the Irish Tests on tour in 1967 and 1968 and were beaten on their own turf in both 1967 and 1979, the two 1979 Tests being Mike Gibson's final appearances for his country.

MUNSTER HUMBLE THE TOURISTS

Munster had given various touring teams a hard time over the years, and when they gave the 1967 Wallabies their second defeat in Ireland they became the first Irish province to beat a southern hemisphere country. The first Irish win of all over one of the great southern hemisphere powers had come in 1965, however, when the Springboks arrived on a short tour. Combined Irish Universities, with several of their best players being rested in advance of the Test four days later, won a remarkable 12-10 victory. It was a finely judged piece of selection, for the full Ireland side completed the double with a 9-6 success, their only win to date over the South Africans. The 8-8 draw with the Springboks in Dublin five years later was also a significant date in Irish rugby

Above: Flying wing Simon Geoghegan, one of the most exciting players of the 1990s, rounds Tony Underwood to score the only try of Ireland's 13-12 win at Twickenham in 1994.

history. It was the first game in Fergus Slattery's long and effective international career and the first game in which Ireland had an official coach, the former hooker and Ireland and Lions captain Ronnie Dawson.

Munster confirmed their great reputation by taking a draw off the All Blacks in 1973, and Ireland were ever so close to going one better in the Test a few days later. Tom Grace just won a frantic chase to touch down an equalising last-minute try deep in the in-goal area and only centimetres in from touch. Barry McGann, faced with a horribly difficult conversion to give Ireland a first-ever win over New Zealand, struck his kick well, only to see it slide a fraction outside the post. The All Blacks were back in 1978, and it was left to Munster to claim that first Irish victory. Flanker Christy Cantillon got the try, Tony Ward kicked the goals and the whole team made tackle after tackle roared on by an ecstatic Thomond Park crowd. The final score was 12-0, and the pubs in Limerick had a busy night.

DAD'S ARMY

Ireland's great stars of the 1960s and 1970s had only a single outright home championship in 1974 to show for their efforts. By the early 1980s, Ireland's forwards in particular looked to be a little bit long in the tooth, but in 1982 they

proved it was too early to write them off as 'Dad's Army'. Moss Keane, Willie Duggan, Phil Orr and Fergus Slattery were still very much around to hustle and chase the opposition into errors, and Ollie Campbell was at the height of his kicking powers at fly-half. Campbell wrapped up the Triple Crown and championship with six penalties and a dropped goal against Scotland, but a win in Paris proved too much to ask, and the Grand Slam went astray. Most of the oldest faces had finally dropped out by the 1984-85 campaign, but Phil Orr was still around to enjoy a second Triple Crown under Ciaran Fitzgerald's leadership. This time Philip Matthews and Nigel Carr did the spoiling in the back row, and Keith Crossan, Trevor Ringland, Brendan Mullin and Michael Kiernan made up one of Ireland's finest-ever three-quarter lines.

STRUGGLES IN THE NINETIES

Unfortunately for Irish fans, the 1982 and 1985 successes were isolated incidents and have not been repeated, either in the Five Nations or in competition with the southern hemisphere. In fact, Ireland have increasingly struggled in world rugby ever since. In an attempt to lift standards, a proper All-Ireland Club Championship was set up in the 1990-91 season. This has certainly been a success as far as Munster clubs have been concerned. Cork Constitution took the title in the first year, and since then it has stayed firmly in Limerick, with Garryowen, Young Munster and Shannon each taking a turn.

Whatever improvements this increased domestic competition may have brought, they have not paid off in international success. Ireland have had a couple of upset wins over England in the 1990s, but little more of note. And with the opening of the professional era, more and more top Irish players are being signed by the richer English clubs. All four Irishmen in the original 1997 Lions party were exiles.

Irish rugby may face difficult times, but it also has much to offer. Protestant and Catholic and Unionist and Republican have played together and against each other amicably enough throughout Irish rugby's history. Irish rugby players have seldom seemed like peacemakers to their foreign opponents over the years, but the 1996 Peace International played between Ireland and the Barbarians in Dublin was a small but valuable token of the positive role that rugby continues to play in Ireland's troubled situation.

Below: *Munster's Mick Galwey (centre) and Peter Clohessy (left) in action against Welsh club Swansea in the 1995-96 Heineken European Cup. Munster won this pool game 17-13.*

CHAPTER SEVEN

· NEW ZEALAND ·

New Zealand on the move against South Africa in the final match of the 1996 Tri-Nations. Robin Brooke has the ball, supported by brother Zinzan, Sean Fitzpatrick and Olo Brown. Ian Jones (left) looks on, while Josh Kronfeld (on ground) finds time for a chat.

Various types of football were being played in New Zealand by the 1860s, but the first true game of rugby did not take place until 1870. A young New Zealander called Charles Monro, whose father was Speaker of the New Zealand House of Representatives, had been sent to school in England, where he played and learned the Rugby School rules. When he returned home to Nelson, at the northern tip of South Island, he introduced the locals to the game and quickly organised teams from the town football club, founded in 1868, and the local senior school, Nelson College. They played New Zealand's first Rugby School rules match on 14 May 1870, with the town winning by two goals to nil.

Although he was only 19, Monro did not leave it at that. He travelled across the Cook Strait to North Island, to New Zealand's capital Wellington, and contacted the local

football club to arrange a fixture. Monro also arranged transport for the Nelson team, no doubt using his official connections to hitch a ride on a government steam ship. On 12 September 1870, Nelson duly won New Zealand's first inter-club match by three goals to nil.

Besides Monro, other arrivals from England also played a significant part in establishing what was quickly to become New Zealand's national sport. One A. StG. Hamersley, who played in the first-ever international – Scotland *v* England in 1871 – was one of the leading lights in getting Canterbury rugby going in 1875. And an old boy of Rugby School called W.F. Neilson captained the Canterbury team on their first visit to Auckland in 1876. Canterbury was the first New Zealand provincial union to be formed, in 1879, although it was actually begun in Timaru in what is now the separate rugby province of South Canterbury.

Unions soon followed in what would come to be the traditional powerhouses of New Zealand rugby. The Wellington union was established the same year as Canterbury's, with Otago following in 1881 and Auckland in 1883. Football clubs in Otago were formed as early as 1872, but true rugby was first played in Otago in 1875 when a Dunedin clubs' select played an Auckland clubs' team, effectively Otago *v* Auckland. Otago won 9½-½. According to the scoring convention then locally in use a ½ point was awarded for a 'force-down' when a defending team touched down behind their own line!

Conditions in those days were rough and ready to say the least. Grounds were scarcely satisfactory and often hard to find. New Zealanders traditionally describe the playing field as the 'paddock', since that is what many of the early grounds were, often littered with stones and other hazards. One early report for a Wellington match records a ball being caught in telephone wires above the pitch.

Often there were problems even in getting a game started. Communications were slow and uncertain, with teams travelling up and down the coast by sea to matches. Equipment was also scanty. The first match in Wanganui, was organised in 1872 by A. Drew, who had been the Nelson captain in their first game against Wellington, but the game had to be delayed for two weeks until a ball had been obtained. Some sides routinely took their goal-posts with them to away games. More formal aspects of organisation could also be problematic. The Waikato union, now one of New Zealand's strongest, was formed and went out of existence three times from its first establishment in 1887, before being set up on its current basis in 1921.

The national New Zealand Rugby Football Union was formed in Wellington in 1892, with seven provinces joining. Again there was a difficulty, however. Canterbury, Otago and Southland did not affiliate at first, fearing that the new organisation would be overly dominated from Wellington. Within a few years, though, all three had joined.

MAORI RUGBY

One of the players in that first delayed game in Wanganui was called Wirihana and he is reputed to have been the first Maori to play in a rugby match. As rugby quickly spread

Below: *An all singing, all dancing occasion. The climax to the haka at the 1993 New Zealand v Scotland Test at Murrayfield. This Maori war dance is a familiar pre-match ceremony.*

■ NEW ZEALAND ■
■ RUGBY FOOTBALL UNION ■

National colours: black
Year founded: 1892
No. of clubs: 600
No. of provinces: 27
Oldest provincial union:
   Canterbury, 1879
No. of players: 50,000 adults,
   110,000 juniors
World Cup record: 1987
   winners; 1991 third; 1995
   runners-up

among the European, or *pakeha*, people in New Zealand it was also enthusiastically adopted by the Maoris. Since then, Maoris have made an outstanding contribution to the game in their own country and worldwide.

After New South Wales's first visit in 1882, tours by various teams to and from New Zealand soon became a regular feature of the game. One of the most celebrated early tours was by a mainly Maori team, the so-called New Zealand Natives, who visited Britain in 1888-89. Including games played in New Zealand before and after the trip, and 16 in Australia en route, they played an astonishing total of 107 matches in 14 months. They won 78 of these games, including an international against Ireland. They lost to England and Wales.

THE *HAKA* TRADITION

Only 22 of the 26-strong team were actually Maoris, although two of the four *pakeha* players were native-born New Zealanders. The tourists were very popular throughout Britain for their stylish play, but they surprised some of their hosts by performing a Maori war dance, or *haka*, before their matches, setting another tradition that Maori and All Black teams still follow. One of the great players of that Maori team was Tom Ellison, reputedly the first Maori to be called to the New Zealand Bar. Ellison later captained New Zealand and is also said to have invented the 2-3-2 scrummage formation that was an effective New Zealand trademark until the 1930s.

Since that first tour, Maori rugby has remained an important and valuable part of the New Zealand game, existing alongside the entirely integrated regular club and provincial set-up. The Maoris have toured abroad on a number of occasions since that first epic and have also traditionally played matches at home against major touring

teams, including the British Isles, France and South Africa. Maori encounters with the last-mentioned, however, have been controversial.

In 1921 the Maoris played the first Springbok side to visit New Zealand, losing 9-8. The game was rough and unpleasant, but was nothing compared with the scandal that followed when an offensive South African report on the match was published, recording Springbok disgust at being forced to play a non-white team. Although Maoris continued to play against South African teams in New Zealand, the New Zealand RFU shamefully agreed not to select any Maori players for the next three All Black tours to South Africa – in 1928, 1949 and 1960. Maori players were included for subsequent visits, but until the end of the apartheid era they had to be classed degradingly as 'honorary whites' – one example among many that gives the lie to those who claim that playing rugby in or against South Africa in those years was a sporting act entirely free from political connotations.

PROVINCIAL AND DOMESTIC RUGBY

The first inter-province match is usually said to have taken place in September 1871, when Wellington played a Nelson representative team. The first 'Otago' *v* 'Auckland' game noted earlier in this chapter took place in the course of an internal tour of New Zealand by Auckland in 1875, and a Canterbury select team similarly toured the country in 1876. As the provincial unions were established from 1879 through the 1880s and 1890s, regular inter-province matches began to take place.

New South Wales came to New Zealand on tour in 1882 and 1886, and the first British Isles team arrived in 1888. All these teams' matches were against provincial or other local select teams; there were no Tests. New South Wales won four matches and lost three in 1882, while the British team lost two of their matches in 1888. Taranaki scored the first success against the British, winning by a single try to nil, or 1-0 according to the contemporary scoring system. Auckland were the other winners.

Although provincial rugby was clearly flourishing in New Zealand before the end of the nineteenth century, there was no formal competition in existence. In 1901 the Governor-General of New Zealand, Lord Ranfurly, offered to donate a trophy for a provincial competition to the New Zealand RFU. The trophy was ordered from England, but when it arrived it was found to feature soccer goal-posts in its design. It was quickly altered. The trophy, which was also a shield rather than the expected cup, was officially named the Ranfurly Shield, but in New Zealand it is usually simply described as 'the Shield' or 'the Log'. The first recipients were Auckland, who had been the outstanding team in 1902, the trophy's inaugural season.

The Shield is a challenge trophy, with the holders defending it against various opponents in turn. The usual rule has been for matches to take place at the home ground of the holders, who retain the trophy in the event of a draw. The first challenge to Auckland was in 1904, when Wellington beat them 6-3. Since then various other teams have also given up the Shield to the first challengers, but the real highlights in Shield history have been the periods when one province has mounted a long run of successful defences.

AUCKLAND'S EPIC RUN

The longest run by far was the Auckland sequence of 61 defences from 1985 to 1993, before they finally succumbed to Waikato. But there have been several other series involving 20 or more defences over a period of several seasons. Auckland saw off 23 opponents between 1905 and 1913, while Hawke's Bay were in charge from 1923 to 1927 with 24 defences. That Hawke's Bay team featured such All Black greats as George Nepia, the superb Maori full-back, and the brothers Cyril and Maurice Brownlie in the forwards. Otago had a great run after World War II, defending 18 times from

1947 to 1950. This series included six games in 1949 when 11 Otago men were away with the All Blacks in South Africa. Vic Cavanagh was the Otago coach in those years, and he and his teams virtually invented the fast and aggressive rucking that is still at the heart of New Zealand rugby.

Before the Auckland marathon of the 1980s and 1990s the record of 25 defences was jointly held by Auckland (1960-63) and Canterbury (1982-85). Fittingly, the latter run came to an end when Canterbury agreed to meet Auckland for the 26th match, which could have established a new record. The game was a classic, Auckland running away to a 24-0 lead and Canterbury clawing back to a nail-biting 28-23 at the death. That win set Auckland on their way to their record, but appropriately they in turn gave Canterbury the chance to stop them in their 26th defence. Auckland also broke with tradition during their great run by playing some of their matches away from their stronghold at Eden Park.

Auckland's dominance through that era was so absolute, even when they played away from home, that plans were laid to change the format of the Shield

Below: *Auckland second five-eighth Lee Stensness takes off during the 1994 national championship final against North Harbour, which Auckland won 22-16.*

competition into a more conventional knockout. These plans have not yet come to fruition, and the three changes of titleholder in 1996 prove that the Ranfurly Shield still has the special competitive edge it has always had.

THE NATIONAL CHAMPIONSHIP

In 1976 the New Zealand RFU decided that the eight or ten Shield defences that took place in most years did not supply sufficient competition so they instituted a proper national championship, with all 27 unions competing in three league divisions. The Shield still retains its traditional appeal, but there is no doubt that the National Provincial Championship is now New Zealand's premier domestic competition.

■ EDEN PARK, AUCKLAND ■

Test series played in New Zealand are usually shared between several venues, but Eden Park in Auckland is now always the choice for the final and possibly deciding match. The ground also had the honour of being the venue for the first World Cup final in 1987.

Much of the Eden Park site was originally a lake, but the land was reclaimed in 1910. The ground's first Test was the second match of the 1921 series against the Springboks. South Africa won 9-5 with the decisive score being a long dropped goal by Gerhard Morkel. Crowd control was rather haphazard, however. Some of the spectators ran on to the field to congratulate Morkel by offering him a beer – which he drank.

Despite the ground's watery origins, conditions for that match and many others played there have been fine and dry. In 1975, however, there was the nearest thing yet to an underwater rugby international. Scotland were due to play the only Test of their 1975 tour when a torrential storm left most of the ground several centimetres under water. The game went ahead anyway, and New Zealand splashed to a 24-0 victory, but there were real fears that a player trapped at the bottom of a ruck might drown.

Other All Black home Tests are usually played at Athletic Park in Wellington, Carisbrook Park in Dunedin and Lancaster Park in Canterbury, but there is no doubt that Eden Park was host to New Zealand rugby's greatest day – the 1987 World Cup triumph.

Bay of Plenty, who have never won the Shield, were the first to celebrate, winning the national title in 1976. Auckland have been the dominant force in the competition, however, just as they have in the Shield in recent years. They have won the championship in 11 out of the 21 seasons to 1996. Other winners include Counties in 1979, with All Blacks Andy Dalton and Bruce Robertson to the fore. Manawatu were the winners in 1980, led by their powerful and aggressive forwards, including prop Gary Knight and flanker Mark Shaw. Otago in 1991 and Waikato in 1992 were the most recent sides to break the Auckland monopoly.

Besides domestic provincial matches there is also a long history of games between the New Zealand provinces and their counterparts in Australia and South Africa. This was put on a formal basis with the establishment of the Super 10 competition in 1993, which was succeeded by Super 12 in 1996. New Zealand's provinces also have a proud record in matches against international touring teams. Only the 1937 and 1981 Springboks and the 1971 Lions have come through a long tour with a perfect record in their provincial games.

NEW ZEALAND AND INTERNATIONAL RUGBY

However well the provinces may have played, the real measure of New Zealand rugby prowess has been the achievements of the national team, the All Blacks. New Zealand representative teams played a number of matches and two full internationals before the name All Blacks was coined. The first New Zealand team was selected for a visit to New South Wales in 1884. It was not a properly chosen side, but was made up of a set number of players from each of the four major unions. Nonetheless they had a successful trip, winning all eight of their games. There was no Test, since Australia did not then field a national team. The New Zealanders played in dark blue with a gold fern badge.

A properly representative New Zealand team went to New South Wales again in 1893. The side was captained by Tom Ellison, who was also the originator of the proposal that New Zealand should play in black with a silver fern emblem (although at first shorts were white). The first home New Zealand game was an 8-6 win over New South Wales in 1894. The development process was completed with New Zealand's first true international in 1903, a 22-3 win over Australia in Sydney that helped the tourists complete a perfect ten-match record. Since then there have been more than 100 New Zealand *v* Australia encounters.

That win in Australia was not enough to impress the game's traditional powers in the northern hemisphere, but they began to notice the emerging strength of New Zealand rugby when the 1904 British Isles touring team lost both Tests and drew one provincial match on the New Zealand leg of their trip. The opening scorer in the first Test of that pair, as he had been in the first game with Australia, was the great New Zealand full-back and wing Billy 'Carbine' Wallace, who was to amass 379 points in all matches for New Zealand, a record that stood for some 50 years.

In July 1905 the first New Zealand touring party to the northern hemisphere set off by boat for the long journey to Britain. When they arrived, reporters asked what colours the team played in and got the simple answer 'all black' – the nickname and the team colours have never changed since.

THE ORIGINALS

The 'Originals', as the 1905 side have become known, were also one of the most successful of All Black touring teams, winning 31 of their 32 matches in Britain. Their only loss was a 3-0 defeat by Wales, and as every New Zealander will still tell you their centre Bob Deans had a perfectly good try disallowed by a Scottish referee who was miles behind the play. The match against Scotland was the closest of the three other internationals against British sides, but was marred by an off-field dispute about the New Zealand players' expenses and the distribution of the gate money. The Originals went on to beat France 38-8 in Paris, and played a few successful games in California on their way home.

This tour and other results in the years before World War I suggested that New Zealand and South Africa had become the two strongest nations in world rugby. Australia

AGES, WEIGHTS, & HEIGHTS.							
BACKS.				**FORWARDS.**			
	Age.	st.	lbs	ft. in.			
W. Wallace	... 27	..12	0	..5 8	D. Gallaher (Capt.) 29 ..13 0..6 0
E. Harper	... 27	..12	7	..5 11	W. S. Glenn ... 27 ..12 12..5 11
E. Booth	... 26	..11	10	..5 7½	S. Casey ... 22 ..12 4..5 10
G. W. Smith	... 33	..11	12	..5 7	A. McDonald ... 22 ..13 0..5 10
H. Abbott	... 23	..13	0	..5 10½	W. Johnstone ... 23 ..13 6..6 0
F. Roberts	... 23	..12	4	..5 7	C. Seeling ... 22 ..13 7..6 0
R. Deans	... 21	..13	4	..6 0	G. Nicholson ... 26 ..13 10..6 3
J. Hunter	... 26	..11	8	..5 6	G. A. Tyler ... 26 ..13 0..5 10
S. Mynott	... 29	..11	9	..5 7	J. Corbett ... 25 ..13 9..5 11
W. Stead	... 28	..11	0	..5 9	F. Newton ... 23 ..15 0..6 0
G. Gillett	... 28	..13	0	..6 0	F. Glasgow ... 25 ..13 3..5 10
H. D. Thomson	... 24	..10	9	..5 8	J. O'Sullivan ... 22 ..13 7..5 10
R. McGregor	... 23	..11	3	..5 9	W. Mackrell ... 23 ..12 7..5 10
Manager—MR. DIXON.					W. Cunningham ... 29 ..14 6..5 11

Above: *A section from a tour programme for the 1905 All Blacks in Britain. In terms of size, the forwards would not look out of place in a modern international back division.*

won only two of 14 games against the All Blacks in this period. The 1908 'Lions' struggled in New Zealand, and the Springboks proved equally tough opponents for the British both at home and away. The first showdown between the All Blacks and the Springboks for the then mythical world championship was in New Zealand in 1921. That three-match series ended in a draw as did the return in South Africa in 1928.

Interspersed with these titanic struggles and the ongoing series with New South Wales and Australia were visits by the All Blacks to Europe and by the British Isles to

Below: *The 'Originals', who toured the northern hemisphere in 1905-06, still hold the New Zealand record for most points scored on an overseas tour – 868 in all matches.*

Above: *Wilson Whineray (right) leads the All Blacks out at Dunedin for the First Test against the 1959 Lions. Full-back Don Clarke kicked six penalties in an 18-17 New Zealand win.*

New Zealand. Tours by individual northern hemisphere countries did not come until much later. France did not tour New Zealand until 1961, and in 1963 England became the first of the four home unions to visit.

THE INVINCIBLES

The 1924-25 All Blacks went one better than their predecessors in Britain and France, winning all 30 of their games. Full-back George Nepia was one of the stars and amazingly he played in every match. Only two things spoiled an otherwise perfect tour. Cyril Brownlie was sent off during the 17-11 win over England. By all accounts he deserved it, but several other players on both sides could easily have joined him. The second shortcoming was that the 'Invincibles', as Cliff Porter's team were soon named, did not play Scotland because of an organisational squabble and so had no chance of recording a Grand Slam. This was especially unfortunate since it might have been quite a match. Scotland won a Grand Slam of their own in the Five Nations later that season.

Later All Black teams naturally struggled to match the 100 per cent record of the Invincibles. The All Blacks have twice won all four Tests of a home series with the Lions – in 1966 and 1983 – and England, Wales and France each lost all

of their Tests in New Zealand in various visits in the 1960s. On tours to the northern hemisphere, meanwhile, perfection continued to be elusive. Occasional games were lost against club and provincial teams, while Wales and England won against the Third All Blacks in 1935-36, and Wales beat the Fourth All Blacks in 1953-54.

THE FIFTH ALL BLACKS

Wilson Whineray's Fifth All Blacks got agonisingly close to the long-awaited Grand Slam in 1963-64. They lost 3-0 early in their tour to Newport in Wales but won the Irish, Welsh and English international matches. Scotland, who have never beaten the All Blacks, stood firm in Edinburgh. There were near misses by both sides in a match that ended in a nil-all draw. The All Blacks duly rounded off their tour with a win in France and a spectacular 36-3 success in the finale against the Barbarians.

One unusual feature of the Barbarians match was that a member of the All Black party actually played, and even scored, against his own team. Prop Ian Clarke, brother of goal-kicking full-back Don, was the first All Black to visit Britain on two full-length tours and so was offered Barbarians selection when he did not make the New Zealand line-up. Early in the match he claimed a mark from a drop-out and knocked over a very neat dropped goal, the only points the Barbarians scored that day.

Brian Lochore's 1967 team are reckoned by many good judges to have been one of the finest All Black line-ups ever. They had an immensely powerful pack, but they did not allow that to dominate their tactics. Their backs got plenty of chances and scored plenty of tries, too. One low point of the tour was the sending-off of Colin Meads in the Scotland game. There was only one draw (with East Wales) to spoil the perfect record, which included four Test wins. Frustratingly there was no possibility of a Grand Slam, since the scheduled Ireland game had to be cancelled.

The 1972-73 tour was troubled by various off-the-field incidents. The All Blacks also suffered five defeats, but won against Wales, Scotland and England. The tourists could manage only a 10-10 draw against Ireland in Dublin, with fly-half Barry McGann just missing the conversion of the equalising Irish try with only a few minutes to go. One of the tour games that the All Blacks lost was the finale against the Barbarians, that special match that opened with the classic try begun by Phil Bennett deep in his own 22 and finished by Gareth Edwards's dive into the corner.

The long-awaited Grand Slam of wins over the four home unions was finally achieved in 1978. Flanker Graham Mourie led the team. Mourie was a mobile and intelligent player and, in a highly distinguished field, ranks as one of New Zealand's finest captains ever. The final match of the four was at a drenched Murrayfield. Scotland were three points down but pressing hard towards the end of the game when a dropped-goal attempt that could have gained a draw was charged down. New Zealand hacked the ball to the other end, Bruce Robertson won the chase and his try was converted to give the All Blacks a welcome 18-9 win.

Future All Blacks may not get the chance to equal the 1978 Grand Slam, since tours now tend to be shorter; indeed they were already becoming shorter by the 1970s. That fact, combined with other, more recent changes in the game, makes it unlikely that tours will again include a complete programme against all four home unions – either with or without an additional game against France.

IN THE WORLD CUP ERA

International rugby in the 1980s and 1990s has of course been dominated by the World Cups, but tours in both directions, although shorter than the traditional epics, have continued, with England being the only British Isles country to pick up even an occasional win. Scotland came close to their first success against the All Blacks in the second game of a two-match series in New Zealand in 1990, only to be foiled principally by the immaculate goal-kicking of Grant Fox. The Lions, too, lost their latest Test series in New Zealand in 1993, and in fact the most consistent northern hemisphere success against the All Blacks in recent years has been achieved by France. Many France *v* New Zealand games have been played in an atmosphere of the fiercest commitment. The two-match series in France in 1986 and 1995 were both shared, but in 1994 France did the unthinkable – they won both Tests down under to join the select group of teams to have won a series in New Zealand.

The best way to sum up All Black rugby is to say that in the table of wins and losses they are on a par with South Africa (in fact exactly equal at the time of writing), but against every other rugby nation the All Blacks are miles ahead. There sometimes seems to be a special spirit and determination that the men in black pull on along with their jerseys. One thing is sure in rugby's uncertain future – it will always take a very special effort to beat an All Black team.

Below: *All Black half-back Jon Preston strikes an acrobatic pose during New Zealand's 30-13 defeat of the 1993 British Lions in the deciding Third Test at Eden Park.*

CHAPTER EIGHT

· SCOTLAND ·

The supremely gifted Gregor Townsend takes off during Scotland's memorable 19-14 Five Nations victory over France at Murrayfield in 1996. Michael Dods, brother of 1984 Grand Slam full-back Peter, scored all Scotland's points, including two tries.

Historians of Scottish rugby will quickly tell you that England has no monopoly of involvement in the old-style informal town or school games that preceded the creation of true rugby in the nineteenth century. There are numerous Scottish historical references, going back as far as 1424, to football being played and often banned because of the public disorder it created or because it interfered with Sunday worship. Games were traditionally played in several of the Border towns that are now at the heart of Scottish rugby, and various schools, notably those for the sons of the better-off in Edinburgh, also had their own forms of football by the mid-nineteenth century.

One of the most famous early matches was a game organised near Selkirk in 1815 by the writer Sir Walter Scott. There were evidently several hundred players, and at one point one of those involved somehow worked the ball out of a maul and threw it to a noted runner who was standing some distance off so that he could sprint with it towards goal. It would be stretching a point to claim this as an early example of the 'distinctive feature of the Rugby game' because rules were so informal that the speedy 'winger' was ridden down by a mounted spectator – although this annoyed the crowd so much that the horseman had to make his escape. Handling and carrying, however, did feature in various of the games played by school and university students. The High School of Edinburgh certainly had these aspects in its football games by about 1810.

Although the general principles of the handling game were therefore widely familiar before the 1850s, direct connections with the Rugby School form of football in that decade took the development further. Schoolmasters who had learned the game during studies at Oxford University and boys who had had part of their education in England moved to Edinburgh and brought their knowledge of the Rugby laws to the schools there.

THE FIRST GAMES

Merchiston School and Edinburgh Academy were major pioneers, and former pupils of the Academy formed the first adult club, Edinburgh Academicals, in January 1858. The club's constitution specifically stated that it would play according to the Rugby School rules. When they formed, the Academicals were in the process of winning a 25-a-side match against Edinburgh University, which was played for the best of seven goals over four Saturdays in December 1857 and January 1858. Although various rugby-like games had gone before, this can perhaps be counted as Scotland's first true rugby match. There is no doubt which is Scotland's, and the world's, oldest rugby rivalry, for on 11 December 1858 Merchiston School played Edinburgh Academy, a fixture that still takes place annually.

Other adult clubs were soon formed in the cities of Glasgow and Edinburgh and in some smaller towns, and schools and the universities in both cities and in St Andrews also took up the game in the 1860s. Several of these clubs got together in 1868 to produce a standard set of laws, known as the Green Book. The Green Book probably provided the laws used in the first international that was shortly to follow, although unfortunately no copy of the work has survived to the present day.

CHALLENGING ENGLAND

The Football Association staged an England *v* Scotland soccer international in London in 1870, but all the Scotland players were London residents, and some of their Scottish connections were highly tenuous. Scottish rugby men thought this was unsatisfactory, especially since there were only four Association clubs in Scotland at that time, so in December 1870 a group of them had a letter published in a London sporting newspaper challenging 'any team selected from the whole of England, to play us a match, twenty-a-side, Rugby rules, either in Edinburgh or Glasgow on any day during the present season…we can promise England a hearty welcome and a first-rate match.'

The challenge was taken up by leading members of the Blackheath club in London, and it helped inspire them to form England's Rugby Football Union the next month. The first international duly took place on 27 March 1871 at the Edinburgh Academicals ground in Raeburn Place. England were disappointed to discover that the pitch was very narrow (only about 50 metres/55 yards wide), since they

thought that their backs had more pace, and became even more unhappy at the way Scotland obtained what proved to be the winning score. Scotland won by one goal and a try to a try. The Scottish goal was a conversion kicked following the 1871 equivalent of a pushover try from a five-metre scrum, with the English claiming that Scotland had pushed before the ball had been grounded (allowing the ball to touch the ground was the requirement in those days). Despite this dispute, relations between the two sides must have been reasonably amicable, for several of the Scottish clubs quickly joined the Rugby Football Union, and a return match was arranged for London the next year.

ADMINISTERING THE GAME

An independent Scottish Football Union (SFU) was formed in 1873. (It was renamed the Scottish Rugby Union – SRU – in 1924.) The founder members were six Glasgow and Edinburgh clubs, all dominated by former pupils of the various private schools and by other similarly prosperous men. A second group soon affiliated that was made up of various town clubs from the Border area. The Langholm, Hawick, Gala, Kelso and Melrose clubs were all established in the 1870s and, unlike the city clubs, drew their players and supporters from all classes in their respective towns. For many years, the Scottish game's administrators remained drawn from the city and former pupils' clubs and rather tended to look down on the Borderers. The first Border player was not capped until 1890, when Adam Dalgleish of Gala was selected for the Wales match. The first Border captain of Scotland was T.M. Scott of Hawick in 1900.

England were Scotland's only opponents until 1877, when the first game against Ireland was played in Belfast and easily won by the Scots. This was the first 15-a-side

▪ SCOTTISH RUGBY UNION ▪

National colours: dark blue
Year founded: 1873 (as Scottish Football Union)
No. of clubs: 283
Oldest club: Edinburgh Academicals, 1858
No. of players: 13,000 adults/32,000 juniors
World Cup record: 1987 quarter-finals; 1991 fourth; 1995 quarter-finals

SCOTTISH RUGBY UNION

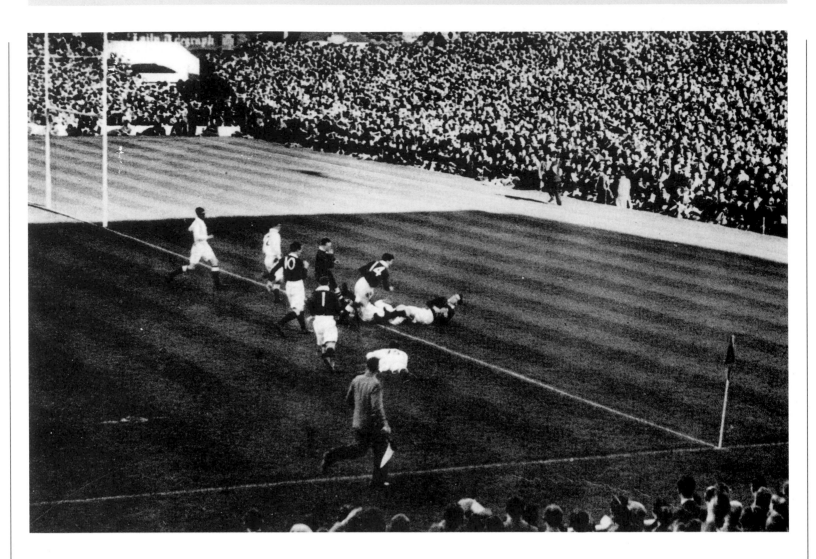

Above: *W.N. Renwick scores Scotland's first try of the 1938 Calcutta Cup game at Twickenham. That day's 21-16 win over England gave the Scots the championship and Triple Crown.*

match Scotland played, although the England *v* Ireland game earlier that season was the first such international. The first Scotland *v* Wales game was in 1883 and the first Scotland *v* France match in 1910. In each case Scotland was the last of the established nations to add the newcomer to the fixture list. This was only one respect in which the Scottish rugby authorities were perhaps the most conservative of any nation (which is saying something). Both then and for many years to come, they were resistant to change and especially fierce in their persecution of the slightest hint of professionalism.

In the early years, the Scottish administrators were extremely suspicious of the Border clubs. The Melrose club invented sevens in 1883, and their tournament was joined on the rugby calendar by others at Gala in 1884 and Hawick in 1885. The union quickly put a stop to prizes being given to tournament winners and were always very vigilant regarding travelling expenses and similar matters. There were also several instances in the 1880s and 1890s when individual Border players and even whole clubs were suspended for rough play and for abusive behaviour by players and spectators towards referees.

The union also found time to quarrel with the other home nations on a number of occasions. Contested rulings on the laws of the game brought various disputes and several cancelled internationals, so Scotland, Ireland and Wales formed an International Board in 1887 to rule on these matters. They then refused to play England for two seasons because the English would not join too. Later, in the 1890s, there was a fierce quarrel with Wales because of a testimonial payment raised for retiring Welsh star Arthur Gould. And following the first All Black tour in 1905-06, the Scottish union was horrified to learn that the New Zealand players had been paid three shillings (15 pence) a day in expenses. The Scots had the International Board make a ruling that such an abomination must not occur again.

A QUESTION OF NUMBERS

Hidebound attitudes also made themselves apparent in on-field matters. For example, Scotland did not wear numbered jerseys until 1933. The reasoning was that the game should be for players and that numbering was only pandering to the unnecessary and intrusive involvement of spectators. At an international in the late 1920s, King George V asked James Aikman Smith, virtual dictator in Scottish rugby from 1890 until the early 1930s, why numbers were not worn. 'This is a rugby match, not a cattle auction,' Aikman Smith rudely replied. Scotland also persisted with the 3-2-3 scrummage formation for many years after every other country had switched to 3-4-1. The old style was better suited to the traditional Scottish tactic of wheeling the scrum and breaking away with the ball at the feet, while the crowd encouraged their team with the equally traditional cry of 'Feet, Scotland, Feet.'

CLUB AND DISTRICT RUGBY

At club level there was more of a pioneering spirit. Langholm played the first 'international' club match against the northern English club Carlisle in 1873, the game being abandoned with no score when it got dark. To dispel such gloom, Melrose, Hawick and Kelso each experimented with floodlit matches in 1879. Perhaps because the Border clubs did not always see eye to eye with the authorities, five of them were independent minded enough to establish an annual league competition in 1901-02. The original five – Hawick, Gala, Jed-Forest, Langholm and Melrose – were

joined by Kelso and Selkirk in 1912, and the format has not changed since, with the fixtures being maintained even though the clubs are now in different divisions of the national leagues. The rugby authorities are said to have been generally disapproving of the Border League from the start, so it is rather surprising that the Scottish union contributed part of the cost of the trophy when one was purchased for the 1906-07 season.

In the early days the union certainly did not support the idea of a national club competition, but fans and the press were soon speculating on who the national champions might be. Such predictions were being made as far back as the 1860s, and from the 1890s newspapers took to publishing a table of 30 or so leading clubs and their percentage of success in fixtures against the others. It was far from scientific, since none of the clubs had fixtures against all the others, and occasionally this led to a 'wrong' result, with a clearly middle-of-the-road team ending up with the best record and the title. But one consolation for the clubs having a poor season was that at least they would not be relegated.

Below: *George 'Doddie' Weir on the rampage for Melrose against Gala in a 1994 national league game. Weir joined Newcastle in 1996-97 and was selected for the 1997 Lions tour.*

▪ MURRAYFIELD ▪

Scotland's was the first national rugby union to own its home ground. Inverleith in Edinburgh was used for all Scotland's home games from 1899 to the start of 1925, apart from the 6-0 win over South Africa in 1906. By the 1920s, the capacity at Inverleith was clearly inadequate, and in 1922 the SFU bought land at Murrayfield, formerly used by the Edinburgh Polo Club, and set about building a ground.

The stadium was ready for the final international of the 1924-25 season, a match against England with a Scotland Grand Slam beckoning. The game was fast and exciting with Scotland coming back from 11-5 down to win 14-11 with a late dropped goal by fly-half Herbert Waddell.

For the modern generation of Scottish fans, Murrayfield's best day came in 1990 when England were once again the opponents. This time both sides had the chance of a Grand Slam, and England were overwhelming favourites. But from the moment that Scottish captain David Sole led his men slowly out onto the field it was clear that they meant business. England were knocked out of their stride early on, lost their tactical pattern, and the Scots held on to win 13-7 and take the full house of Calcutta Cup, Triple Crown and Grand Slam.

Murrayfield has been totally rebuilt in recent years as a fully modern stadium, but for almost 40 years one aspect of the facilities set a trend that many other sports grounds have taken a long time to catch up with. Various matches had to be postponed over the years because of hard frosts, but from the summer of 1959 this became a thing of the past at Murrayfield when the famous 'electric blanket' was laid. This network of cables under the pitch kept the ground playable whatever the weather and has enabled numerous games to go ahead that would otherwise certainly have been cancelled.

This cosy system was all very well, but by the 1950s it was clearly failing to give leading players the competition they required to develop their skills. For many years before this, the various Scottish districts had fielded combined sides on occasion, such as against major touring teams (a nil-all draw with the 1931 Springboks was one notable South of Scotland result). In 1953-54 this practice was put on a formal basis with the creation of an Inter-District Championship. There were four participating teams until 1970, when a Scottish Exiles team joined the competition. Edinburgh won the first title, in 1954; South of Scotland the second – and those two sides have generally been the strongest up to the present day, with only an occasional success by Glasgow, North and Midlands, or the Exiles.

Scottish rugby lived up to its conservative reputation in 1971, when there was a unanimous vote against introducing official national club leagues. The decision was nonetheless reversed the next year, and leagues were introduced from 1973-74, making Scotland the innovators among the home unions by over a decade. Hawick were the champions for the first five seasons, and there have been only three years since then when the title has strayed outside the Borders. Heriots and Boroughmuir have each taken the crown to Edinburgh, and the third intruders into the Border monopoly were Stirling County. When the leagues started, Stirling were down in the lower reaches – in Division 7 in 1976 – but they were successively promoted, eventually reaching the top division in 1989 and taking the championship in 1995. This remarkable rise to fame is probably unique in world rugby and was accomplished not by chequebook recruiting but by committed club officers and coaches determined to progress by nurturing local talent and enthusiasm – a lesson perhaps for clubs and players everywhere.

The range of club and district competitions has been expanded still further in recent years. The first national cup competition was held in 1996, when Hawick took the title in a closely contested final with Watsonians, and in 1996-97 Scottish districts participated in the second staging of the Heineken European Cup. All were eliminated in the pool stages, reinforcing long-held fears of low standards in the Scottish domestic game. Some clubs, however, saw another problem. Led by Melrose, league champions in 1996 and 1997, these argued that Scottish rugby would be better represented in the European competition by clubs, since these were better equipped to generate the loyalty and cohesion needed to make a creditable showing. Whether this view prevails or not, Scottish domestic rugby obviously faces many problems raising the finance necessary in the professional era from the limited support it enjoys in a soccer-mad country.

THE INTERNATIONAL SCENE

The Calcutta Cup has been the prize for the annual Scotland v England match since 1879, and if reports of the first game are accurate it was as fiercely contested and enthusiastically supported as Scotland v England matches are today. The 1879 match, played in Edinburgh, was a draw, with a

Scotland dropped goal equalled in the values of the time by a converted English try. An English player was roundly booed for cowardice because he deliberately stepped behind his own line to touch down when in difficulty. Scotland full-back Bill MacLagan, who went on to be 'Lions' captain in 1891, was cheered for beginning counterattacks several times in similar situations and for his powerful tackling.

Unfortunately for Scottish fans England are comfortably ahead in matches won in the long rivalry. Ireland are now the only major opponent against whom Scotland have a positive record overall. Nonetheless Scotland have had 13 outright and eight shared wins in the Five Nations tournament over the years, so there has been plenty for the fans to cheer about, with the Grand Slams in 1925, 1984 and 1990 at the top of the list.

THE OXFORD 'SCOTS'

By all accounts the 1925 Grand Slam was the most spectacular of the three, with the stars of the team being the Oxford University three-quarter line of Ian Smith, Phil Macpherson (who missed the Ireland game but was captain in the other three), George Aitken and Johnnie Wallace. Scotland scored 17 tries in the four games, with wingers Wallace and Smith getting 14 between them. Aitken had captained the All Blacks in two games against the Springboks in 1921, Wallace would be back in Britain in 1927-28 as captain of the Australian Waratahs and Smith had been born in Australia, although his Scottish parents had brought him home soon after. Then as now, Scotland were quick to search out players with Scottish connections, especially to fill the tight five positions in the scrum, where they have often been weakest.

While the 1920s were particularly good for Scottish rugby, Scotland had a reasonable share of success in every decade until World War II. After the war it was a different story. From 1946-47 to the 1984 Grand Slam, Scotland won only one championship, a shared title with Wales in 1964, and there were sequences of very poor results in the 1950s, when 17 consecutive Tests were lost between 1951 and 1955. The 1970s were also a unsuccessful decade for the Scots.

Left: *The Oxford University three-quarter line that played* en bloc *for Scotland in the 1925 Grand Slam season. From the left, Johnnie Wallace (New College and Sydney, NSW), George Aitken (St John's College and New Zealand), Phil Macpherson (Oriel College) and Ian Smith (Brasenose College). Macpherson was injured for the Ireland v Scotland game in Dublin and was replaced by J.C. Dykes.*

Above: *Ian Paxton finds Jim Calder during Scotland's 21-12 win over France at Murrayfield in 1984. John Rutherford (No 10), Roy Laidlaw (No 9) and David Leslie provide back-up.*

There was some light amid the gloom, however. Even though the clubs briefly turned down the idea of national leagues in 1971, that year did see one notable innovation when the SRU finally admitted the necessity of coaching at the top level. Old ideas died hard, though, for the old guard insisted that Bill Dickinson, who got the job and did it well, was not a coach at all but merely an 'adviser to the captain'. It took a while for such foolishness to be swept away finally and for the increased competitiveness of the league system to feed through into increased national success.

The long-awaited breakthrough came in 1984. Scotland had fine away wins in Cardiff and Dublin and a comfortable home success in the Calcutta Cup game. But France had looked more impressive in their three wins and were favourites for the decider, even though it was to be played at Murrayfield. In the first half France were on top but could not build a significant lead. Scotland spoiled effectively, in the Frenchmen's eyes bending the laws far more often than the referee penalised them, and in the second half Scotland took hold of the game as French discipline fell apart. Gala prop Jim Aitken was the skipper, and joining him in a formidable front row were Colin Deans and Ian Milne, but many would say that half-backs Roy Laidlaw and John Rutherford were the real inspirations of the success.

Since then Scotland have had mixed results in early season matches against touring sides but have generally pulled themselves together to look fit and well prepared when it has come to the Five Nations. Championships have still been thin on the ground, with Scotland's last win at Twickenham being back in 1983, and the 1995 success in Paris now confirmed as Scotland's only win at the Parc des Princes (the stadium closed in 1997). The glorious exception, when it all worked out just right, was 1990.

Remarkably that season's matches led to the first occasion on which Scotland and England met on the final weekend with both having the chance of a Grand Slam. Scotland had beaten France comfortably at Murrayfield but had looked shaky in their two away wins against Wales and Ireland, whereas England had looked in magnificent form throughout, with a record score against Wales and a devastating display of exciting rugby in Paris. The pundits gave Scotland little chance but, roared on by the crowd, they showed their commitment from the start and established an early lead. They kept in front to half-time with some inspired defending and judicious scrummage collapses, and after Tony Stanger pinched a try at the start of the second half England never really looked like catching up.

AGAINST THE SOUTHERN HEMISPHERE

The Maoris in 1888 were the first overseas team to play in Scotland. They played only one game, however, beating Hawick by a goal to a try. Since Hawick were a Border club, some concession was made to the needs of the spectators, with players being identified in the programme – not by numbers of course, but by the colour of the garters with which they kept their stockings up.

Scotland have never beaten the full All Blacks team, but have had two draws with them at Murrayfield in 1964 and 1983. Both games were played in very poor weather, and rather surprisingly those who saw both matches generally say that the 0-0 game in 1964 was a better one than the 25-25 in 1983. Probably the closest that Scotland came to landing that first elusive success against New Zealand was when the 1990 Scottish Grand Slam team went on tour. They had no answer to the New Zealand line-out supremacy in the First Test in Dunedin but were clearly the better side in the Second in Auckland. But too many errors and infringements in the last quarter gave Grant Fox just enough chances to secure a 21-18 New Zealand win.

Scotland were the first of the home nations to mount a short tour of a major southern hemisphere country, going to South Africa in 1960. They did not quite get things right, however, for the Test was scheduled as the first game. Scotland lost that one 18-10 but have quite a good record against the Springboks overall, with wins in 1906, 1965 and 1969. In 1951, however, during that horrible run of 17 defeats, the Springboks coasted to a 44-0 walkover at Murrayfield. It was reportedly after this match that a bitter Scottish fan first used the now-famous condemnation of a woeful performance, '…and they were lucky to get nil.'

Scotland's recent competitiveness in the Five Nations has been reflected by solid performances in the World Cup tournaments. Scotland have certainly won every game that they were expected to and have played some fine rugby in the process. There have been real thrillers in 1987 and 1995 against France, and the 28-6 defeat of Western Samoa in 1991 was probably a finer performance than is generally credited. But slightly disappointingly Scotland have not yet found the inspiration to win that extra unexpected game. In the professional era, with southern hemisphere rugby striding ahead and England and France with massively greater player and financial resources, Scotland fans must worry that even the occasional underdog win against the really big guns will be increasingly difficult to achieve.

Below: *A moment to break English hearts. A delighted Tony Stanger (facing No 4 Chris Gray) has scored for Scotland in the 1990 Grand Slam decider at Murrayfield.*

CHAPTER NINE

· SOUTH AFRICA ·

South Africa skipper François Pienaar hoists the Webb Ellis Trophy after his side had beaten New Zealand 15-12 in 1995's cliffhanging World Cup final. The Springboks had triumphed in front of their home crowd and a delighted President Mandela (left).

August 23, 1862, is usually given as the day that South African rugby began. The place was Green Point Common in Cape Town and the match was Civilians *v* Military. It is not absolutely certain whether this game can really be called rugby, or whether it was some other type of football, but since the player who kicked off for Civilians at the start of the match was Adriaan van der Byl, who had captained Merchiston School in one of Scotland's first games four years previously, it is quite likely that something close to Rugby School rules was used.

Other types of football were also beginning to be played in South Africa around this time. In 1861, Canon G. Ogilvie was appointed Principal of Diocesan College in Cape Town and began encouraging his students to play football based on the version of the game established by Winchester College in England, which was similar to, but slightly different from, the Rugby School game. This form of football became quite popular in the Cape Town area under Ogilvie's influence and became known as 'Gog's game' from the three letters that were evidently the only legible parts of Ogilvie's signature.

THE FIRST CLUBS

Clubs playing Gog's game or other hybrid types of football soon appeared. The Swellendam club may have been formed in 1865 or even before, but the evidence is inconclusive. The oldest club for which there is definite proof is Hamilton, formed in 1875 to play Gog's game. Villagers followed later in 1875 or early in 1876 and played a scoreless draw against Hamilton on 1 July 1876. Hamilton switched over to playing rugby in 1878, probably at the suggestion of a new member of the club that year, W.H.

Milton, who had been capped by England in 1874 and 1875. Villagers swopped to rugby in 1879, and other clubs in the Cape Town area quickly came into existence, notably Stellenbosch University in 1882 and South African College (later known as University of Cape Town) in 1883.

The Hamilton club called a meeting with five others from the Cape Town area in May 1883 to form the Western Province Rugby Union, the first provincial union in the country. Twelve teams played in the first Western Province club tournament the same season, with Hamilton winning the title. A Cape Town Clubs select (effectively a Western Province team) played and beat a team from the diamond-mining town of Kimberley in 1884. The Griqualand West union, based in Kimberley, was founded in 1886, with Eastern Province following in 1888 and Transvaal in 1889. Rugby had been played in Transvaal between Johannesburg and Pretoria teams since at least 1886, with five clubs making up the Transvaal union initially. The first Transvaal championship was played in 1889, Pretoria having a one try to nil victory over Pirates in the final. A more important advance that also took place in 1889 was the formation of the South African Rugby Board (SARB). The original four provinces then went on to hold a tournament in Kimberley that same year, with Western Province coming out winners.

NEWLANDS

The Western Province union took another big step forward in 1889 when it bought the lease to a ground at Newlands, just outside Cape Town. In other respects things were not quite so slick, however. After the Western Province team had been selected for the second inter-provincial tournament in 1892, the first in which the Currie Cup was actually at stake, an announcement was placed in the Cape Times newspaper, 'Members of the team who find it convenient are requested to go to Newlands by the 4.10 p.m. train from town this afternoon to indulge in practice.' There is no record of how many turned up.

The first major touring team to visit South Africa were a British Isles XV, who toured in 1891. Although the party was far from being composed of the best British players, it showed that South African rugby had a lot to learn at that early stage. The 'Lions' won all their 20 games and conceded only one point in all matches – from a try (worth only a single point then) in the first game, against a Cape Clubs XV. The scorer was Charles 'Hasie' Versfeld, one of four brothers playing against the 'Lions' that day. Hasie's brother Loftus (R.L.O. Versfeld) was in the side. He had had a hand in establishing both the Eastern Province and the Transvaal unions. It is after him that the stadium in Pretoria is named.

The three Tests against the 1891 'Lions' were South Africa's first – all were lost. One feature of the series never likely to be repeated was that Herbert Castens captained South Africa in the First Test, did not play in the Second, but was back for the Third – as referee.

THE CURRIE CUP

The British team had been given a cup by a shipping tycoon called Donald Currie to present to the team that gave them their hardest game. Griqualand West duly won the prize after their 3-0 defeat by the British and passed the cup on, as intended, for use as South Africa's inter-provincial trophy. The first few Currie Cups were all competed for at irregular intervals in a tournament based in a single centre. Later, partly because of continuing travel difficulties, the trophy was usually contested every other year, with additional breaks in seasons when South Africa was hosting an incoming Lions or All Blacks tour. The Currie Cup competition has been held annually only since 1968. Western Province won the first six titles and continued to dominate the scene until World War II. For years, old-timers would insist that the finest team they had ever seen was the 1914 Western Province side, captained by W.H. 'Boy' Morkel.

Although the South Africans learned quickly from that first British tour, they were still generally outclassed by the next British side to tour in 1896. The British won 19 out of 21 games. The one game that was drawn was against Western Province, and that result seems to have been not so much a credit to the Western Province team as owed to the fact that most of their opponents had had too much to drink at the pre-match lunch. There was genuine cause for celebration, however, when South Africa claimed their first international win in the Fourth Test, even if the British protested furiously

■ SOUTH AFRICAN RUGBY UNION ■

National colours: green and gold
Year founded: 1889 (as South African Rugby Board)
No. of clubs: 913
Oldest club: Hamilton, 1875
No. of players: 46,000 adults/194,000 juniors
World Cup record: 1987 & 1991 did not compete; 1995 champions

SA RUGBY

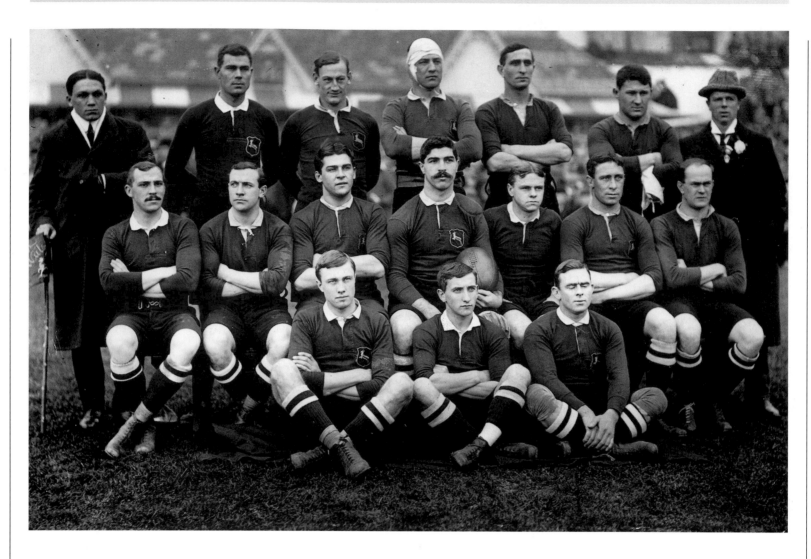

Above: The 1906 Springboks who beat Wales 11-0. Paul Roos is seated, with ball; Arthur Marsberg is standing third from left; and Bob Loubser is second from left in the middle row.

that the South African try should have been disallowed and that the referee had been biased against their scrummaging methods throughout.

GREEN IS THE COLOUR

South Africa's captain that day was Barry Heatlie, and he arranged for his team to wear jerseys from the Old Diocesan club. Heatlie played in the First and Third Tests against the 1903 British team as well, being reinstated as captain for the second of these games. For this match he once again supplied the team with jerseys from the Old Diocesans, even though that club was defunct by then. Once again South Africa won, to take the series 1-0 after the first two matches had been drawn. Perhaps because South Africa's sole victories to date had been recorded in Old Diocesan green, this was the colour officially chosen by the SARB in 1906 for the national team's jerseys. Colours of shorts, socks and jersey collars have varied over the years, but gold collars, green socks and white shorts have been the rule since 1949.

The green shirts were worn by the first South African team to tour overseas, who set off for Britain shortly after the decision on the colours was taken. The badge on the shirts showed a leaping springbok, and captain Paul Roos told the British press on arrival that the team wished to be known under this name, which, of course, has stuck ever since. It was a successful trip, with 25 of the 28 matches won and one drawn. Full-back Arthur Marsberg and wing J.A. 'Bob' Loubser, who scored 21 tries in his 24 games, were probably the stars. Many of the matches were played in terrible weather, including both the defeats. Ireland, Wales, England and a France XV were all beaten, but only after Scotland had won the first of the internationals. That game was played on a sodden Hampden Park in Glasgow. The Scottish forwards were far too experienced in the mud and stuck successfully to their traditional foot rush attacks while the South Africans fumbled their attempts at handling moves. The other loss, late on in the trip, was in similar conditions against the Cardiff club.

A series win for the Springboks over the 1910 'Lions' confirmed the strength of South African rugby, and the 1912-13 Springboks proved equally powerful on their tour of Britain and France. They lost three of the club and provincial games, with Newport being presented with the springbok head trophy that every South African party gives to the first team to beat them, but all five internationals were won. The Springboks gained an emphatic 16-0 revenge for the 1906 defeat by Scotland and did even better against Ireland, the 38-0 result being a record score for a major international for many years to come.

New Zealand had been similarly impressive in their contacts with the British teams before World War I. The long rivalry between the Springboks and All Blacks began in earnest after the war, when South Africa visited New Zealand in 1921. That series was drawn, as was the return in South Africa in 1928, but South Africa got their noses in front with a 2-1 series victory in New Zealand in 1937. South Africa also first played in Australia in 1921, with Australia making the return trip in 1933. This rivalry has produced many fiercely contested games, with South Africa clearly having the upper hand until the 1990s.

MR MARK, BENNIE AND DANIE

Three personalities came to dominate South African rugby in the inter-war years: A.F. Markötter, Bennie Osler and Danie Craven. August Friedrich Markötter never played for South Africa but did captain the first South African provincial team to beat a major touring side – a Western Province Country XV v the 1903 'Lions' – before he had to give up playing because of a cricket injury. Known simply as 'Oubaas Mark' (or 'Mr Mark' in English) he was Springbok coach and selector from 1921 to 1938. There were always other selectors on the panel, but Mr Mark was effectively a law unto himself, time and again plucking players out of third-team obscurity, perhaps ordering them to change playing positions, and then literally kicking them up the backside regularly until suddenly they blossomed into Springbok stars.

Bennie Osler first made his name with the University of Cape Town in the early 1920s and in 1924 made the first of his 17 consecutive Springbok appearances, against the 'Lions'. Osler was a skilled runner and distributor of the ball, but he is remembered first of all as one of the greatest of the kicking fly-halves, expert at gaining the big South African forwards the field positions they needed to grind their opponents down. Above all, Osler was a winner. He never played in a losing Test series, and Western Province and the various clubs he played for were all dominant in their respective competitions during his time.

Danie Craven was one who benefited greatly from Markötter's patronage and advice, owing both his Stellenbosch debut and Springbok selection in 1931 to Mr Mark's advocacy. Craven is best known as a scrum-half, but he was an astonishingly versatile player, appearing in five different positions for South Africa in all. He was also quickly recognised as one of the team leaders, although he captained the side only in his last international season in 1938. After World War II, he continued as Springbok coach and manager before eventually becoming the long-serving

Below: *Coach Danie Craven (on left in blazer) puts the 1951 South African tourists to Britain, Ireland and France through their paces. Craven had toured Europe as a player in 1931.*

▪ ELLIS PARK ▪

South African rugby has several great cathedrals in which its devoted fans worship their heroes. Newlands at Cape Town, Loftus Versfeld in Pretoria and King's Park in Durban have each seen great rugby occasions, but Ellis Park in Johannesburg has surely played host to the greatest of them all – the 1995 World Cup final triumph.

The Ellis Park ground dates back to 1928, when Transvaal faced the All Blacks in the stadium's first big game. Transvaal won 6-0, the first of many famous victories they would record on this their home turf, although New Zealand avenged this defeat when they won the First Test, also played at Ellis Park, a week later.

The crowd for that game was 38,000, which was then a record in South Africa, but Ellis Park was soon developed to give it a considerably larger capacity. Perhaps as many as 100,000 packed into the ground for the First Test against the British Lions in 1955 and were rewarded with one of the greatest games ever. The Lions led 23-11 well into the second half, but South Africa came back to 23-22 with an injury-time try. The conversion looked straightforward, but the pressure was too much for Jack van der Schyff, and as his kick flew outside the left-hand post, the referee's whistle went for no-side.

Ellis Park was rebuilt in the 1970s, with capacity cut to just over 70,000, although the cost of the improvements caused Transvaal rugby problems in the new stadium's early years. All that was forgotten by 24 June 1995, when all South Africa watched as Nelson Mandela presented the World Cup to François Pienaar, both president and captain wearing the number 6 Springbok jersey.

SARB president, from which position he dictated events just as firmly as Markötter before him, although in a rather different style.

THE FIFTIES AND SIXTIES

After the war, it was back to business as usual for South African rugby at first, a 4-0 series win over the All Blacks in 1949 being followed by five Test wins, including a record 44-0 thrashing of Scotland, on the 1951-52 tour of Britain, Ireland and France. Springbok fans were disappointed that their men could only share the series with the 1955 Lions,

but that was nothing compared to their gloom in 1958, when France achieved the unthinkable. They came to South Africa, drew one Test and won the other to become the first team to win a series on South African soil in the twentieth century.

The 1960s saw mixed fortunes, with the 1960-61 side winning 31 of its 34 matches in Europe, drawing two and losing one. Four of the five Tests were won, with the fifth, against France, being a scoreless draw. The short tour to Scotland and Ireland in 1965 was disastrously different. The Springboks played five games, lost four, including both the internationals, and drew the other. And this was only a beginning to a terrible year, for two Test defeats in Australia and three defeats in the four Tests played in New Zealand were to follow. By the end of the decade, however, South African rugby standards were once again improving, with a comfortable home win over the 1968 Lions and a successful short visit later the same year to France. But other issues were about to come to the fore and overshadow all this.

RUGBY AND APARTHEID

South African rugby had been run on a racist basis from the start – a Western Province Coloured Rugby Union existed in the 1890s – and the first Springboks to go to New Zealand in 1921 had been caught up in a race-related scandal after their game against the Maoris. From then until the 1960s, South Africa occasionally played on tour against teams containing non-white players, but refused to allow such players to visit South Africa. Since there were few non-white rugby players in Britain and Australia, those most affected by this were New Zealand Maoris, with the New Zealand rugby authorities conniving at this discrimination by regarding Maoris as ineligible for selection for tours to South Africa.

Racism in white South African society became institutionalised with the creation and expansion of the apartheid system in the 1950s and 1960s. In rugby terms, this meant that only white players and white teams belonged to the main South African Rugby Board, which was the body affiliated to the International Board. In line with the absurdities of apartheid generally, there were separate organisations for 'coloureds' and 'blacks', the South African Rugby Federation (SARF) and the South African Rugby Association (SARA) respectively. And of course white players monopolised the available funding, had all the decent facilities, and were the only ones considered for selection to representative teams.

The first sign that the rest of the rugby world found this unpalatable was when New Zealand refused an invitation to tour South Africa in 1967 because it was made clear that Maoris still could not be included in the team.

Next the Springbok tour to the British Isles in 1969-70 was met by furious anti-racist protests, as was the visit to Australia in 1971, after which it was clear that there would be no further Springbok tours to either of these countries while apartheid remained in place. In due course the Springbok tour to New Zealand in 1981 was met by even fiercer demonstrations, with the same consequences.

In 1970, however, New Zealand did play in South Africa, with players of Maori and Pacific Island descent prominent in the party, and in 1971 France came on a short tour with non-white players in the team also. In 1972 England played a SARF and a SARA team in the course of their tour. Although the British Lions toured once again in 1974 and various other club and representative teams continued to visit regularly, opinion outside South Africa was increasingly hostile to such contacts. In 1977, therefore, the SARB was amalgamated with SARA and SARF (although a fourth, mainly black body, SARU, remained resolutely opposed to such a move) and began to consider a few non-white players for representative sides and make further token changes. In 1981 Errol Tobias, a fine fly-half or centre, became the first non-white player to represent South Africa, when he played against Ireland.

Above: *Some of the stars of the ill-fated 1969-70 Springbok tour of the British Isles. From left, Don Walton, skipper Dawie de Villiers, H.O. de Villiers, Tom Bedford and Frik du Preez.*

Rugby opinion outside South Africa was divided on how to proceed. Some wanted a complete boycott of South Africa. Others believed that to cut off relations was to bring politics into where it did not belong, while others thought that maintaining contact was the best way to influence South Africa to change for the better. And some worried – with good reason in the late 1980s, as the 1986 New Zealand Cavaliers tour showed – that South African money would buy many of the best foreign players and ruin the world game if official contacts were not kept up.

CHANGING TIMES

SARB president Danie Craven was heavily criticised by white conservatives in South Africa when he participated in talks involving the African National Congress in 1988, but that was the way wider events were moving. South Africa's government began the process of change in 1990, and in 1992 a new rugby governing body, the South African Rugby Football Union (SARFU), was formed on a non-racist basis.

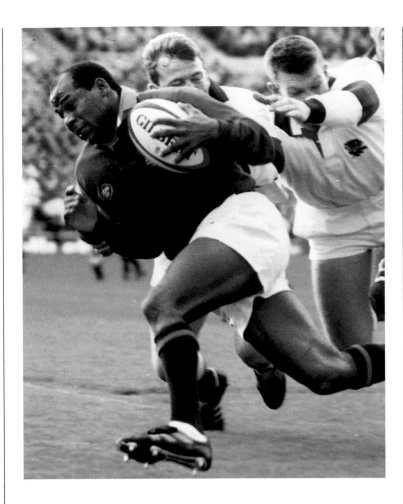

remarks that he had made. Perhaps so, but this could also be taken as a sign of progress, for the idea that such an outcome would follow such an offence would have been ludicrous in South African rugby only a handful of years before.

Whatever problems there may have been off the field, there were many exciting developments and much fine rugby. However, despite the various 'World' and invitation teams that had been lured to South Africa in the 1980s, it was very clear in the first proper internationals in 1992 and 1993 that the Springboks were some way off the pace – one win in France and one in Australia being the only successes in the first ten games. The 1994 series in New Zealand was lost, too, with the sending home of prop Johan le Roux for a biting incident one of several low points.

WINNING WAYS AGAIN

The tide began to turn, perhaps, with a series of comfortable wins on the 1994 tour to Scotland and Wales, which was followed in early 1995 by a 60-8 thrashing of Western Samoa

Below: *Johan Roux in action in the 1997 Super 12. Scrum-half Roux plays for the Gauteng Lions, who were formerly known as the Transvaal Golden Lions.*

Above: *Chester Williams bursts for the line against England in 1995. Williams's touchdown was disallowed this time, but he still scored two in the Springboks' 24-14 Twickenham win.*

South Africa's return to international rugby did not go entirely smoothly, with difficulties, for example, over whether the old or new anthem, or both, should be played before games. There was controversy, too, over whether the national team should keep the traditional green and gold colours and the Springbok name and badge. In the end the colours and the springbok remained, but with the addition of a protea flower to the badge.

By the 1995 World Cup, many such problems had been smoothed over by the diplomacy of President Mandela and the enlightened attitudes of some senior figures in South African rugby, notably Morné du Plessis and François Pienaar. It did no harm that a black player, Chester Williams, was on hand to feature in the publicity and, since he was clearly a world-class winger, he was obviously selected on merit and not for appearances' sake. The changes in South African rugby were much more than superficial ones, as some critics claimed, but the situation was still far from perfect. Some took it as evidence of continuing problems that Springbok coach André Markgraaf was forced to resign in 1997 because of allegedly racist

in a warm-up game for the World Cup. During the World Cup campaign South Africa never matched the spectacular scoring of the All Blacks, but no one defended better, and it was this quality above all that earned them their historic victory in the final.

PROVINCIAL RUGBY

Even in the years of isolation South African domestic rugby remained as fiercely fought as ever, with great sequences of Northern Transvaal wins in the Currie Cup in the 1970s being followed by Western Province supremacy in the 1980s. Natal took the title for the first time in their history in 1990, with a series of strong drives by flanker Wahl Bartmann inspiring their comeback in the final.

Northern Transvaal took the 1991 Currie Cup with a comfortable 27-15 win over Transvaal in the final, but they only got there courtesy of one of the strangest-ever rugby events in one of the earlier group matches. Orange Free State were playing Western Province and, if they had won, it would have put Northerns out of the reckoning. Late on, a Free State player made a storming run into the Western Province 22 and looked set to score the decisive try when he was tackled, not by an opponent but by a streaker from out of the crowd. The referee gave a scrum, Western Province pinched possession in the subsequent play and immediately raced to the other end for a breakaway try to win the game.

Transvaal were back at the top in 1993 for the first time in over 20 years and also took the Super 10 title that year, beating Auckland in the final. The Super 10 and now the Super 12 have clearly played a part in helping the development of rugby in South Africa, with the Springboks looking far too strong for all the northern hemisphere sides they met from their World Cup win up to the 1997 Lions tour. South Africa even threatened to complete a World Cup double in 1997, when they raced into a big early lead in the World Sevens final before being overhauled by Fiji. The first Tri-Nations tournament in 1996 and the later All Blacks tour to South Africa showed that the Springboks cannot expect to have things all there own way, in southern hemisphere competition at least. Even so, there is no doubt that South Africa are back at the heart of the rugby world, and it would be foolish to rule them out for the 1999 World Cup.

Below: *Joost van der Westhuizen, believed by many to be the best scrum-half in world rugby, bursts from the base of the scrum in South Africa's 1996 Second Test victory over France.*

CHAPTER TEN

· WALES ·

Number eight Scott Quinnell dips the shoulder to charge at the Scottish defence during Wales's 34-19 triumph at Murrayfield in 1997. Quinnell, son of former Welsh forward Derek, was one of a number of returnees from rugby league to play for Wales that year.

In common with other parts of the British Isles, Wales had a long history of various types of football game before the formal beginnings of rugby in the nineteenth century. A game known as *cnappan* was especially popular in Pembrokeshire from at least as early as 1600. These rough-and-ready football matches continued to be played into the nineteenth century, so there was fertile ground when the influence of true rugby began to be felt.

Rugby began to develop in Wales in the 1850s in various colleges and schools. The Reverend Rowland Williams was one important figure in this period. He had been involved in early Cambridge University rugby and in 1850 became Vice-Principal of St David's College, Lampeter. Llandovery, Christ's College, Brecon, and Monmouth School were also pioneers. Lampeter played Llandovery at a 12-a-side version of football in the 1860s, and the Brecon school

had games against a town team in the same decade, although neither of these forms of football could really be called rugby. Young Welshmen who had been educated at English schools also brought their knowledge of various types of football back home to Wales with them.

CLUB RUGBY BEGINS

It is hard to say which was the first adult club in Wales. Neath in 1871 was certainly the first to be formed of what are now the senior clubs, but Blaenau Gwent and Chepstow, among others, probably existed before then. Neath's founders included both Llandoverians and an experienced Scottish player, Dr T.P. Whittington, who became the first Welsh club representative to be capped, when he played for Scotland in 1873. All of the other major towns of South Wales acquired clubs in the 1870s, usually inspired by a similar mixture of home-grown enthusiasts, imports and returnees. Old boys of Cheltenham College in Gloucestershire were important in the parent clubs of the present Cardiff (formed by an amalgamation in 1876), and Old Rugbeians were involved at Llanelli (1872), but the native Monmouth influence predominated at Newport (1874). Newport and Swansea (1872) began life as soccer clubs, but they soon switched to rugby.

The leading members of all these clubs – and of the many others that soon sprang up – were almost invariably reasonably well-off business and professional men, but rugby quickly caught the imagination of miners, dockers and steel-workers as well and soon became Wales's national game. Some early clubs were connected with churches or chapels, and Anglican clergymen were prominent among the early enthusiasts – there were three in the first Welsh team. Rather more predictably there were many clubs based in pubs and inns. The latter connections, and the on- and off-field violence that soon came to be associated with the game, also brought some religious opposition to rugby's development, but this did not have much effect. When the Reverend Alban Davies, Welsh captain in 1914, was criticised for his association with men who used rough language on the field, he said that he never heard any because he always wore a scrum-cap.

THE WELSH RUGBY UNION

The first Welsh players knew that they had some way to go to catch up with the standard of the better-established English game, so in 1875 the South Wales Football Club was set up as an invitation team to play county and club sides in the English Midlands and West Country. They played their first game against Hereford in December 1875 and won by a goal to nil.

The South Wales Football Club was reformed in 1877 as the South Wales Football Union. In March 1880, under the leadership of Richard Mullock of Newport, representatives of nine clubs met in the first step towards establishing a Welsh national union and creating a national team. The outcome was Wales's first international match, on 19 February 1881, when a team travelled to Blackheath to play England. They lost by seven goals, six tries and a dropped goal to nil. It was just as well that a points-scoring system had not yet been introduced – that lot adds up to 82-0 using modern values.

Critics at the time slated the team as little more than a private venture by Mullock, with West Walians being unfairly excluded, and so there was a second meeting, this time attended by 11 clubs and held at the Castle Hotel in

Neath on 12 March 1881. This meeting agreed to set up the Welsh Rugby Union (WRU), which has remained the governing body of Welsh rugby to this day.

As well as helping inspire a national organisation, the South Wales Football Club also helped develop the domestic game when it established a cup competition in 1877. This was soon fiercely contested on the field and regularly accompanied by crowd trouble off it. There were also complaints from various clubs about player-poaching and the fielding of players who did not meet the residence qualification that was one of the rules of the competition. Rivalry became especially intense from 1880, when the competition was structured to ensure that the final was always an East Wales v West Wales affair. Newport won the first title and five in all, and the other winners up to 1887, when the senior clubs withdrew from the cup, were Swansea, Cardiff and Llanelli, who were quick to establish their status along with Newport as the 'Big Four' of Welsh rugby. The cup continued to be contested by junior clubs and second XVs but was scrapped before the outbreak of World War I.

EARLY INTERNATIONALS

After that February 1881 walkover, England dropped the fixture against Wales for the next season. Wales did play and beat Ireland in 1882, but the Irish did not take the game very seriously, with a number of the original selection not turning up and others walking off in disgust during the match. Two Welshmen had to make up the numbers for Ireland in the second game, in 1884, and it was 1887 before the match became an annual fixture. Wales resumed matches with England in 1883 and also began to play Scotland the same

▪ WELSH RUGBY UNION ▪

National colours: **red**
Year founded: **1881**
No. of clubs: **372**
Oldest senior club:
Neath, 1871
No. of players: **25,000 adults/56,000 juniors**
World Cup record: **1987 third; 1991 & 1995 eliminated in pool stages**

WRU

year. Wales did not beat Scotland until 1888 and had to wait for their first win against England until 1890, when they triumphed at Dewsbury.

Although it took a little while for the national team to make its mark, the club game in Wales quickly flourished. At least 60 clubs were in existence by 1890, and the largest ones had begun charging at the gate in the late 1870s and began using the revenue to pay players' 'expenses' soon after. Senior clubs regularly drew up to 20,000 spectators and played fixtures with leading English sides at home and as far afield as Yorkshire and London. The economy and population of South Wales were growing rapidly at this time on the back of the successful coal industry. Wales attracted many immigrants in those days, drawn by the relatively high wages available, and they and the established work force had both leisure time and money to spend on watching rugby, coupled with strength and fitness from their everyday work if they wanted to play the game themselves.

THE FIRST TRIPLE CROWN

The real breakthrough for Welsh rugby began in Cardiff in January 1893, with the so-called 'Brazier Game' against England. Hard frost threatened the postponement of the

match, but a collection of night-watchmen's braziers was placed all over the ground the night before and constantly fed with Welsh coal by an army of small boys. The match went ahead and Wales won it 12-11, with the scores including two tries from Arthur Gould and a crucial late dropped goal from Billy Bancroft. The result of the match was calculated by the scoring values established by the International Board, which was fortunate, since the normal Welsh domestic method of the time would have made it 14-14. Wales then beat Scotland comfortably in Edinburgh and claimed their first-ever Triple Crown with a 2-0 success against Ireland. Bert Gould, brother of Arthur, scored a second-half try in what would prove to be the last home international played at Llanelli's Stradey Park.

An interesting feature of that season's play was that it confirmed Wales's switch to a four three-quarter formation with eight forwards from the previously customary three three-quarters and nine forwards. The Cardiff club had been the first to use this line-up, in 1884, under the influence of

Below: *The Welsh national team photgraphed in January 1892. The side was captained by the great Arthur Gould (with ball in centre of middle row), who played for Newport.*

one of their centres, Frank Hancock. Hancock captained the club the next season, when they won 27 of the 28 games they played and conceded only four points in total. Hancock was actually English, from a Somerset brewing family that had moved to Cardiff, but he played four games for Wales. In the last of these, the Scotland match in 1886, Wales tried the four three-quarter system for the first time, although without success because of the strength of the Scots forwards.

Arthur Gould of Newport, who played 27 times for Wales from 1885 to 1897, was easily the biggest star of the day. Although he took some time to be won over by Hancock's new-fangled back formation, he was certainly the greatest influence in developing the running, attacking style of rugby that was to remain a Welsh trademark until after World War I. Early in 1896, in appreciation of his great role in Welsh rugby, a public subscription, to which the Welsh RU contributed, raised enough money to buy him a house. When the other unions heard about this there were howls of protest about professionalism. Ireland refused to play Wales the next season, and Scotland withdrew from their Welsh fixture for the next two years, but England turned a blind eye because too many English clubs relied on the large gates from their Welsh fixtures to be too fussy about such matters. Gould retired, and the affair was gradually swept under the carpet after much hypocritical posturing and self-justification all round. The truth seems to be that, both then and later, Welsh rugby was run by relatively prosperous men who were prepared to overlook laxity with expenses and similar matters, provided it was all reasonably discreet. Of course they were not alone in world rugby in doing this.

Gould in fact retired on the eve of a golden age of Welsh rugby. One contemporary wrote, 'in 1897 there was introduced into the Welsh pack what became known as the Rhondda type of forward…a man who could stand rough handling…and give as good as he received'. Players from valley clubs, like Mountain Ash and Llwynypia, helped provide the national team with a hard core that only Scotland regularly challenged in the first decade of the twentieth century. And there were classy backs like Tommy Vile at scrum-half and Rhys Gabe in the centre to provide the handling and running skills.

BEATING THE ALL BLACKS

Even including the six triple Crowns (three of them also Grand Slams) between 1900 and 1911, Wales's greatest moment of that period was the 1905 clash with the First All Blacks. They arrived in Cardiff unbeaten on their tour and with victories over the other home unions already under their belts. There was little detailed pre-match planning

then, but the only score of the game, a try by Welsh left-wing Teddy Morgan, was made from a called move involving a dummy run to the right by fly-half Percy Bush and one of the Welsh centres. After the match, players from both sides seemed to think the 3-0 Welsh win a fair result, but then the sensation-seeking *Daily Mail* newspaper reopened one particular incident in which All Black centre Bob Deans had been tackled close to the Welsh try-line. The controversy 'Did Deans score?' has fuelled many arguments since. There is obviously no saying now what the truth of the matter was, and it certainly seems that the Scottish referee (a young, fit man, but wearing street shoes) was some way behind play when he disallowed the try. Players from both sides predictably backed their own cause in later recollections, but the few neutrals that did have a reasonable view seem to have thought that it was a perfectly good try. But before New Zealanders claim they were robbed, it is worth remembering that the same neutral observers generally said that Wales deserved to win on the day.

Below: *Three of the Welsh XV that triumphed over the First All Blacks in 1905. From the left, W. M. Llewellyn, H.T. Winfield and E.T. 'Teddy' Morgan, who scored the Welsh try.*

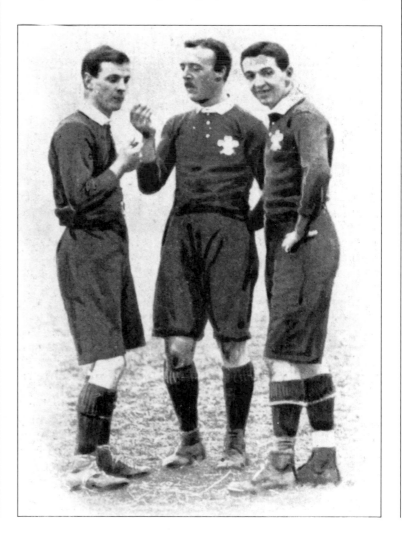

▪ CARDIFF ARMS PARK ▪

Cardiff Arms Park has been the spiritual home of Welsh rugby since the first international was played on the ground in 1884. Wales beat Ireland that day and won 104 of the 172 internationals played at the ground until it closed for reconstruction in 1997.

The site was originally a piece of open land beside an inn called the Cardiff Arms. Players in the first recorded match on the ground, a club game in 1874, changed in the Cardiff Arms, then simply walked over the road to play, a custom that continued for many years, even for internationals. There have been numerous developments since the first 300-seat stand was built in 1881, especially between 1968 and 1984. This rebuilding was overtaken in turn by the need for a completely new stadium to improve safety for spectators, to provide better off-field facilities and to create a fitting setting in which Wales could host the 1999 World Cup. The final Five Nations match at the original Arms Park in 1997 unfortunately could not give the old stadium a fitting send-off, being marked instead by an English win and Triple Crown success, although Wales scrum-half Robert Howley had the honour of crossing for the last try scored at the ground. Jonathan Davies converted.

The new Cardiff Arms Park, the Millenium Stadium (below), will be open in time for the World Cup. The pitch will be entirely relaid at 90 degrees to the present surface – all the fittings and the original turf have been sold off in souvenir pieces – and the 75,000 spectators will have every modern facility for sports matches and other events, even including a retractable roof over the pitch. (*Picture courtesy of Lobb Sports Architects*)

After 1911, Wales did not win the Triple Crown again until 1950, and, as this statistic suggests, the years between the two world wars were very difficult for Welsh rugby. Tactics had changed, with forwards increasingly specialising in particular positions, and Wales were slow to adjust. Even after the 'Big Five' selection committee system had been set up in 1924, team selection was inconsistent, especially in the backs for some reason, and results were accordingly mixed throughout the 1920s. Then came the Depression. This hit the industrial areas of Britain devastatingly hard and the South Wales coal fields probably hardest of all. In the rest of Britain, the soccer heartlands suffered most, while the rugby-playing and rugby-supporting population was predominantly middle class and better equipped to ride out these problems. This was not the case in Wales, with numerous rugby clubs forced to seek help from the WRU when most of their players and members were unemployed and their supporters unable to afford the gate money. Hundreds of thousands of Welshmen sought jobs in England. Some then played for English clubs and were not entirely lost to the game, but many of the finest players found that they had no option but to accept the offers of the rugby league scouts and 'go north'.

POLICE PRESENCE

A feature of these years was the number of policemen playing for the senior clubs and in the national team – the police force at least offered job security in difficult times. Up to the present day about one in twelve of all Welsh internationals have been policemen. Police officers made up more than half of Cardiff's first XV on average in the inter-war years, and there were six policemen in the Welsh pack in 1926, for example. Newspaper cartoons of the time often showed well-known police players 'arresting' opponents, but this phenomenon had its sombre side, too. The industrial disputes of the time threw up many unpleasant incidents between police officers and workers. The grudges thus raised sometimes resulted in grim violence when the parties concerned met again on the rugby field.

Not all was quite so gloomy, however. Aberavon fans enjoyed a run of success in the 1920s, when the 'Wizards' won four consecutive Welsh unofficial club championships, a feat that Cardiff nearly matched with three in a row just before World War II. Wales won the international championship outright in 1922, 1931 and 1936. In 1933 there was the joy of the first-ever win at Twickenham, and in 1935 Wales achieved a second win over the All Blacks.

SUCCESS IN THE FIFTIES

Times changed for the better after World War II, and in the early 1950s Wales were once again at the top. The club game was especially healthy, with large crowds flocking to matches – 30,000 at Newport and 40,000 at Cardiff were not unusual attendances. There was new blood on the club scene, too. Maesteg, Newbridge, Pontypool and Ebbw Vale were all admitted to the unofficial championship table shortly after the war, with Maesteg becoming champions in 1950 and Ebbw Vale lifting the title four times in the ten years after that.

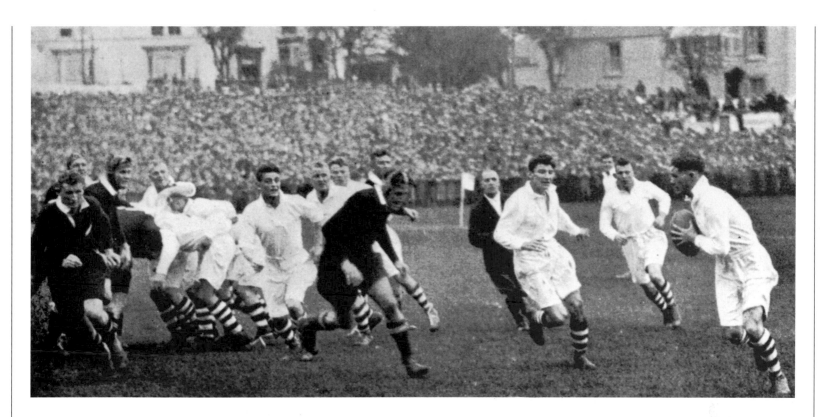

There were many great players as well. Fourteen Welshmen travelled with the Lions in 1950 after Wales had completed a well-earned Grand Slam earlier that season. Some of the stars of that era got their starts in slightly odd ways, however. After a 19-0 loss at Murrayfield in 1951, the Big Five named five A.N. Others in their next side. A typical selectors' muddle perhaps, but one of those gaps was in the fly-half position and was filled in the end by an up-and-coming youngster called Cliff Morgan, who duly played a vital part in another Grand Slam in 1952 and delighted rugby fans everywhere until his retirement in 1958.

Unfortunately Morgan's was not the only retirement around the end of that decade, and with the passing of a generation of great players some of the spark went out of Welsh rugby for a time. In the Five Nations, Wales had no real answer to the big ball-playing forwards that France were fielding in those days, and in the space of a few years Wales lost games at home to all three major southern hemisphere nations. Even worse was the heavy Test defeat on Wales's first major tour to the southern hemisphere in 1964, a 24-3 loss to the Springboks.

The first answer to the problem was a wholehearted adoption of the idea of coaching. In 1961, Newbridge became the first Welsh senior club to appoint an official coach. Coaches were appointed for the national team for the first time in 1967-68, and the next season Wales even took the then unheard-of step of starting national squad sessions. This was so radical that it was referred to the International Board, who duly gave their approval a few months later.

Above: *The national team were not alone in beating the 1935 All Blacks. Swansea did it, too. Here their scrum-half Haydn Tanner (third from right) has just handed on to fly-half Willie Davies. Both were schoolboys when they played in this match.*

Below: *Wales clash with Ireland at the Arms Park in 1971. Denzil Williams releases to Gareth Edwards as Mervyn Davies (white headband) tries to prevent Ireland's Willie-John McBride (No 4) from spoiling. Wales won the game 23-9.*

Above: Pontypridd wing Geraint Lewis beats Neath's Chris Higgs to the line to score his side's third try in the 1996 SWALEC Cup final. Pontypridd ran out 29-22 winners.

The greatest Welsh coach of the period was without doubt Carwyn James, who sadly never had the honour of coaching the Wales team. His success with the 1971 Lions clearly speaks for itself, but there is no doubt either that his greatest day at home in Wales was that famous October afternoon in 1972, when the Stradey Park scoreboard read 'Llanelli 9, Seland Newydd 3'.

TRIUMPHS IN THE SEVENTIES

Delme Thomas, Derek Quinnell, Tom David, Phil Bennett and J.J. Williams were among the heroes in that Llanelli team, but not even they, great players as they all were, would be certain of selection in a 'best' Welsh XV of the 1960s and 1970s. From 1965 to 1979 Triple Crowns and Grand Slams seemed almost routine, with stars like Gareth Edwards, Mervyn Davies, J.P.R. Williams, Gerald Davies, Graham Price and others all contenders for every 'all-time greats' team.

Inevitably, perhaps, there came a time when their successors in the national side could not match this astonishing standard, and fortunes slumped. Wales had half a dozen bottom-of-the-table finishes in the 1980s and 1990s and suffered embarrassing whitewashes in 1990 and 1995, the only occasions this has happened to Wales. World Cup results were no better. Wales did reach the semi-finals in 1987 but only by courtesy of woeful Ireland and England performances. The 49-6 defeat against the All Blacks in those semi-finals was a truer reflection of the state of affairs. Then there was the 63-6 debacle in Australia in 1991, followed by defeat against Western Samoa and another heavy loss to the Wallabies in the 1991 World Cup. At least the ultimate nightmare, defeat in the qualifying matches for the 1995 tournament, did not materialise.

Welsh rugby could do little about one aspect of the problem – that a selection of the best players were lured away, in difficult economic times, to demonstrate their skills as stars in the rugby league world. But one reason why they were so readily persuaded to defect was the poor management and internal bickering that beset much of the Welsh union game. Several leading players announced that they were unavailable for Wales or quit playing altogether well before their time, and even referees (who have to be pretty thick-skinned and uncomplaining) decided to go on strike briefly in 1996, unhappy at the way they were being treated by the authorities.

Certainly the top players play far too many matches and their familiarity with each other's play all too often results in grim and sterile games, with a levelling down of standards rather than a levelling up. But even when levelled down, Welsh domestic rugby is still powerful and impressive. Cardiff only just lost out to Toulouse in extra time after an epic struggle in the first European club championship in 1996, and later that year the Pontypridd *v* Neath SWALEC Cup final was an exciting, quality game well worth anyone's admission money.

There have been various false dawns when it has seemed that Welsh rugby would harness such resources to recover its pride and strength. Wales won the Five Nations in 1994 and even had a shot at the Grand Slam in the finale against England, only to come a cropper the next year and

fail to progress beyond their pool in the World Cup. Again in 1997, heartened by the return of some former stars from league, Wales began with a spectacular win at Murrayfield, only to make a mess of seemingly the easiest task of all and go down to Ireland in Cardiff in the next match.

As in the other countries of the Celtic fringe, coping with the advent of professionalism has not been easy for the game in Wales. Numerous leading players have taken the money on offer from English clubs, getting themselves out of the distracting internal politics that still bedevil Welsh rugby into the bargain. Also, the senior Welsh clubs are struggling to make ends meet, and no one is very happy with the league structure or the organisation of the season. Despite all this, it is still hard to believe that Wales will not dig deep and live up to their past reputation by making a real show as hosts of the 1999 World Cup.

Below: *Wales's Robert Howley takes on the Irish in the 1997 Five Nations game at Cardiff. Howley made his Wales debut in 1996 and was quickly hailed as the best scrum-half in Britain.*

CHAPTER ELEVEN

· THE RUGBY WORLD ·

Western Samoan threequarter Timo Tagaloa on the charge during the Pacific islanders' win over Argentina in the 1991 World Cup.

Rugby is one of the most widely played sports in the world today. At the end of March 1997 a total of 76 countries were members of the International Rugby Board (usually known simply as the International Board, or IB). These rugby-playing nations ranged from England with 2000 clubs and half a million players of all ages to Andorra with two clubs, 53 registered adults and one referee. Even these 76 countries do not represent the whole rugby world. Mexico played their first-ever international in 1996, against Colombia. Neither of these is an IB member, and there are certainly quite a number of other countries outside the IB where rugby has been played, taking the true total of rugby-playing countries to over 100.

For many years the British authorities asserted a right to control the game, and only in 1949 did they grudgingly allow Australian, New Zealand and South African representation. Even France, who had formed the rival *Fédération Internationale de Rugby Amateur* (FIRA) in 1934, were not given a voice or a vote until 1978. This short-sighted policy of exclusiveness changed in the late 1980s, with 30 countries joining the IB in 1987-88. The policy now is the more sensible one of bringing the whole of rugby under one governing body, and it is to be hoped that a decent proportion of the profits from World Cups and of other revenues flowing into the game will be devoted to development outside the traditional strongholds of rugby.

The table on page 101 lists the International Board's members as at March 1997. With there being so many, it is unfortunately impossible to cover all of them in detail. Instead, the remainder of this chapter will focus on the 11 'minor' nations that have so far appeared in the final stages of the World Cup.

ARGENTINA

Year founded: 1899 *Joined IB:* 1987 *No of clubs:* 250
No of players: 10,000 adults / 15,000 juniors

The first recorded rugby match in Argentina was played in 1873 by British expatriates of the Buenos Aires Football Club. It was an internal game, the teams being selected on the basis of Banks *v* City. The first rugby club to be formed, the Buenos Aires Cricket and Rugby Club, did not come into existence until 1886 and, as its other sporting interest suggests, it too was largely made up of expatriates. The first club catering principally for native-born players is believed to have been formed at Buenos Aires University in 1904.

The River Plate Rugby Union – the parent body of the present Argentinian Rugby Union – was set up in 1899 and affiliated to the English RFU, thus continuing British links. Also in 1899, the inaugural Argentinian club championship was played. Four clubs took part, and the title was won by Lomas. The most frequent winners of the national club championship to date have been Atletico San Isidro.

The first important touring team to visit Argentina arrived in 1910. It was a British select of similar strength to the 'Lions' teams of the time and won all six games. Numerous other teams visited between the two world wars, including two more British Isles selects in 1927 and 1936 and the Junior Springboks in 1932. All were unbeaten.

Below: *The powerful Argentinian forwards in possession against England in the 1995 World Cup. England managed a 24-18 victory, but Argentina scored the game's two tries.*

France were the first major nation to play Argentina at full international level, winning two Tests and seven other games on their 1949 tour. An Ireland XV did not fare as well in 1952. The Argentinians lost one 'Test' but gained a well-merited draw in the other.

The first major overseas tour made by the Argentinians was to South Africa in 1965, when they won 11 of 16 games, including the big one against the Junior Springboks. It was on this tour that the nickname 'Pumas' was coined by Rhodesian journalists. The name has stuck, even though the animal on the Argentinian badge is not a puma but a jaguar.

Games with other countries very quickly followed. Between 1968 and 1978 Argentina had wins or draws against Scotland, England, Ireland and Wales, albeit none of them in games recognised as cap internationals by the home nations. In 1978, they had a hard-fought 18-18 draw with France in a full Test, and the following year the Pumas chalked up their first Test win, beating Australia 24-13 in Buenos Aires, with Hugo Porta kicking three dropped goals in his 16-point tally.

The 1980s saw two more especially notable results for the Pumas. Predominantly Argentinian squads toured South Africa as 'South America' in 1980, 1982 and 1984. On the second of these tours, they took a Test off the Springboks 21-12. Hugo Porta was the mastermind. He scored all his team's points with a try, the conversion, four penalties and a dropped goal. Three years later, Argentina gained a thrilling 21-21 draw at home against the All Blacks.

Since then, although they have recorded some good results, Argentina have never quite lived up to their potential. In all three World Cups, they have disappointed

by failing to progress beyond the pool stages, even in 1995 when their scrummaging was clearly the most powerful in the tournament. That year, the Argentinian authorities also decided to try to keep their domestic game amateur, while the big boys of the rugby world were turning professional. This action led a number of Argentina's best players to move abroad. However, other developments of the modern era may help Argentina by giving more regular international competition, including the Latin Cup and the Pan-American championship involving Canada and the United States.

CANADA

Year founded: 1929 Joined IB: 1986 No of clubs: 175
No of players: 16,000 adults/25,000 juniors

Canada have been perhaps the one 'minor' nation to return home from each World Cup with an enhanced reputation, a remarkable achievement bearing in mind the difficulties the game has faced in Canada over the years. The sheer size of the country and the weather that forces a winter break in the season have together posed many problems.

The details of exactly how the game got started in Canada are uncertain, but the earliest recorded game is believed to have been between an army team and McGill University in Toronto in 1863. Another Toronto educational establishment, Trinity College, is known to have drawn up a set of rules in 1864 and may have formed a club then also. Other reports say that Montreal Football Club is the oldest in the country and that it was formed in 1865.

Rugby also came early to western Canada. A. StG. Hamersley, a noted rugby pioneer, arrived in British Columbia in the early 1880s and was instrumental in setting the game up there. The British Columbia Rugby Union was formed in 1889, and ever since then the greatest strength of Canadian rugby has been concentrated in this province, only a handful of wins by Ontario spoiling a British Columbia monopoly in the inter-provincial championship.

Incoming and outgoing Canadian tours were soon staged. A Canadian side played 23 club and district games in Britain in 1902 and won eight of their matches. There were also games against visiting New Zealand sides before World War I (some of them played in California) and an exchange of tours with Japan in the 1930s. After World War II, major touring teams began to come to Canada more regularly, and Canadian rugby accordingly developed. A Canadian Rugby Union had formed in 1929 but subsequently folded. It was reformed in 1965 and was rewarded the next year with its first Test, when the Lions stopped over on their way home from New Zealand. The Lions won the international 19-8, but British Columbia succeeded in overcoming the tourists in the other game.

Since then, Canada has built up a programme of incoming and outgoing tours and more regular inter-provincial and other domestic competitions. There has been at least one annual match with the United States since 1977, with Canada comfortably ahead in this Can-Am series to date. Canada also won the inaugural Pacific Rim tournament in 1996. In full Tests against the traditional rugby powers, they have so far had one win, a 26-24 success against Wales in Cardiff in 1993.

In the 1987 World Cup, Canada claimed a creditable win against Tonga before being beaten by Wales and Ireland. In 1991 they had good wins in the pool games against Romania and Fiji before going down 29-13 to the All Blacks in a rain-sodden quarter-final that was much closer than the score suggests. In 1995 Canada were unfortunate to be drawn in the same group as both Australia and South Africa, but they gave both very tough matches – too tough in the case of the South African game, which was marred by a huge brawl and multiple sendings-off.

Left: *Ecstatic Canadian players celebrate as the final whistle blows at Cardiff Arms Park in 1993. Canada had just beaten Wales 26-24 through a last-minute try by lock Al Charron.*

The Canadians' problem now will be to make the transition from being a team that can give the top sides a good game to one that can beat them from time to time. Modern methods have obviously made travel and communication in their massive country easier, but the professional era has already seen leading Canadian players being lured abroad to ply their trade. How Canadian rugby will emerge from all this remains to be seen.

FIJI

*Year founded: 1913 Joined IB: 1987 No of clubs: 600
No of players: 30,000 adults/50,000 juniors*

It is no surprise to learn that rugby in Fiji began with the arrival of the British in the nineteenth century. Fiji's first recorded match was at Ba in 1884, when a team of British soldiers played against a team of local soldiers. The oldest known Fijian clubs date back to 1904, when Civil Service and Police teams were formed. They started a club competition in and around the capital, Suva, in the same year, but at that time these clubs would have comprised

Below: *Fijian skipper Waisale Serevi, possibly the best sevens player of all time, on the attack in the early rounds of the 1997 Sevens World Cup in Hong Kong. Fiji won the tournament.*

mostly European players. Native Fijians were taking up the game, however, especially those who had worked or been educated in New Zealand and learned to play there.

Development was rather sketchy until 1913, when a Kiwi plumber called Paddy Sheehan happened to be working on the construction of a hotel in Suva. He was a former captain of Otago and helped form one Fijian club and inspire the foundation of two more. The colonial governor of the islands donated a trophy called the Escott Shield, which is still competed for by clubs in Suva, and the Fiji Rugby Union was formed. This was still mainly the preserve of expatriate players, and two years later, in 1915, a Native Rugby Union was also set up. The two bodies eventually amalgamated in 1945.

International action came to Fiji as early as 1913. That year, Sheehan's club, Pacific, were heavily beaten in an unofficial match against an All Black team who called in on their way back from a North American tour. Fiji's first formal international match was away against Western Samoa in 1924. Fiji won 6-0. The Fijians were on their way to Tonga, where they played a three-match series, winning one game, losing one and drawing the other. Until the mid-1980s, Fiji had by far the best of their many matches against both of these opponents, but have lost more frequently in recent years.

The first major team to come to Fiji were the Maoris in 1938, and Fiji had an undefeated nine-match visit to New Zealand the next year, drawing one and winning eight games, including the 'Test' against the Maoris. Australia were the first major nation to give an international against Fiji full Test status, which they did when the Fijians toured in 1952. The Fijians lost the First Test but came back to take the Second 17-15. This tour, and a second visit to Australia in 1954, were enormously popular, with big crowds clamouring to watch the Fijians' exciting running.

Fiji's first European tour, to France and Wales in 1964, was also hugely popular, but Fiji lost both the big games, against a Welsh XV and a full France side. Besides Australia, whom they have played 15 times, Fiji have had only one or two full internationals against each of the major nations and the only big scalp they have taken (besides Australia) has been that of the British Lions. Fiji beat the 1977 side 25-21 on the way home from the Lions' troubled New Zealand tour.

By the early 1980s, Fiji were clearly the strongest of the South Pacific teams but this status has slipped. They reached the quarter-finals of the 1987 World Cup, where they gave France a tough game, but in 1991 they were bottom of their pool while Western Samoa were doing great things in their matches. Even worse was their failure to reach the 1995 tournament, after a defeat by Tonga in the qualifying games.

Below: *Italian scrum-half Alessandro Troncon gets the ball away against Wales in Rome in 1996. Italy lost 31-22 that day, but have often shown they could compete in a 'Six Nations'.*

Economic and political troubles in Fiji have not helped Fjian rugby nor has the poaching of leading players, notably by Australian teams. A particular reason for the comparative decline in the standard of the Fijian national XV, however, has been the emphasis that Fiji have placed on sevens. Fijian teams have always revelled in individual running, passing and tackling skills, and the country has produced a range of dazzling sevens stars. They won the Hong Kong Sevens seven times in the first 21 years, more than anyone else, and were semi-finalists in the first Sevens World Cup. In 1997, they took the Sevens World Cup – the Melrose Cup – with a 24-21 win over South Africa in the final.

ITALY

Year founded: 1929 *Joined IB:* 1987 *No of clubs:* 430
No of players: 10,000 adults / 17,000 juniors

Students educated in France brought rugby home to Italy, with the first game probably being played there in 1910. Rugby was a rather low-key affair for some years, however, but around ten clubs had been formed by the mid-1920s. They got together to found the Italian Rugby Federation in 1929 and started a national championship the same year. Ambrosiano Milano were the first winners. Italy also played their first international in 1929, losing 9-0 away to Spain.

Other internationals followed in the years up to World War II. In 1935, Italy played their first match against a French XV, losing 44-6 in Rome, and there was an equally disappointing result in the first game against Germany, who were quite strong in rugby terms in the 1930s, Italy going down 18-9 in 1936. It was to be a long time before Italy beat France, but they have not lost to Germany since 1939.

Italy were founder members of FIRA, the French-led body that came to govern Europe's 'minor' rugby nations. Through FIRA Italy developed a good range of fixtures in the 1950s and 1960s against the likes of Spain, Romania, the USSR and France, although from the late 1960s until recent years Italy played French XVs rather than full Test teams. The Italian national side grew in strength and the domestic game flourished, helped substantially by significant corporate sponsorship of the top clubs. The Padua and Milan sides have won the national title most times to date, with Rovigo and Treviso their most frequent rivals.

From the late 1970s, leading southern hemisphere players and top coaches from northern hemisphere nations also began to play and teach regularly in Italy. Andy Haden, David Campese (who is of Italian descent), and Rob Louw were just three examples among the players; Carwyn James and Pierre Villepreux were among the coaches.

Italy really began to make a mark in the wider rugby world in the 1987 World Cup when they only failed to reach the quarter-finals on an inferior try count. They topped the European qualifying table for the 1991 competition and although they could not match England and New Zealand in the pool games, they had a good win over the United States. In 1995 it was a similar story, with a fine win over Argentina and a disappointing defeat against Western Samoa.

The prospect of Italy being drafted in to make the Five Nations into a 'Six Nations' is now increasingly being discussed, and on the field the Italian national team are doing plenty to back this up. They gave Australia a fright in Brisbane in 1994 before going down by three points but then beat Ireland in Italy in 1995 in a warm-up match for the World Cup. This was their first win over a major nation in a full international and was followed a few months later by a win over a Scotland XV that was a full-strength side in all but name. In 1997 Italy recorded another win over Ireland, in Dublin this time, followed by a first-ever success against France. The game in Italy would benefit enormously from the impetus of playing in a regular international competition like an expanded Five Nations, even if, as seems likely, Italy do not win the championship for some time.

IVORY COAST

Year founded: 1961 *Joined IB:* 1988 *No of clubs:* 40
No of players: 1000 adults/10,000 juniors

West Africa's Ivory Coast were a real surprise as qualifiers for the 1995 World Cup tournament. They were introduced to rugby by France and have retained a rugby connection with the one-time colonial power. A separate Ivory Coast Rugby Union was formed in 1961 following independence in 1960, but for some time, many rugby players in the country continued to be French expatriates.

Ivory Coast played their first international, against Tunisia, in 1976, winning 22-6. When they entered the preliminary competition for the 1991 World Cup they came bottom of the African qualifying group, but in 1995 it was a different story. Many of the Ivory Coast players now had experience of senior club rugby in France, and this helped them see off Tunisia, Morocco, Namibia and Zimbabwe, all of whom had a stronger rugby reputation. Predictably, in the tournament proper, the Ivory Coast team were no real competition for Scotland or France, although they did hold

Right: *Ivory Coast's Thierry Kouame in action against Tonga in the 1995 World Cup. The Africans went down 29-11, but this was far from a disgrace against a more senior Test nation.*

Tonga to a creditable 29-11 margin. Tragically, in the early minutes of this match, Ivory Coast wing Max Brito was severely injured and paralysed.

JAPAN

Year founded: 1926 *Joined IB:* 1987 *No of clubs:* 4800
No of players: 88,000 adults/72,000 juniors

The British introduced rugby to Japan in the second half of the nineteenth century, initially playing the game among themselves for their own recreation. The first mainly Japanese club was founded at Keio University in 1899. Two teachers at the university, Edward Clarke and Tanaka Ginnosuke, were the prime movers. Clarke and Tanaka had known each other as youngsters – Clarke was British but had been born in Yokohama and had his early education there before going to Cambridge University, where he learned the game. Keio University played its first fixture

against an expatriate team from the Yokohama club in 1901, losing 35-5. Other Japanese universities and prestigious high schools soon took up the game.

The 1920s were a successful era for rugby in Japan. Various regional unions were formed, and the Japanese Rugby Union itself was established in 1926. University matches were regularly watched by crowds of 20,000 or more. Japanese teams are known to have toured in Canada in 1930 and 1932, with return visits from Canadian sides taking place over the next two years. In 1934, a team of Australian students toured Japan.

With the rise of militaristic governments in the approach to World War II, traditional Japanese martial arts were emphasised and rugby and other foreign pastimes officially frowned on. Rugby obviously had a hold on its enthusiasts, though, for it continued up to, and even to some extent during, the war years. It was renamed, however, with a wholly Japanese title meaning 'the fighting game'.

Rugby began to revive when the war ended, with the occupying Allied powers encouraging non-Japanese sports. Major companies began to form rugby teams, partly as a marketing and publicity tool and partly to give some of their workers recreational opportunities. Kobe Steel was the first such team, in 1945, but others quickly followed. Rugby also revived in universities and high schools, and tours from Oxford and Cambridge and other foreign universities in the 1950s renewed Japanese rugby's overseas contacts.

Modern Japanese domestic rugby is still dominated by these two classes of teams, the company sides and the universities. Japan actually has the largest number of clubs of any country in the world, but most of them run only a single team. One domestic showpiece is a play-off game between the champion company side and the champion college, although this is a rather predictable affair almost invariably being won comfortably by the company team.

Internationally, Japan was the main organiser of the Asian championship, which was first played in 1969. Japan has won this tournament more often than any other country, with Korea providing the major competition in recent years. Japan's first contact with a major nation was when they played an England XV in Tokyo in 1971 and lost only 6-3, although they had beaten a strong Junior All Blacks side 23-19 in New Zealand three years earlier. In 1973, France became the first leading country to award full international status to a match against Japan. The game took place at Bordeaux during a Japanese tour, the French winning 30-18. Scotland toured Japan in 1989, and Japan won the Test 28-24, although the Scots had nine players absent on Lions duty.

Unfortunately the World Cup has not been such a happy hunting ground for Japan. A 52-8 win over Zimbabwe in 1991 has been their only success in nine matches in the final stages, and in 1995 there were heavy defeats against Wales and Ireland and that horrible 145-17 rout by the All Blacks. Japan is hosting the 2002 soccer World Cup. Poor international rugby results will not help the Japanese game resist that challenge.

ROMANIA

Year founded: 1914 *Joined IB:* 1987 *No of clubs:* 65
No of players: 1100 adults/3300 juniors

Historically Romania had close cultural connections with France, and it was through this link that rugby in the country began. Romanian students who had been educated in Paris brought the game back with them just before World War I. All the early rugby-playing clubs in the country were in and around the capital city of Bucharest, with the first to play the game being the Romanian Tennis Club Bucharest in 1913. They were also the winners of the first national club championship, which took place the next year.

The Romanian Rugby Federation was also founded in 1914, when there were probably only about 100 players in the country. Numbers grew slowly in the 1920s and 1930s to something over 1000 in the 1940s. International rugby also began between the wars. A Romanian national team played

Left: *British expatriates ruck and maul at Yokohama in 1874 as curious Japanese look on. The game soon took hold of the locals, however, particularly in educational establishments.*

a French XV in 1919, and Romania played internationals against France and the United States during the 1924 Olympics, suffering heavy defeats. In 1927, Romania also began matches against Czechoslovakia, to whom they have never lost, and in 1936, they began playing Germany. Romania were also founder members of FIRA, the French-led alternative to the British-dominated International Board.

Romanian rugby prospered from the 1950s to the mid-1980s. In 1957, a full-strength French side only just scraped an 18-15 last-minute win in Bucharest, and the Romanians notched up their first win against France in 1960. Since then Romania have played France every year except 1985, recording seven wins and two draws from the 38 games.

Romania widened its horizons during the 1970s with trips to Argentina and New Zealand as well as to Britain. By the start of the 1980s Romanian rugby was clearly strong enough to warrant full international status from the established countries. In 1981 they lost to Scotland by six points in Edinburgh and to the All Blacks at home by eight – both performances won them considerable respect. In 1983 they claimed a comfortable 24-6 win over Wales in Bucharest. To confirm this result was no fluke, in 1984 they beat Scotland, fresh from a Five Nations Grand Slam.

From this high point, the Romanian game went into a steep and rapid decline. The corrupt and incompetent Ceaucescu government led the county into chaos, and since rugby was state run and state funded, standards plummeted. Then came the 1989-90 revolution that toppled the communist regime. Tragically, several leading Romanian rugby personalities were killed during the uprising. Despite all this, rugby has continued in Romania. There are now about a third as many clubs as there were during the game's high point in the late 1970s, but there have still been some important international successes.

Romania have played in the final stages of all three World Cups, with wins in 1987 over Zimbabwe and in 1991 over Fiji. They also beat Wales in Bucharest in 1988 and Scotland, also at home, in 1991. Even better was their first away win against France in 1990. Domestic problems continue to hit Romanian rugby hard, however, and Romania have now clearly been overtaken by Italy as Europe's leading 'minor' nation.

Below: *Romania score against Scotland at Bucharest in August 1991. The home side won the game 18-12 and went on to beat Fiji later in the year in the pool stage of the World Cup.*

Above: The Tongan team perform their version of the haka *before their World Cup match against Ivory Coast in 1995. The Tongans came third in their pool behind France and Scotland.*

TONGA

Year founded: 1923 Joined IB: 1987 No of clubs: 600
No of players: 30,000 adults/50,000 juniors

Rugby was first played in Tonga in about 1900, when it was introduced by Australian teachers employed in a number of Tongan colleges. Gradually, other Tongans learned the game while working or studying abroad. The Tongan Rugby Union was formed in 1923, and it was then, despite the earlier games, that organised rugby in Tonga really took off.

In 1924, Fiji arrived to play a Test series. Tonga won the first game 9-6, Fiji took the second 14-3 and the third was a tense 0-0 draw. Fiji won the return series two games to one in 1926 and have generally had the upper hand since. Tonga's first game against Western Samoa was in 1956, and the Tongans remained well on top in this series until the 1980s, since when Western Samoa have been dominant.

In 1954, an Australian XV became the first side from a major rugby-playing country to visit Tonga, and the Tongans' first Test against opponents other than fellow Pacific islanders was on a visit to Australia in 1973. The Tongans had mixed results in the early part of their tour and

lost the First Test 30-12, but they turned the form book upside down in the Second Test, scoring four tries to two in a 16-11 win.

Tonga made an effective showing in the 1987 World Cup, although they did not win any of their pool games. They might have done better in their game against Canada but were compelled to play on a Sunday, which they never do at home for religious reasons, many Tongan clubs in fact being part of local churches. They did not qualify for the 1991 World Cup but were delighted when they edged Fiji out for a place in the 1995 final stages. Again they won only one match, against Ivory Coast, the unfortunate game in which Ivory Coast wing Max Brito was so seriously injured.

UNITED STATES

Year founded: 1975 Joined IB: 1987 No of clubs: 850
No of players: 28,000 adults/2000 juniors

Various American universities played rough-and-ready football-type games as far back as about 1840, but they must have been violent affairs, for the game was banned at Harvard in 1860. Rutgers and Princeton Colleges played a 25-a-side game in 1869 that has been described as America's first rugby match, but it would be more accurate to regard it as the first-ever game of American football. Harvard did play Canada's McGill University in a genuine rugby match in 1874, while the Canadians were on what was perhaps the first overseas rugby tour. In 1880, American football rules were formalised, and the two games began to diverge.

Aspects of the rules of American football made serious injuries and even fatalities quite common in the early days, however, and President Theodore Roosevelt threatened to ban the game in 1905 unless rule changes were made. The rules were duly modified, but in California, football was still forbidden for some years. Colleges took to rugby instead. From 1905 to 1913 there were regular domestic matches as well as tours both to and from Australia and New Zealand. New Zealand sent a full-strength All Blacks squad to California in 1913, and they were unbeaten in 13 games. These one-sided matches are said to have helped turn the Californians back towards American football.

Some American rugby was played after World War I, however, especially in the Olympic Games. The United States took the Olympic gold in 1920, beating the only other entrant, 'France', in reality a Paris select team, 8-0 in Antwerp. In 1924 Stanford University formed the US team to defend the title in France. There were only three entrants, and the Americans beat Romania 39-0 and then France 17-3 in the final. Rugby then ceased to be an Olympic sport, and as reigning champions and two-time winners the United States is the top Olympic rugby nation.

These were one-off successes, though, and rugby remained a minor sport. Nonetheless, enthusiasts kept the game going and in 1975 formed a national union. Since then

rugby has grown in popularity. A national club competition was set up in 1983 and was first won by Old Blues of California. Women's rugby, largely based in colleges and universities, is especially strong in the United States.

The United States have also developed a regular rivalry with Canada, with matches played every year since 1977. The United States won the second Can-Am game in 1978, but Canada are comfortably ahead in the series. Other than in the Olympics, the United States have not yet beaten a major Test side, but they did appear in the first two World Cups, beating Japan in the final stages in 1987. Argentina edged them out in the qualifying rounds for the 1995 tournament. Regular competition can only be beneficial, and in 1996 the United States played nine internationals in the new Pacific Rim and Pan-American Championships, with wins over Canada, Uruguay, Japan and Hong Kong.

WESTERN SAMOA

Year founded: 1927 *Joined IB:* 1988 *No of clubs:* 124
No of players: 6500 adults/7500 juniors

Western Samoa was a German colony until the end of World War I and was then administered, until independence in 1962, by New Zealand. It is therefore no surprise that much

Below: *The Americans move the ball during their match against Ireland at Dublin in 1994. The United States held the Irish to a very creditable 26-15 margin.*

of Western Samoa's rugby development is owed to that connection. Western Samoa's rugby union was originally founded in 1927 as the Apia Rugby Union (Apia is the capital) and was affiliated at first to the New Zealand union.

By then the Western Samoans had already played their first international, however, against a visiting Fijian side in 1924, losing 6-0. Over the next 30 years, Western Samoa's international experience was limited to a number of matches against opponents like the Cook Islands and the Solomon Islands. It was 1954 before Western Samoa played Fiji for the second time, and a further two years before their first meeting with Tonga. Western Samoa won the South Pacific Championship for the first time in 1971, although Fiji and Tonga did not play that year, and in both 1982 and 1985 they confirmed their growing strength by winning a three-team tournament, with Fiji and Tonga the other participants.

The New Zealand Maoris gave the Western Samoans their first contacts with the wider rugby world when they toured Western Samoa in 1960, but it took until 1976 for Western Samoa to make the return trip. Western Samoa's first major European opponents were Wales, who played one Test against them during a South Pacific tour in 1986. Wales won comfortably. Western Samoa then toured a number of European rugby-playing countries in 1988 and 1989 but without wins in any of the big games.

The 1991 World Cup was a different story. Western Samoa beat Korea, Tonga and Japan in the qualifying matches and then claimed their biggest scalp in their opening game of the tournament proper, when their thunderous tackling reduced Wales to incoherence and a 13-16 defeat – at Cardiff Arms Park of all places. Next they held

Above: *Matthew Vaea of Western Samoa tussles with the Welsh forwards as his side upsets the form book and defeats Wales 16-13 on their home turf in the 1991 World Cup.*

eventual champions Australia to 9-3, before comfortably defeating Argentina to earn a place in the quarter-finals. They could get no further than that, however, falling to a well-prepared Scotland team who now knew what to expect. It was still the finest performance yet by a World Cup outsider, made possible by the 24 players out of the squad of 26 who had played first-class rugby in New Zealand.

The New Zealand connection has been a mixed blessing for Western Samoan rugby, however. Many top players of Samoan descent have been lost to the All Blacks over the years, among the best-known being 1970s wing Bryan Williams, 1990s threequarter Va'aiga Tuigamala and flanker Michael Jones. Western Samoan rugby has lost a number of its stars to league in recent years also. Together, these factors, combined with economic and other problems on the islands, have meant that Western Samoan teams have had extreme ups and downs as the 1990s have proceeded. In 1996, for example, they lost 60-0 to Fiji but came to Britain at the end of the year and beat Ireland 40-25.

Western Samoan teams have also had problems with discipline on the field. Their aggressive tackling often crosses the line and becomes dangerous and illegal. They were involved in various rough games in the 1995 World Cup, for example, and had a player sent off in the semi-finals of the Sevens World Cup in 1997. But, if and when they can assemble their full rugby strength, Western Samoa will certainly be able to give anyone a run for their money.

ZIMBABWE

Year founded: 1895 *Joined IB:* 1987 *No of clubs:* 40
No of players: 900 adults / 5000 juniors

Rugby is believed to have been played in what is now Zimbabwe since the arrival of the first European settlers in the so-called Pioneer Column in 1890. By 1895, five clubs existed, two in Salisbury (modern-day Harare) and three in Bulawayo. That year, these clubs got together to form the Rhodesia Rugby Football Union. From those earliest times until the creation of a fully independent Zimbabwe in 1980, Rhodesia played under the auspices of South African rugby.

Rhodesian 'national' sides played in the Currie Cup from 1898, their entry that year meaning a six-month 'tour' of South Africa for the team. Almost equally arduous was the travelling involved in Rhodesia's first provincial match between Salisbury and Bulawayo in 1901. Bulawayo, won 16-0, but had a 400-kilometre, three-week round trip by ox-cart to fulfil the fixture.

As inhabitants of a South African 'province', Rhodesian players were also regarded as eligible for Springbok selection. Rhodesia were also often given fixtures against major touring teams visiting South Africa. The first such match was in 1910 against the British Isles, who won 24-11. Rhodesia never beat the Lions in nine attempts, but they did have success in two matches against New Zealand in 1949, beating the All Blacks 6-5 in the first match and holding them to a draw in the second. Almost as creditable was a draw four years later against the Wallabies.

■ INTERNATIONAL BOARD MEMBERS ■

Andorra	Latvia
Argentina	Lithuania
Australia	Luxembourg
Austria	Madagascar
Bahamas	Malaysia
Barbados	Moldova
Belgium	Morocco
Bermuda	Namibia
Bosnia Herzegovina	Netherlands
Botswana	New Zealand
Brazil	Norway
Bulgaria	Papua New Guinea
Canada	Paraguay
Chile	Poland
China (People's	Portugal
Republic)	Romania
Chinese Taipei	Russia
(Taiwan)	St Lucia
Cook Islands	Scotland
Croatia	Singapore
Czech Republic	Slovenia
Denmark	South Africa
England	Spain
Fiji	Sri Lanka
France	Sweden
Georgia	Switzerland
Germany	Tahiti
Gulf RFU	Thailand
Guyana	Tonga
Hong Kong	Trinidad and Tobago
Hungary	Tunisia
Ireland	Ukraine
Israel	United States
Italy	Uruguay
Ivory Coast	Wales
Jamaica	Western Samoa
Japan	Yugoslavia
Kenya	Zambia
Korea	Zimbabwe

In the 1960s and 1970s, Rhodesia also recorded wins against Argentina, Italy and the United States. In the years immediately before and after independence in 1980, however, many top players, including two Springboks of the time, Ray Mordt and David Smith, chose to continue their rugby careers in South Africa. For this and other reasons the strength of the game in Rhodesia/Zimbabwe declined.

The government and the rugby authorities have since begun successful programmes to develop the game in schools and among the black population generally. In international terms, Zimbabwe have remained weak, however. Invited to play in the first World Cup, their best result was a one-point defeat against Romania. This was followed by three heavy defeats in 1991 and a failure to qualify for the final stages in 1995.

Left: *Smiles all round as Western Samoa win the Hong Kong Sevens in 1993. In 1997, they got to the semi-finals of the World Sevens before being put out by eventual winners Fiji.*

· COMPETITIONS ·

All Black prop Craig Dowd in determined mood in the Third Test of the Lions 1993 tour. New Zealand won the match 30-13 and the series 2-1.

There are many long-standing rivalries in rugby, yet not so long ago formal international competitions were few. Indeed, until fairly recently the northern hemisphere home unions regarded the Five Nations as a series of friendlies. The arrival of the World Cup and the move to professionalism, however, has led to the emergence of new competitions – for women as well as men – at national, provincial and club level. The old rivalries still exist, but now prize money may be at stake as well as national pride.

CHAPTER TWELVE

· THE WORLD CUP ·

New Zealand captain David Kirk (left) and his predecessor Andy Dalton hold up the Webb Ellis Trophy after the 1987 final.

Rugby was one of the last major sports to establish a world championship tournament. Traditionalists at the top of the game, especially in the British unions, feared that creating such a tournament would merely be the thin end of a wedge driving the game towards professionalism and domination by television and other commercial interests. In the 1950s, there had even been a resolution passed by the International Board forbidding countries from organising a world championship tournament. By the 1980s, views had changed, however. Both Australia and New Zealand actively supported a world cup, and in 1985 the International Board gave the go-ahead.

Of course the traditionalists were proved right, since the establishment and then success of the Rugby World Cup have been the most important factors that have moved the game towards its present position on professionalism. On the other hand, the traditionalists cannot argue with the fact that, on the field at least, the three World Cups to date have justified all their proponents' hopes and given the game a dazzling and attractive centrepiece.

It is also possible that the creation and development of the World Cup have assisted the political changes that have taken place in South Africa since the late 1980s. South Africa was excluded from the first two World Cups, a correct and surprisingly brave decision considering the previous weakness of the other leading rugby nations in the face of clear evidence of both professionalism and racism in South African rugby. This exclusion can have been only a small, albeit useful, addition to the pressures for change brought to bear on South Africa's rulers in these years. However, the atmosphere of good sense and goodwill created around the 1995 World Cup by President Nelson Mandela – with the notable assistance of South Africa's captain, François Pienaar – said much about the role rugby can play in reuniting a formerly divided nation.

THE WORLD CUP DOWN UNDER

Sixteen nations competed in the 1987 World Cup tournament, which was jointly hosted by Australia and New Zealand. All the teams that played in the competition did so by invitation, there having been no qualifying matches. The participating teams were the two hosts, the five leading European nations, plus Argentina, Canada, Fiji, Italy, Japan, Romania, Tonga, the United States and Zimbabwe. These were clearly the leading playing countries of the time, with the exception of South Africa, although Korea, Spain and certainly Western Samoa might have challenged the claims of their respective regions' representatives.

New Zealand and Australia were both tipped in the pre-tournament assessments – New Zealand especially, since the participants in the 1986 rebel Cavalier tour to South Africa had been allowed to return to the official All Black party. France arrived on the back of a Five Nations Grand Slam and 1986 victories over the All Blacks. Scotland, in the same pool as France, looked the best of the British teams.

The tournament burst into vibrant life in the first match. Hosts New Zealand laid down a challenge to all their opponents with a crushing 70-6 win over Italy. All Black

Below: *John Kirwan, the All Blacks' all-time leading try-scorer and most-capped wing, runs at the Argentinian defence during New Zealand's 46-15 pool match win in 1987.*

▪ JOHN GALLAGHER ▪

| John Gallagher | *Full-back, born 1964* |
| *Wellington & New Zealand* | *18 Tests 1987-89, 13 tries* |

One of the most potent weapons in the All Black armoury at the 1987 World Cup was full-back John Gallagher. Gallagher, brought up in England but of Irish descent, went to New Zealand for the first time on holiday in 1984 and stayed on. In England, he had played mainly junior rugby, but by the 1987 World Cup he was first choice All Black full-back and made his full New Zealand debut in the first match against Italy.

Gallagher went on to score four tries in the pool match against Fiji, showing great pace, brilliant timing of attacking runs and excellent choice of running angles. After sharing in the 1987 triumph, Gallagher starred in the All Black line-up for two more years before departing to rugby league. Sadly, he never re-created in his new sport the form that had taken him to the top in rugby union.

wing John Kirwan scored an utterly astonishing try. Kirwan took a pass from his captain, scrum-half David Kirk, well inside his own 22 and set off. By the time he reached the Italian 22, Kirwan had swerved and powered his way past about eight defenders and he made the try-line before the last despairing efforts of the Italian cover. New Zealand easily saw off Fiji and Argentina in their other pool matches, with Fiji coming second in the group on points difference.

In the other pools, Australia beat England, and Wales edged ahead of Ireland, but with none of the four looking desperately impressive in the process. Scotland and France

played the most dramatic match in the pool stages. The Scots built up a good lead by the middle of the second half, despite the loss through injury (for the whole tournament as it turned out) of their principal playmaker, the great stand-off John Rutherford. France turned the tables, only for Scotland to snatch a draw with an injury-time try. France outscored Scotland in their other pool games, and so Scotland, having finished second, faced the harder quarter-final against the All Blacks.

Scotland hoped to trouble New Zealand in the scrummages. They did nothing of the sort, and New Zealand calmly accumulated a 30-3 win. Meanwhile, France cruised past Fiji in their quarter-final, and Australia began to justify their tag as pre-tournament favourites with a decisive win over the Irish. The Wales v England match was, to say the least, indifferent, with seemingly little commitment and even less skill on show from both sides. Wales won by 13 points.

BLANCO STUNS AUSTRALIA

One semi-final was the best match of the tournament; the other was a debacle. The former was played in Sydney before a disappointingly small crowd, even though it featured Australia's attempt to reach the final. The few who turned up to watch were rewarded with a classic. Four Michael Lynagh penalties and converted tries from David Campese and David Codey were countered by a penalty from Didier Camberabero and tries from second-row Alain Lorieux, centre Philippe Sella and flying wing Patrice Lagisquet. France were behind three times in the match, and at 9-0 and 15-12 Lynagh had relatively simple kicks to extend Australia's lead – he missed both. With moments left on the clock, the score stood at 24-24. Then France created one of the great scores in international rugby history. Back row, centres and wings combined in a seemingly endless move that finally gave full-back Serge Blanco just enough room to sneak over in the far left corner, just ahead of a despairing Australian tackle. Camberabero kicked the conversion and France were in the final.

MIXED FORTUNES FOR WALES

The next day, New Zealand destroyed Wales 49-6 in the second semi-final. Wales were without several of their best forwards, but even with them they would have been no match for one of the great All Black teams, who had now knitted together a fierce combination of power and technique. Following an altercation near the end of the

Below: *France's Serge Blanco, one of the great running full-backs of the modern era, crosses in the corner to extinguish Australia's hopes of reaching the 1987 final.*

match, Welsh lock Huw Richards had to be picked up woozily off the floor only to be sent off for the punch that had started it all, rounding off a day of misery for Wales. All Black number eight Wayne Shelford, otherwise one of the players of the tournament, was lucky to remain on the pitch for his part in retaliating for the original offence. In the third-place match, Wales surprisingly came back to beat Australia 22-21 with an injury-time conversion by full-back Paul Thorburn. Australian forward David Codey was sent off early in a lacklustre game.

After the brilliance of the Sydney encounter, the final in Auckland was disappointing for neutrals – but not for New Zealand fans. Apart from short periods, the All Blacks had just too much control. They dominated the match up front, with French captain and hooker Daniel Dubroca unable to inspire his men to the same level of passion as they had reached in the semi-final. Unfortunately the All Blacks showed little enterprise outside the pack. Fly-half Grant Fox kicked 17 points but did little to set his backs running. Nonetheless, New Zealand notched three tries. The first was scored by flanker Michael Jones, whose form throughout the

Below: *David Kirk races away to score New Zealand's second try in their 29-9 victory over France in the 1987 final. Michael Jones and John Kirwan also got on the All Black score sheet.*

Above: *Wales scrum-half Robert Jones spins out a pass during the 1987 third-place play-off against Australia. Wales won 22-21 after Paul Thorburn converted a late Adrian Hadley try.*

tournament had been sensational. Jones had been capped by Western Samoa in 1986 and had made his All Black debut in the first World Cup match against Italy. A devoutly religious man, Jones had not played in the semi-final because the match took place on a Sunday. Half-back and skipper David Kirk also ran in a try and had a hand in the other before, in the final minute, Pierre Berbizier registered a consolation score for France.

It is perhaps asking too much to get a great game in the final when so much is at stake. But when David Kirk marched up the steps in the Eden Park grandstand to hoist the Webb Ellis Trophy, it was not hard to see that he and most of New Zealand were more than happy with the result. And even more important for the future, every one of the leading countries left the tournament convinced that this was the way forward for the game and determined that next time they would give New Zealand a real contest for the prize.

THE WORLD CUP HEADS NORTH

For the 1991 tournament, the World Cup moved to the northern hemisphere, with matches shared between the four home unions and France. The split of matches between Australia and New Zealand had been unsatisfactory in 1987, and the dispersion of games in 1991 was also unfortunate, although it did guarantee that each of the Five Nations sides

played most of their matches before partisan home support. The tournament was played in October and November in the first half of the northern hemisphere 1991-92 season.

This time a qualifying competition had taken place, contested by 15 teams in four regions. This yielded a total of eight qualifiers to join the eight quarter-finalists from 1987. The bookmakers made Australia slight favourites over the All Blacks, with England and France, and then Scotland, the only outsiders given any realistic chance of winning.

The opening match was at Twickenham and saw England, Grand Slam winners in 1990-91, take on the reigning world champions, New Zealand, in Pool 1. It was not a great game, with only one try to accompany the 26 points scored from kicks, but New Zealand were able to win more possession and so give Grant Fox just enough chances at goal to secure the match. New Zealand won 18-12, with the All Black try-scorer Michael Jones once again showing his quality in everything he did all around the pitch. As expected, New Zealand and England proved too strong for the other teams in the group, Italy and the United States.

ENTER WESTERN SAMOA

Pool 2 came down to the predicted showdown between Scotland and Ireland, won 24-15 by Scotland. France won all three of their matches in Pool 4, although they were pushed hard by Canada, who claimed a quarter-final spot with fine wins over Romania and Fiji. Pool 3 was dominated by Australia, but it also supplied the first great upset of the tournament. In their first game, Wales came up against Western Samoa. Most Welshmen would have been pushed to find Western Samoa on the map, but many of the latter's team lived in New Zealand and had been hardened in the fires of New Zealand rugby. They put in a barrage of crunching tackles that knocked the Welshmen back time after time. The Western Samoans may have been a little fortunate to have been awarded their first try, but they held on for a famous 16-13 victory.

The Welsh were at least able to joke for a time that it was just as well they hadn't been playing the whole of Samoa, but they had little to smile about after their final pool game against Australia. Wales were never in contention in the first half and conceded five tries in the second to lose 38-3. For long periods one of the world's finest rugby nations, Wales would now have to face matches with the European minnows to earn qualification for the next World Cup.

Left: *Phil Davies of Wales runs into Western Samoan centre Frank Bunce in the 1991 pool phase. Bunce went on to play for New Zealand and featured in their 1995 World Cup campaign.*

All the winning quarter-finalists had to work hard for their successes. Scotland saw off Western Samoa 28-6 at Murrayfield, and the All Blacks beat Canada 29-13 in a rain-sodden match at Lille, France. France and England's match took place in the deafening atmosphere of Parc des Princes in Paris. France were too fired up for the game, and their discipline and organisation suffered. Referee David Bishop from New Zealand had his work cut out keeping the match under control, and afterwards, when France had lost 19-10, he was involved in an unpleasant incident with French coach Daniel Dubroca. England controlled the match through the power of their forwards. One enormous tackle from flanker Micky Skinner that snuffed out a dangerous French attack was one of the high points of the match.

IRELAND OH SO CLOSE

There was if anything more drama in the fourth quarter-final in Dublin. Favourites Australia were expected to post a routine success over Ireland – but the Irish would have none of it. Ireland competed all the way and entered the last six or seven minutes only 15-12 down. Australia had always looked the better side and had scored both the game's tries up to that point, but Ireland were not finished. Suddenly flanker Gordon Hamilton found himself clear but with over 40 metres to go to make the line. His desperate sprint was roared on by the Lansdowne Road crowd, and he had just enough pace and strength to keep ahead of the Australian cover. Ralph Keyes kicked the conversion, and Ireland were three points in front with scarcely five minutes left.

Now Australia really showed their quality, mounting a last-chance attack without a sign of panic or unnecessary haste. They drove down the left into the Irish 22, and their forwards won possession again. The ball came out to fly-half Michael Lynagh who had the option of a drop at goal for the equalising points but instead spun it wide. The Irish cover scrambled across but could not quite close down centres Tim Horan and Jason Little, who made ground before moving the ball on to David Campese on the wing. Campese was tackled short of the line but was able to give the pass on to the supporting Lynagh, who just made it home in the corner. Australia 19, Ireland 18 was the final score.

SHOWDOWN IN EDINBURGH

The first semi-final was Scotland v England at Murrayfield. Not only was a place in the final at stake, but England were also fiercely determined to reverse the result of the last Murrayfield encounter between the game's oldest enemies, in which Scotland had denied them the 1990 Grand Slam. It proved to be a dour and tense struggle.

Above: *Straining every sinew, Irish flanker Gordon Hamilton charges up the Lansdowne Road pitch, cheered on by thousands of his compatriots and with one of the game's speed merchants, David Campese, in pursuit. Hamilton hung on to reach the line first. Ireland were within moments of dumping Australia out of the 1991 tournament, only for Michael Lynagh to snatch victory for the Wallabies with a last-gasp score.*

Below: *Dublin proved a happy hunting ground for Australia in the semi-finals, too. Here All Black centre Craig Innes is stopped by Wallabies Lynagh (bottom) and Simon Poidevin.*

England had the better of the play for the first 60 minutes, but were unable to get in front. The score midway through the second half stood at 6-6. Then a rare Scottish attack ended with the award of the simplest of penalties virtually in front of the English posts. Gavin Hastings, who had been in towering form all through the tournament, stepped up from full-back to take the easy three points – and sent the kick wide. The English effort was revived. Instead of allowing a game they ought to have been winning begin to slip away, England dominated the rest of the match and finally clinched victory with a Rob Andrew dropped goal.

The second semi-final, which took place in Dublin the next day, saw Australia score a well-deserved 16-6 win over the All Blacks. Quite simply, Australia looked the better team. They were committed to lively, attacking rugby and inspired by the genius of David Campese. Australia scored the only two tries of the match, and in the final stages it even looked as though they were coasting a little – a luxury that few opponents of the All Blacks have ever enjoyed.

New Zealand beat Scotland 13-6 in the third-place match, which was, as in 1987, a rather subdued affair. Perhaps the most amusing moment was when All Black prop Richard Loe had the indignity of being bounced backwards when trying to tackle Gavin Hastings.

Below: *Australia's John Eales (No 5) palms the ball back towards the waiting Nick Farr-Jones (No 9), as the Wallabies defeat England on their home turf in the 1991 final.*

▪ THE CAMPESE MAGIC ▪

Some people said that the real final of the 1991 World Cup was played out a week early in Dublin between Australia and New Zealand. Australia were victors, thanks to two moments of David Campese magic. Campese scored the first try himself. Australia won a ball well inside the New Zealand 22, out towards the left wing. Instead of spinning the ball to the open side, scrum-half Nick Farr-Jones sent his pass further left, and up popped Campese off the right wing to slant into the corner to score.

Australia's second try was scored by centre Tim Horan but was made completely by Campese. He snapped up a bouncing kick from under the All Blacks' noses, took it on at pace and, when the cover closed in, flicked a delightful pass over his shoulder for Horan to score.

The tournament's climax took place at Twickenham, and England naturally had most of the support in the ground, but the Australians had a few unexpected fans – most of the Scottish team turned up to watch wearing Australian colours! Bizarrely, England, with the strength of their forwards plain for all to see, tried to alter their game plan and develop a more open style. If, as some people have suggested, this was inspired by Australian criticism of the established England style, then there can scarcely ever have been a more effective piece of sports kidology. This is not to say that England would inevitably have won if they had played their usual game, but they certainly did not improve their chances by this last-minute change of mind.

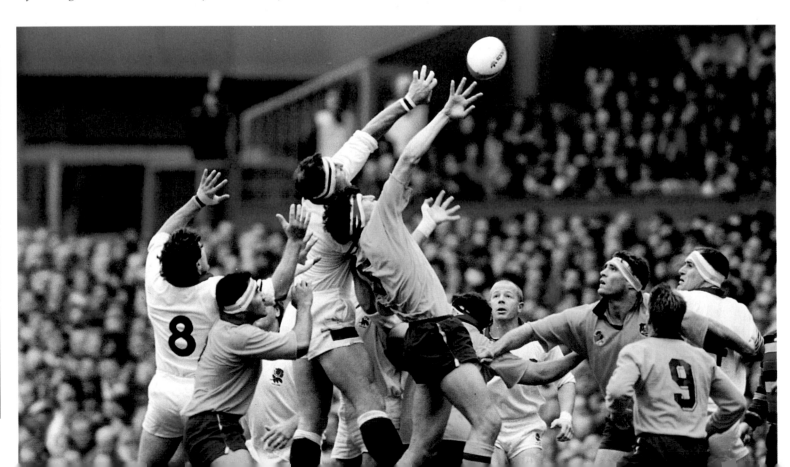

Australia kicked the opening penalty, and then midway through the first half scored the only try of the match. Flanker Willie Ofahengaue won a line-out ball close to England's line, and the Australians drove it on. The pile collapsed over the England line with a delighted prop Tony Daly at the bottom to claim the score. England had to wait until the second half before they got on the scoreboard with a Webb penalty, only to see Lynagh make it 12-3 to Australia soon after. Then came the most controversial incident of the game. England worked what looked to be a clear overlap on the left, when David Campese dived in to block the final pass to Rory Underwood. There could have been no question in Welsh referee Derek Bevan's mind that it was a deliberate knock-on and therefore a penalty – but was there a case for a penalty try? It was a horribly difficult decision. Underwood had some space at first, but would he have beaten the Australian cover to the corner? Bevan awarded a penalty, and Webb knocked it over. Try as they did, though, England could manufacture no more scoring opportunities, and the Wallabies ran out 12-6 winners.

THE RAINBOW WORLD CUP

Great political changes began in South Africa in 1990 with the release from prison of Nelson Mandela. The country's reintegration into the rugby world soon got under way, and the new South Africa played its first internationals in 1992. In rugby terms the rehabilitation process was completed with South Africa's appointment as host nation of the 1995 World Cup. With the aid of many important rugby personalities, notably Springbok captain François Pienaar and manager Morné du Plessis, the event was used to foster feelings of 'rainbow nation' togetherness and to begin healing some past wounds. It was a happy coincidence that wing Chester Williams was on hand to feature in the publicity campaigns. With his talents, there was no question of his being included as some sort of token black.

The qualifying process for the 1995 tournament was the most extensive yet, with 43 countries participating. There were comparatively few surprises, and the more fancied teams generally made their way to the final stages. In the last of the qualifying matches, Argentina beat the United States to clinch the Americas place, and Tonga beat Fiji in the Pacific. Wales meanwhile calmed their fans' worst fears by topping the final European group, followed by Italy and Romania. Ivory Coast surprisingly saw off Namibia, Zimbabwe and Morocco for the African spot, while Japan won the Asian play-off against Korea. A bunch of world records for an international match were set in the Asian qualifiers when Hong Kong beat Singapore 164-13.

Above: *Referee David McHugh dismisses South Africa's James Dalton (centre left) and Canada's Gareth Rees (centre right) at Port Elizabeth. Canada's Rod Snow was also sent off.*

Setting aside supporters' own national allegiances, most rugby fans would have agreed before the tournament that the 'correct' final in what was rugby's first true world championship ought to be between South Africa and New Zealand, historically the game's two strongest teams. But Australia, England and France, and perhaps even Scotland on their day, would all have something to say about that.

THREE GET MARCHING ORDERS

The big guns were in action from the start, with South Africa facing Australia in the opening pool match. The pre-match ceremonies were dazzlingly colourful and contributed substantially to what in rugby's eyes was already a great occasion. South Africa did not let their fans down. Although the teams scored two tries apiece, South Africa seemed to have the greater commitment and were able to give fly-half Joel Stransky enough kicking chances to see them through to a 27-18 win. The other teams in the group, Canada and Romania, had shown disappointing form in the build-up, but Canada at least improved enough to give the top two a real work-out. The final game in the group was the Canada v South Africa clash, won 20-0 by South Africa. Unfortunately this was marred by an unseemly brawl late on. Three players were sent off and two more were subsequently cited and banned for foul play.

In the second pool, England were clear favourites and duly won all three games. They performed best against Western Samoa in their final match, having struggled hard against Argentina and Italy earlier on. Argentina had a

Left: Emile N'Tamack sets up victory for France in their 1995 pool match against Scotland. The win gave France a quarter-final against Ireland; Scotland got New Zealand.

ferociously powerful scrummage and could easily have won all three of their games but ended up with three defeats. Western Samoa claimed the second qualifying spot.

LOMU CUTS LOOSE

New Zealand played in the third group. The All Blacks had been rather unsettled in their preparation for the competition. Even so, their qualification for the quarter-finals was expected to be a formality, with Wales and Ireland fighting it out for second place, and Japan marked down as the whipping boys. As anticipated, New Zealand won all three of their games, but in far from routine fashion. New Zealand's opener was against Ireland, who played with all their traditional passion and actually scored the first try. Then the All Blacks unveiled the player who was to become the sensation of the tournament, Jonah Lomu. Lomu scored two tries and played a big part in a third, scattering Irish tacklers behind him whenever he got the ball. Wales, too, were swept aside by the All Blacks, but at least they managed to keep Lomu off the score sheet. One of the All Black scorers against Wales was flanker Josh Kronfeld, who was playing a vital role in creating for New Zealand the continuity of play that every team was trying to establish.

The Wales *v* Ireland match was scrappy and unconvincing, only coming to life near the end. Ireland built up a solid lead, and Wales gradually hauled them back in the final stages. Ireland just held out 24-23. But spare a thought for poor Japan – 57 points conceded against Wales, 50 more given away against Ireland, and then in the most astonishing match of all, 145 points were amassed against them by what was essentially the All Black second XV. Mark

Ellis scored six tries, and Simon Culhane kicked ten conversions. And Japan were far from being a hopeless side.

In the fourth pool, Scotland and France were the real contenders and met in the group's final match. Scotland if anything had the advantage, having won their Five Nations match in Paris earlier in the year. They had also registered a record 89-0 win over Ivory Coast eight days before. Captain Gavin Hastings was in talismanic form, and there was plenty to play for with the losers set to face the rampant All Blacks in the quarter-final.

The outcome was one of the games of the tournament. Scotland started the stronger, with a fierce forward effort sustained throughout the first half. France fought back, breaking Scottish hearts with an injury-time try by Emile N'Tamack, which, when converted, gave them a 22-19 win. Tonga and Ivory Coast tried hard in this group but ended up also-rans. And tragedy struck when they played one another – Ivory Coast wing Max Brito was carried off and subsequently found to be completely paralysed.

Three of the quarter-final matches seemed easy to call, and turned out as expected. France had too much strength for Ireland and dominated the game up front. They scored only two tries in their 36-12 win, but Thierry Lacroix was in expert form with the boot, kicking one conversion and eight penalties. South Africa also saw off Western Samoa comfortably enough – on the scoreboard at least. The match was rough, with many Western Samoan tackles being high and dangerous. Equally unpleasant were the (emphatically denied) allegations that the South African scrum-half, Joost van der Westhuizen, had made racist comments.

In the Scotland *v* New Zealand game, the Jonah Lomu story continued. The Scotland defence simply could not cope with his power. The Scots were disappointed with a couple of the scores they conceded as the All Blacks ran up a 45-16 lead. They rallied and recovered to 48-30 at no-side, but New Zealand went marching on.

BATTLE OF THE BOOTS

The outcome of the fourth of the quarter-finals, which would see one of the favourites for the trophy drop out, was harder to predict. As it turned out, the England *v* Australia match was hardly a classic, with only two tries scored, but even for neutrals it was nail-bitingly close. The English forwards powered ahead from the kick-off and dominated the first half. The England try, however, came from an

Australian error deep in the English half. The English backs snapped up the loose ball, and well-timed passes sent Tony Underwood scampering up the right wing on a long sprint to the try-line. He had just enough space – and pace – to elude his pursuers. At half-time, England led 13-6, but in the first minute of the second half, Australia grabbed a try through Damien Smith to level the scores. From then on it was up to the respective fly-halves and goal-kickers, Michael Lynagh and Rob Andrew.

The score went from 13-13 to 16-16, to 19-19, and then 22-22. Two minutes into injury time, England had a line-out just inside the Australian half. The giant second-row Martin Bayfield took the catch, and England drove forward, trying desperately to get Andrew into range for a final dropped-goal attempt. When the ball emerged, scrum-half Dewi Morris's pass to his stand-off was spot on, and Andrew's kick sailed over from some 45 metres out – 25-22 to England.

FRANCE HELD AT BAY

The first semi-final, featuring South Africa and France, was nearly a wash-out. Supposedly, torrential rain never falls in Durban in June, but it did, and as kick-off time approached,

Below: *South African flanker Ruben Kruger powers over for the only try of the 1995 South Africa* v *France semi-final, which was played on a rain-soaked pitch at Durban.*

part of the ground was under water. It was a terrible responsibility for the referee, since if the match had been abandoned without a try being scored, hosts South Africa would have gone out of the competition because of the sending-off and citing they had incurred against Canada. In the event, the game got going one and a half hours late, only for already poor conditions to be made worse by a return of heavy rain early in the first half.

It was not the fine test of rugby skills that everyone hoped for from a match of this stature. But there was no doubting the commitment shown by all 31 players who eventually appeared on the pitch. The Springboks scored the only try through flanker Ruben Kruger, who was having an excellent tournament. The other notable feature of the match was the resilience of the South African defence in the dying stages against the fiercest French attacks. Abdelatif Benazzi was stopped centimetres short of the South African line, and a sequence of crucial scrums followed. South Africa held out against the French drive for a push-over and then cleared the danger with decisive tackling when the French tried to move the ball wide.

ENGLAND PUT TO THE SWORD

The talk before the England *v* New Zealand game was mostly about Jonah Lomu. It took him about one minute of action to make his mark on the game. Lomu picked up a

kick in space well out on the left wing and proceeded to the England try-line without noticeable hindrance from Tony Underwood, Will Carling or Mike Catt, who were all well placed to make the tackle.

Within 20 minutes of the start of the match, New Zealand were out of sight. To add insult to injury, All Black number eight Zinzan Brooke dropped a goal, a virtually unknown feat for an international forward. To their credit, England stemmed their obvious panic and knuckled down to prevent total humiliation. England even outscored their opponents in the second half to finish 45-29 down, but there could be no question that the All Blacks were the superior side. In that first dreadful spell, Lomu seemed to terrify England in everything that he did, but he was far from a one-man band. New Zealand were stronger and quicker all through the team.

Despite automatic qualification for the 1999 tournament being at stake, the third-place play-off was the usual woeful affair, with an uninterested France beating a weary and fed-up England 19-9. The third-place match never really has any value for the tournament or the teams. It surely should not take place in future.

Left: *Jonah Lomu shrugs off Tony Underwood on the way to scoring the first of his four tries in New Zealand's 45-29 demolition of England in the 1995 semi-finals.*

Above: *South Africa's full-back André Joubert (No 15) congratulates his fly-half Joel Stransky, who has just dropped the goal that won the 1995 World Cup final.*

The final was played at Ellis Park, Johannesburg, in front of 63,000 spectators. There were no tries in a match that was dominated by the teams' defences. The Springboks proved that Jonah Lomu's remarkable physique could be tamed. They hit him hard and early, and he was unable to make the same impact as he had in the earlier games. The All Blacks were 9-6 down at half-time, but had the better of the territory and possession in the second half. They drew level with the Springboks, but could not land the decisive score, fly-half Andrew Mehrtens missing a final dropped-goal attempt just before the 80 minutes were up.

And so the World Cup final went into extra time. Mehrtens and Stransky exchanged penalties in the first ten minutes, and then, half-way through the second period, Stransky got the ball in dropped-goal range. His right-footed kick soared over. New Zealand tried everything to get back on level terms, but South Africa had enough left to hold out. South Africa's captain and number six, François Pienaar, received the cup from a delighted President Mandela, who was also wearing a Springbok number six shirt for the occasion.

Pienaar credited the South African success not just to the fans in Ellis Park but to the country's entire population of 43 million. One of the features of the game was the at times inspired defence of the South Africans, no doubt assisted by the sense of occasion that their fans so greatly enhanced. However, it is possible that the South African win

was owed partly to outside interference. Most of the New Zealand players were stricken with food poisoning or some similar complaint in the hours before the match. Reports have since suggested that this episode was related to the activities of a betting syndicate but, whatever may be the case, the All Blacks have declined to adopt this as an excuse.

After the final, a little bit of the gloss was taken off the occasion by the behaviour of the South African rugby president, Louis Luyt, who denigrated the efforts of the previous World Cup winners and insulted Ed Morrison, the English referee who controlled the final. Nonetheless, the terrible injury to Max Brito apart, it had been a superb World Cup. The best team of the tournament did not win the championship, but all in all perhaps the right one did.

FORWARD TO 1999

Qualifying matches for the 1999 World Cup are already well under way as this book is being written. Hosts Wales are rebuilding their national stadium in Cardiff to create a fitting setting for the final, and all the top teams are already preparing their strategies and developing their young stars in the quest to get their names on what is now undoubtedly rugby's most treasured trophy. And preparations for the 2003 World Cup are also beginning, with the host nation to be chosen during 1998.

Below: *President Mandela presents the Webb Ellis Trophy to South Africa's François Pienaar. Faced with a highly talented All Blacks outfit, the Springboks simply refused to lose.*

CHAPTER THIRTEEN

· THE FIVE NATIONS ·

Centre Christophe Lamaison on the attack against England at Twickenham during France's Grand Slam campaign in 1997. England built up a 20-6 lead, only to see it turn into a 23-20 deficit by the final whistle. Lamaison contributed 18 points, including a try.

Until only a few years ago, rugby purists used to insist that there was no such thing as the Five Nations championship, even though England, Scotland, Ireland and Wales had been playing each other regularly since the 1880s, with France joining in the fun in the early years of the twentieth century. They would tell you instead that each team merely happened to have annual friendly fixtures against all the others without there being any formal tournament.

Of course, rugby enthusiasts have been compiling championship tables almost since the first complete set of fixtures between the home unions in 1883. England won all three matches that year, but it was not until 1899 that the term Triple Crown was coined, when it was used to describe the Irish success that season. France first had a complete set of fixtures in 1910, and Wales became the first country to

win all four matches in a season in 1911. Once again the term for this feat took a long time to devise, with the first success to be called a Grand Slam being the England triumph in 1957. Even as late as then, most British commentators called the tournament the 'International Championship' and rather regarded the games against France as supplementary to the real business of Triple Crowns. The term 'Five Nations' has been in common use only in the most recent years. And to prove that the first hundred or so years of matches had not been part of any tournament, it was only in 1993 that a trophy was first awarded to the winners – with a system using points difference being established to prevent titles being shared.

The idea that there was no formal tournament was reflected in the way fixtures were scheduled. The current system is for two matches on a weekend, roughly every other week from mid-January to mid-March, with the sequence of fixtures altering according to a rota. But this has only prevailed since 1973-74. For most years before then, the various fixtures had traditional dates in the season, weather permitting. Scotland *v* France was almost always the first match of all, whether in Edinburgh or Paris, and the Calcutta Cup was similarly fixed on the third Saturday in March. This situation had consequences for the type of rugby that was played. Cardiff Arms Park was notoriously poorly drained in the 1950s and 1960s, and as a consequence the Wales *v* England game (always in January in those days) was virtually certain to be a muddy struggle in odd-numbered years, while those same seasons would see Wales toil in Paris on a warm spring day in March or early April.

GREAT DAYS AND UPSETS

One of the best features of the Five Nations is its unpredictability – it is a very unusual season indeed that does not have at least one significant upset. But equally, the best-remembered times in the Five Nations' history have been the eras when one team has been very much on top and given all the rest a real target to aim at. Wales and Scotland

Below: *Action from Wales's 22-0 victory over England at Swansea in 1907. Wales won six championships outright between 1900 and 1911 and shared a seventh.*

were the top dogs in this way in the first decade of this century, with England taking over as the team to beat in the 1920s. France had their first spell of domination at the end of the 1950s and have generally been strong ever since, but not strong enough to overshadow Wales in the 1970s and England in the 1990s.

It is also very noticeable how much better every team usually does on its home ground. Scotland, for example, have won at Twickenham only four times in 38 attempts since 1911. It is no surprise then that nine of Scotland's ten Grand Slams and Triple Crowns have been won in years when the Calcutta Cup match was played in Edinburgh. The rare exception was in 1938, when Scotland were inspired by fly-half Wilson Shaw and scored an unprecedented five tries at Twickenham. England fans might prefer to remember 1973 or 1975, when victories at Twickenham denied Scotland a Triple Crown, or 1995, when power up front and 24 points from Rob Andrew's boot gave England a Grand Slam that Scotland had hoped to claim for themselves.

The Parc des Princes in Paris has been another notable home fortress. Ireland never won there at all. The last time they won in France was at the old Stade Colombes in 1972, and they have not even beaten France in Dublin since 1983. Scotland have had almost as hard a time in Paris in recent decades. They won three times in the 1960s at Stade Colombes but lost every game at the Parc in the 1970s and

Above: Ireland's one and only Grand Slam to date was in 1948. Skipper and tactical mastermind was Karl Mullen (with ball), while Jack Kyle (seated front on left) was the playmaker.

1980s. Scotland finally broke their duck with Gavin Hastings's dramatic late try and conversion for a 23-21 victory in 1995, but France more than avenged this insult with a record 47-20 rout to complete their 1997 Grand Slam.

THE CARDIFF HOODOO

For Englishmen, Cardiff Arms Park was the place where it seemed for years as if they could not win. After their 13-6 success in Cardiff in 1963, there was almost 30 years of English gloom, with hammerings like 30-9 in 1969 and 27-3 in 1979 relieved only by a solitary 13-13 draw in 1983. Even in the late 1980s, when England looked easily the stronger side, they somehow contrived to throw games in Cardiff away. In 1987, English indiscipline cost them dear in a notoriously dirty match, and in 1989 Rory Underwood had a day he would surely like to forget, gifting Wales the only try of the game with a wayward and completely unnecessary pass deep in his own 22. England finally broke the Cardiff hoodoo in 1991 with seven Simon Hodgkinson penalties and

a solitary try – and that an unspectacular forward effort from a maul. Perhaps the long history of failure was the reason why England felt unable to open the game out even when they were clearly the much better team.

After their win there in 1962, Scotland had a similarly grim time in Cardiff through the 1960s and 1970s, but at least when the Scots finally broke this sequence after 20 years they did it in style. It was centre Jim Renwick's 47th game for his country, and amazingly he had never before been on a winning Scottish side away from home. This time he got one of Scotland's five tries as they raced to a 34-18 win, at that time easily the highest score that Wales had ever conceded at Cardiff. The game was also the first Five Nations match Wales had lost at home since 1968.

LOSING AND LOSING

In the early days, France struggled to get playing standards up to the level of the British teams, and accordingly the French sequence of 18 consecutive defeats from 1911 to 1920 (17 in the Five Nations plus one game against the South Africans) is the worst in the history of any of the Five Nations sides. Closely rivalling it is Scotland's sequence of 17 defeats, 15 of them in the championship, in the 1950s.

Scotland had a surprise win over Wales at Murrayfield in 1951 and then lost every match until they once again caused an upset to beat Wales 14-8 in Edinburgh in 1955. The Welsh performance in this game was so poor that when the Welsh players were taken on a sightseeing trip around Edinburgh the next day they were warned that they had better take a good look, since it was the last time that most of them would be there at the Welsh Rugby Union's expense.

Easily the longest losing sequence in recent times has been Ireland's ten championship games without a win from 1991 to 1993. Ireland, however, rounded off the 1993 season with two pleasing and much-deserved successes. First they beat Wales 19-14 in Cardiff and then turned the form book upside down in their last game when they totally outclassed England in Dublin. The Irish forwards dominated the game while Eric Elwood at fly-half kicked beautifully. Elwood put Ireland comfortably in front with two penalties and two dropped goals, and the icing on the cake came from a late Mick Galwey try for a final 17-3 margin.

Below: Left-wing Mike Slemen passes Keith Robertson to touch down for England as they defeat Scotland 30-18 at Murrayfield in 1980. The win gave England the Grand Slam.

▪ BARRY JOHN ▪

Barry John *Fly-half, born 1945*
Llanelli, Cardiff, Wales & British Lions
25 Tests (+5 for Lions) 1966-72.

Barry John had a comparatively short international career and chose to retire long before his best playing days were over, but he is still acclaimed as one of the greatest fly-halves ever to play the game. He came into the Welsh team in 1966 against Australia and did not impress everyone at first. He made a couple of appearances and was then dropped, only to be brought back a few games later. This time he was paired with a new scrum-half, the great Gareth Edwards, and his career never looked back. All of John's later caps, both with Wales and the Lions, were with this same half-back partner, and the two also played many games together as club-mates at Cardiff.

John was an excellent goal-kicker, both of penalties and conversions and of dropped goals, and his tactical kicking was also astute and devastatingly accurate, as New Zealand's Fergie McCormick famously found out in the First Test on the 1971 Lions tour. But what really made rugby fans gasp were John's running skills. He always seemed to have time to give just a little jink or swing of the hips to leave predatory back rows leaden footed and grasping at thin air.

John helped inspire Wales to a Triple Crown in 1969, to a share in the championship in 1970 and then to a Grand Slam in 1971, his efforts that year including a typical, crucial try against France in the decider. He was injured early in the First Test on the 1968 Lions tour and took no further part, but in 1971 in New Zealand he played in all four internationals in the series-winning side. His teammates and British fans called him simply the 'King', and by the end of that trip even the New Zealanders had to admit that they were probably right.

■ SERGE BLANCO ■

Serge Blanco *Full-back/wing, born 1958*
Biarritz Olympique & France
93 Tests 1980-91.

Serge Blanco was perhaps the greatest running and attacking full-back to play the game, and his was the genius that inspired many of France's finest performances in the Five Nations throughout the 1980s. He made his debut for France in South Africa in 1980 and was a leading member of the sides that won two Grand Slams, one more title outright and three shared championships in the decade that followed. Blanco also scored the spectacular last-minute try that won the 1987 World Cup semi-final against Australia, athough he had to be content with a runners-up medal in the final.

Blanco scored a total of 38 tries for France, the current French record, many of them vital – like that 1987 effort – and usually demonstrating great pace allied with balance, determination and intelligent angling and timing of his runs. Blanco and the French teams he played in, and latterly captained, were never afraid to run the ball out of defence, and Blanco regularly featured in glorious running moves from one end of the pitch to the other, as often as not starting them off and being on hand to make the final strike. All of Blanco's later caps were won as a full-back, but he played regularly as a wing in his early career, winning 12 caps in that position.

Blanco is probably the only top-class rugby player to date to have been born in Venezuela, from where he and his parents moved to France while he was a young boy.

Encounters with the leading southern hemisphere nations in recent years have seldom gone well for any of the Five Nations teams. Fans in the five countries have also become increasingly aware that the rugby played in the Super 12 and the Tri-Nations shows levels of skill, pace and commitment that are rarely seen in any European game. It has looked more and more as if England and France alone among the five have the player resources and the money to mount a serious challenge for world honours. The three Celtic nations have had a hard time of it, with only Scotland making anything like the best of their limited resources.

THE FUTURE OF THE FIVE NATIONS

Despite all this, the Five Nations still has a special sense of occasion. Lions tours have the same aura about them and the Tri-Nations will no doubt quickly gain this magical quality, as the World Cup has already done, but other northern hemisphere *v* southern hemisphere games have somehow never matched this. The Five Nations is still truly

Below: *Serge Blanco prepares to hand off a tackler during the France* v *Scotland match in Paris in 1991. Skipper Blanco contributed a dropped goal, as France beat the Scots 15-9.*

competitive as the regular upset results show, and recent talk in England about replacing it with annual games against the All Blacks and Springboks is surely misguided. Such matches might be played in addition to the Five Nations but should not become replacements for it.

This talk was part of the background to the wrangle over television money – largely but not solely provoked by England – that nearly led to the cancellation of the 1997 championship. For the future, perhaps the rugby authorities would do better to remember that much of their revenue still comes from the fans who attend the matches, rather than from those who watch at home. Many of these fans enjoy nothing more than a weekend away in Dublin or Paris for an international. Weekends in Auckland or Cape Town are hardly realistic alternatives. Instead of questioning the future of the championship, why not think of how to make it better and how to please the devoted fans who provide the backbone of the game? A 'Six Nations' tournament and the occasional weekend in Rome will do nicely on both counts.

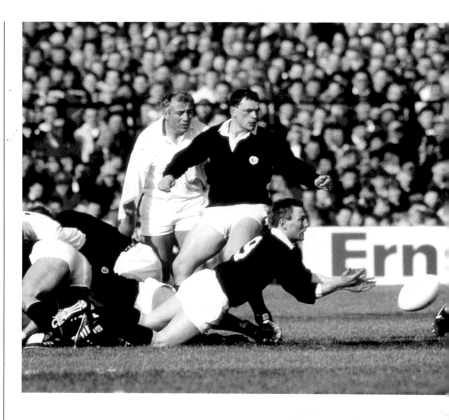

Below: *'Swing Low, Sweet Chariot'. England celebrate their 1992 Grand Slam, a second successive clean sweep for Will Carling's team. There would be another in 1995.*

Above: *It was Scotland's turn in 1990. Here Gary Armstrong ships the ball out against England in the Grand Slam decider at Murrayfield, won 13-7 by a highly motivated Scottish outfit.*

CHAPTER FOURTEEN

· SOUTHERN HEMISPHERE · · INTERNATIONALS ·

Jonah Lomu runs over Australian flanker David Wilson in the All Blacks' 43-6 destruction of the Wallabies in the 1996 Tri-Nations.

Each of the three major rugby-playing countries of the southern hemisphere is involved in a long-running international series against the others. Each series has been fiercely contested even though there has generally been no real southern hemisphere title at stake. There has been one meeting each between the three in the World Cup, and Australia and New Zealand have had the Bledisloe Cup since 1931. But it was only with the inauguration of the Tri-Nations tournament in 1996 that the three met for a definitive competition, all against all, home and away.

NEW ZEALAND *v* SOUTH AFRICA

Results against British teams before World War I had already shown how strong New Zealand and South African rugby was, and appetites for a showdown between the two were whetted in 1919 when a New Zealand Army team made a successful tour of South Africa. The first confrontation for the then-mythical world championship followed in 1921, when Theo Pienaar led the Springboks on a tour of New Zealand.

The team contained five members of the Morkel family, including P.G. (Gerhard) Morkel, who was a star full-back, W.H. ('Boy'), who was a fine prop and actually captained the side in all three Tests, and J.A. ('Royal'), who was one of several giant forwards in the tour party. The Springboks confirmed their strength in the opening provincial matches, a nil-all draw with Taranaki and a narrow loss to Canterbury in bad weather being the only blemishes on their record outside the Tests. There was, however, also a rough and unpleasant game with the Maoris late in the tour, which was followed by a scandal when a racist South African report on the match was widely published in New Zealand.

▪ RESULTS ▪

New Zealand *v* **South Africa**
Played 47, 22 wins each, 3 draws

New Zealand *v* **Australia**
Played 102, New Zealand won 70, lost 27, 5 draws

Australia *v* **South Africa**
Played 35, South Africa won 24, lost 11, no draws

The first-ever Test between New Zealand and South Africa was held on 13 August 1921 at Dunedin. South Africa opened the scoring with a try by wing Attie van Heerden. New Zealand fought back in the second half with three tries, two of them converted, to win 13-5. South Africa took the Second Test 9-5, with the decisive score being a spectacular dropped goal by Gerhard Morkel. In the decider, the wind howled, the rain poured down, and, according to one report, the forwards 'laboured mightily in the mud', but their best efforts could only produce a nil-all draw and a tied series.

The return series in South Africa in 1928 was also shared, this time two matches each. The All Blacks needed to win the last Test to square the series, and skipper Maurice Brownlie told his men beforehand, 'If we don't win this match, we might as well not go home.' The game was played in Cape Town in terrible conditions and is

Below: *Michael Jones on the ball against the Springboks in August 1992. New Zealand won 27-24 in the rivals' first encounter after South Africa's sporting rehabilitation.*

remembered as the 'Umbrella Test'. The All Black forwards responded to their captain's challenge and controlled the game, while fly-half Mark Nicholls dominated the scoring.

In 1937 the third Test series between the two great rivals finally saw one of them slip into the lead. The Springboks, captained by Philip Nel, were unconvincing on the Australian leg of their tour, and the New Zealand pundits predicted that they would lose various provincial matches as well as the Test series. Instead the Springboks won every provincial game and took the Test series 2-1.

'SKRUM, SKRUM, SKRUM'

The All Blacks took the first match 13-7, and the Springboks came back to win the second 13-6. The latter was a tough game in which two or three players on each side finished more or less concussed by opposition punches. The strength of the Springbok team was the power and size of their pack. M.M. 'Boy' Louw was a hugely effective prop, and the rest of the Springbok forwards were all massive men for the time. The laws in 1937 allowed a team to opt for scrummages instead of line-outs, and before the decisive Third Test the South Africans received a telegram from Paul Roos, skipper of the 1906 Springboks. It said simply 'Skrum, skrum, skrum', and the team took the hint. The lighter New Zealand forwards were gradually ground down, and the Springboks ran in five tries to one to win 17-6.

South Africa and New Zealand played seven more international series between 1937 and the end of the apartheid era (eight if the 1986 New Zealand Cavaliers tour is included). Each was won by the home side as successive

generations of All Blacks and Springboks learned just how hard it could be in the contest for rugby's world crown. Many of the matches were fierce, even vicious, and there were also many complaints from both sides about biased home referees. Neutral referees were not used until 1981.

ALL BLACKS WHITEWASHED

The 1949 All Blacks were whitewashed 4-0 in the Tests. Springbok flanker Hennie Muller, still said to be the fastest-ever Springbok forward, hounded their midfield (from an offside position, according to the All Blacks), and prop 'Okey' Geffin kicked the penalties, over-generously given by the local referees in New Zealand eyes. New Zealand struggled at half-back – the likely first choice Vince Bevan was a Maori, and the New Zealand authorities were still prepared to pander to South African racism and regard him as ineligible for selection. There were other problems with the tour management, too, with the New Zealanders leaving clearly their best coach, Vic Cavanagh, at home.

New Zealand got their revenge for this humiliation with a 3-1 series win in 1956. The feeling of there being so much national pride at stake did nothing for the quality of the games, however. The Second and Third Tests (won respectively by the Springboks and All Blacks) featured endless brawls, mainly between the props but also involving other forwards, and even wingers Dixon (for New Zealand) and Johnstone had several ugly tussles in the Second Test.

Above: *Wellington 1994: South Africa's Theo van Rensburg hands on to James Small (No 14) as All Black John Timu closes in. New Zealand won the game 13-9 and eventually the series 2-0.*

Clashes in the 1960s were fortunately less controversial, although still no place for the tender-hearted. South Africa's forwards were just good enough to take the 1960 series at home, but the All Blacks in turn were dominant in New Zealand in 1965. They were even tipped to complete a whitewash in the Tests until South Africa came from 11 points down at half-time to snatch a last-gasp win in the third game of the series.

New Zealand were invited to tour South Africa again in 1967, provided Maoris were not selected once more. The New Zealanders quite rightly refused but did tour in 1970 with Maori scrum-half Sid Going and young part-Samoan wing Bryan Williams among the squad. Williams was one of the All Black stars on the tour, with 14 tries in all, including a beauty in each of the first and last internationals. But it was not enough. The Springboks won the First and Third Tests comfortably. The Second, another notoriously dirty game, was taken by the All Blacks, but the Springboks had just enough left in the tank to hold on for a three-point win in the fourth game of the series.

New Zealand returned to South Africa in 1976 and toured a country riven with riots and other racial disturbances. The spectacle on the field was none too pretty either, with the Third Test in particular being a real bloodbath. In rugby terms neither side matched up to the quality of some of their forebears, but the Springboks took the series 3-1. Springbok goal-kicking was the difference in the decisive final Test, but the All Blacks also complained furiously about the South African referee.

After the troubles that had attended the latest Springbok tours to Britain and Australia, and considering the continuing racism within South African rugby, it was remarkably stupid of New Zealand's rugby authorities to invite a Springbok tour in 1981. Rigorous security precautions and fierce anti-tour protests together made a nonsense of much of the rugby, but for the record the All Blacks took the series 2-1. Then in 1986, after various political and legal interventions, a squad of virtually All Black strength set off for a rebel tour of South Africa. Again for the record, the Cavaliers lost a 'Test' series 3-1 to the Springboks and returned home stoutly maintaining that, of course, they had not been paid to play. Cynics laughed even louder when the players' punishment, with a World Cup coming up, was a brief two-match suspension.

Below: *Springbok flanker Ruben Kruger makes a break in the Third Test at Johannesburg in 1996. South Africa beat the All Blacks 32-22, but the series was already New Zealand's.*

Above: *The All Blacks in possession in the final 1996 Tri-Nations match, which they won 29-18. Sean Fitzpatrick gets the ball with Springbok forwards breathing down his neck.*

Changing times in South Africa were recognised with a five-match All Black tour in 1992. The All Blacks were far the better side in the one Test but could only record a 27-24 win – hardly enough to count as a series victory. Nor could the Springboks repeat the triumph of 1937 when they returned to New Zealand in 1994. The All Blacks won the first two internationals, with Springbok prop Johan Le Roux being sent home after a biting incident in the Second Test. Some Springbok honour was salvaged with a draw in the final game of the series, but it was the All Blacks who seemed better placed for the 1995 World Cup.

That, of course, is not how it turned out, but the All Blacks gained some revenge with their perfect record in the 1996 Tri-Nations competition. When that was completed, Sean Fitzpatrick's men stayed on in South Africa to see if they could be the first to accomplish that long-held New Zealand dream, a series win over the Springboks on their own territory. All three Tests were titanic struggles played at astonishing pace and with huge levels of commitment on both sides. The All Blacks took the first match 23-19, so the Springboks had to put everything into the second to keep the series alive. South Africa opened the scoring, but then New Zealand raced into a ten-point lead at half-time. Twice South Africa clawed their way back to a single point deficit for New Zealand to creep ahead once more. Only a last-minute dropped goal from Zinzan Brooke gave New

Zealand anything approaching a safe cushion and a final result of 33-26. After that, it was all the more remarkable that the final Test was almost equally dramatic, with South Africa summoning up the will to stop the All Blacks' run of victories with a solitary 32-22 win from their five encounters in the season. But the All Blacks had claimed that much-desired series victory, a truly great achievement by a truly great New Zealand team.

AUSTRALIA v NEW ZEALAND

Australia and New Zealand first met in a full international on 15 August 1903 in what was also New Zealand's first-ever Test. If the 'Tests' played by New South Wales in the 1920s are included (they are recognised as internationals by the Australian RFU), then the two have met 125 times to 1996, more often than any other pair of countries. Administrative problems and the competition Australian rugby union has faced from other sports have meant that its strength has waxed and waned over the years. New Zealand rugby has always been strong, so there have been periods when wins over Australia have been overwhelmingly likely.

There have even been times when Australia have been regarded rather as second-class opponents and have played matches against less-than-full-strength All Black teams. New Zealand hosted a Wallaby tour in 1949, for example, and the Australians won both Tests and lost only a single provincial game. The main All Black squad, however, was in South Africa, although Maori players 'ineligible' for South Africa were included in the home New Zealand line-up. The first of these home Tests was played on a day regarded as the blackest in New Zealand rugby history, for, as well as being defeated by Australia, the All Blacks also lost the Third Test and the series in South Africa. However, on other occasions, as in 1905 when the 'Originals' were on tour in Britain, even the All Black second string proved to be too strong for their Australian visitors.

Australia's first win at home did not come until the seventh match, in 1910, and their first success in New Zealand not until the eleventh game, in 1913. The latter victory, however, was against an All Black second XV while the main New Zealand side were in California. The full team had beaten the Australians 30-5 before they left.

Several early All Black tours to Australia had a perfect record both in the Tests and other matches. That was certainly not the case in 1929. By then, Queensland rugby

Left: *A highly delighted Damien Smith helps parade the Bledisloe Cup at Sydney in 1994. Australia had just beaten the All Blacks 20-16 in that year's one-Test series for the trophy.*

Right: *Australian full-back Matt Burke on his way to score against New Zealand in the 1996 Tri-Nations match at Brisbane. Despite his efforts, New Zealand won 32-25.*

had revived after its recess for most of the decade, and several Queenslanders, including the fly-half and captain, Tommy Lawton, were prominent in what was unquestionably an Australian national team once again. Australia won all three Tests, although the final match in Sydney was desperately close, with a last-minute try by centre Syd King needed to give Australia the 15-13 result.

THE BLEDISLOE CUP

The 1931 Australia tour of New Zealand was therefore the first by a full Wallaby side since before World War I. The Australians gained poor results in the provincial matches and crowds were small. Seemingly in an attempt to boost attendance it was announced that the Governor-General of New Zealand, Lord Bledisloe, would donate a trophy to be played for by the two countries. New Zealand predictably won 20-13, with full-back Ron Bush scoring 14 points, which was then a record for an All Black in a Test. It was obviously the wrong thing for him to do – it was his debut match and he was never picked again!

The Bledisloe Cup itself was not ready for that first match, but the trophy duly arrived and has been keenly contested ever since. From that first occasion up to 1996, the Bledisloe Cup has been played for in 37 years. Australia have won the cup only seven times, in 1934, 1949, 1979, 1980, 1986, 1992 and 1994, and there were drawn series in 1951 and 1991. In individual matches Australia are also far behind, with 21 wins out of 84; four games have been drawn. Early on there were gaps of sometimes three or four years between series, but since 1983 the Bledisloe Cup has been an annual contest.

Australian heroes in the earlier matches included tough forwards Aub Hodgson and 'Wild Bill' Cerutti, whose nickname was more than justified. They and successors after the war, like Nick Shehadie in the 1950s and the Catchpole-Hawthorne half-back team in the 1960s, generally could not record more than the occasional consolation win. Even in 1978 when Greg Cornelson scored a remarkable four tries in a Test to give Australia a 30-16 victory it was too late, for the All Blacks had already wrapped up the series with two earlier wins.

By that point, however, Australian rugby was getting much stronger. Mark Ella's 1982 team had a superbly exciting series in New Zealand, with the Australians' version of 15-man rugby only just being overcome by All

Black forward power and effective goal-kicking. In 1986, the Australians joined the very short list of teams who have won a series in New Zealand. Nick Farr-Jones, Michael Lynagh and David Campese were the Wallaby stars.

Buck Shelford led the All Blacks to their revenge in Australia in 1988. He was surprisingly dropped for the home series in 1990, but New Zealand were still too strong, although Australia's win in the final Test did end an All Black run of 23 consecutive international victories.

Great matches continued into the 1990s. One of the most memorable of all Bledisloe Cup moments was the last-minute try-saving tackle by Wallaby scrum-half George Gregan on All Black wing Jeff Wilson that saved the single 1994 Test for Australia. And now the development of the Tri-Nations tournament and the promise of more matches for the Bledisloe Cup can only ensure that this great rivalry will continue to produce more and more games and incidents like that to savour.

SOUTH AFRICA *v* AUSTRALIA

The contests between South Africa and Australia have had a lower profile than the All Blacks *v* Springboks matches and have been far fewer in number than the Bledisloe Cup encounters, but they have been fiercely fought nonetheless. The series started off in a rather low-key way, however, when the 1921 Springboks played five games in Australia on

Left: *South African centre Danie Gerber runs into Australia's Nick Farr-Jones and Tim Horan (No 12) at Cape Town in 1992. Australia beat the re-emerging Springboks 26-3.*

The first Australian tour to South Africa did not take place until 1933, and it quickly became clear in the early provincial matches of the trip that the Test series would be a contest between the Wallabies' speed and mobility and the Springboks' power and weight. This tour is the only time in international rugby history that a Test series has consisted of five matches with, in the event, Springbok power being sufficient to take three of them and the series. The first and second games were particularly rough with repeated brawls, partly because disagreements arose about scrummaging laws and partly because players like 'Wild Bill' Cerutti and 'Boy' Louw, opponents in the front row, rather enjoyed that sort of thing.

Philip Nel's 1937 team played in Australia on their way to their triumph in New Zealand and predictably were too strong for the Wallabies. Once again there were numerous fights, especially during the Second Test. Springbok power was still too great for the Wallabies over the next three tours, in 1953, 1956 and 1961, but in 1963 in South Africa the series was shared 2-2. The South African selectors chopped and changed their side throughout the series, and under the effective leadership of prop John Thornett, the Australian forwards held their own, while Catchpole and Hawthorne at half-back gave them many attacking options.

their way to New Zealand. Their first match was against Victoria, who had to place newspaper advertisements to raise a full team. The South Africans unsurprisingly did not have to try too hard to win 51-0. The three matches against New South Wales (now regarded as Tests by the Australian RU) were closer than that but still comfortable Springbok wins, with Olympic sprinter Attie van Heerden scoring five tries in the opening game.

Below: *Australian centre Tim Horan scorches in to score against the Springboks in the 1996 Australia v South Africa Tri-Nations match at Sydney, which was a 21-16 Wallaby win.*

Right: Springbok prop 'Os' du Randt on the burst in the 1996 South Africa v Australia Tri-Nations game at Bloemfontein. The Springboks won this encounter 25-19.

Dawie de Villiers's 1965 Springboks in Australia and New Zealand gave a series of lacklustre performances on the Australian leg of their tour. Their backs included great players like John Gainsford and Jan Engelbrecht, but the forwards were not up to the traditional Springbok standard. The Springboks complained bitterly about the Australian refereeing but even so were generally outplayed by a well-organised Australian side who won both Tests, their first series win against South Africa.

It was back to business as usual in South Africa in 1969 and in Australia in 1971. That 1971 tour saw the Springboks compile an unbeaten 13-match record, the first-ever by a Springbok touring party anywhere. It was also the first time that a trip to Australia was not tagged on as an addition to more serious business in New Zealand. The brilliant Springbok rugby, however, was overshadowed by off-field troubles between police and anti-apartheid demonstrators that ensured that this would be the last time the two countries met until times had changed in South Africa.

In the event, the next Australia *v* South Africa meeting was in Cape Town in 1992. Australia won easily, and it was clear that South Africa were still coming to terms with world rugby standards after their isolation. However, South Africa visited Australia in 1993 and showed that they had made up much ground. Great South African defence and a touch of Australian over-confidence helped the Springboks to a win in the First Test. Springbok wing James Small, a two-try hero of the First Test, was the villain in the Second, being sent off for dissent. This time it was the Wallabies who made the big tackles, and Nick Farr-Jones came out of retirement to supply the tactical control in a 28-20 Australian win. It was pretty much the same story in the Third Test, a 19-12 Australia win enlivened by a fine Tim Horan try.

THE TRI-NATIONS TOURNAMENT

Although the three top southern hemisphere nations have often been correctly sceptical about the playing standards in the Five Nations tournament, they always agreed that it was a marvellous competition for both players and fans and one that they would like to emulate in their own season. The television money made available from 1995 to support such a tournament made the argument in favour overwhelming, and one of the first developments of rugby's professional era was the creation of an annual southern hemisphere international championship, the Tri-Nations tournament.

The inaugural tournament in 1996 was stunningly successful. The tournament rules provided bonus points for try-scoring and for beaten sides who stayed within seven points of their opponents, but in the event these fancy arrangements were unnecessary, the All Blacks winning all four of their games. The first match was New Zealand *v* Australia in wind and pouring rain in Wellington, and it set the scene for some remarkable rugby. Despite the conditions, New Zealand, especially in the first half, gave an exhibition of fast and fluent handling that was virtually flawless. Jonah Lomu took some stopping as so often before, but he was only one of six All Black try-scorers as Australia were left on the wrong end of a 43-6 scoreline. Australia bounced back to beat South Africa in the next game, and New Zealand ground out a 15-11 success over the Springboks in the next match.

The fourth game was another stunner. The All Blacks were 25-15 down to Australia with barely ten minutes left but then scored 17 unanswered points to win and make themselves uncatchable in the competition. Comebacks and near-comebacks seemed to be standard fare, for in the fifth game Australia only just failed to claw back a 16-point deficit with 12 minutes to go. The Springboks held on to win 25-19. In the final game New Zealand successfully recovered from being 18-6 down to the South Africans early in the second half to win 29-18. After a start like that there is little doubt that the Tri-Nations is here to stay.

CHAPTER FIFTEEN

· BRITISH LIONS TOURS ·

Lions full-back Gavin Hastings about to slot a penalty in the deciding Third Test against Australia in 1989, which the Lions won.

Visits by British Isles teams to southern hemisphere countries have been a highlight of the world rugby scene since 1888. Initial visits were not organised by England's Rugby Football Union (RFU) or any other governing body, and it was not until 1910 that the first 'official' tour took place, when the RFU ran that year's trip to South Africa. The 1924 tourists, also to South Africa, were the first to be known as the Lions, and since the 1950 tour to New Zealand and Australia, organisation has been in the hands of the Four Home Unions Tour Committee, from England, Scotland, Ireland and Wales.

At first the tour parties did not include the best players from the British Isles. Soon, however, South African and New Zealand teams in particular grew stronger. The Test matches and many provincial games were fiercely contested, and wins by the tourists in Test series became a rarity rather than the rule.

The 1899 visit to Australia was the first in which the party included players from all four home countries, but only seven of the 21 had been capped, and the captain, the Reverend Matthew Mullineux (who played only one Test on tour), was never selected for the England side. Almost every later tour has seen several leading players unavailable for selection for business or personal reasons or, in 1974 and 1980, because of opposition to the apartheid policies of the South African government. And there has often been controversy over the actual selections, with critics complaining that weaker players have been included to balance the numbers from each country or conversely that too many players from one country have been included because of bias among the management and selection team.

The 1997 Lions tour to South Africa will be fully professional, managed by former England and Lions prop Fran Cotton and coached by former Scotland and Lions back

◾ LIONS TOURS AND CAPTAINS ◾

1888 Australia and New Zealand, Bob Seddon* (Sco)
1891 South Africa, Bill MacLagan (Sco)
1896 South Africa, Johnny Hammond (Eng)†
1899 Australia, Matthew Mullineux (Eng)†
1903 South Africa, Mark Morrison (Sco)
1904 Australia and New Zealand
              'Darkie' Bedell-Sivright (Sco)
1908 Australia and New Zealand, Arthur Harding (Wal)
1910 South Africa, Tom Smyth (Wal)
1924 South Africa, Ronald Cove-Smith (Eng)
1930 Australia and New Zealand, Doug Prentice (Eng)
1938 South Africa, Sam Walker (Ire)
1950 Australia and New Zealand, Karl Mullen (Ire)
1955 South Africa, Robin Thompson (Ire)
1959 Australia and New Zealand, Ronnie Dawson (Ire)
1962 South Africa, Arthur Smith (Sco)
1966 Australia and New Zealand
              Mike Campbell-Lamerton (Sco)
1968 South Africa, Tom Kiernan (Ire)
1971 Australia and New Zealand, John Dawes (Wal)
1974 South Africa, Willie-John McBride (Ire)
1977 New Zealand, Phil Bennett (Wal)
1980 South Africa, Bill Beaumont (Eng)
1983 New Zealand, Ciaran Fitzgerald (Ire)
1989 Australia, Finlay Calder (Sco)
1993 New Zealand, Gavin Hastings (Sco)

* Seddon was killed in a boating accident during the tour
and replaced as captain by Andrew Stoddart (Eng).
† Hammond and Mullineux never played for England.

Ian McGeechan, who also coached Scotland and the 1989 and 1993 Lions squads. Despite the fact that, at the time of writing, some short-sighted club owners and managements are carping about 'lending' their assets (the players) to international teams, it seems likely that the 1997 Lions will be the first truly representative British Isles team ever.

THE TOURS BEGIN

The first 'Lions' tour, which visited Australia and New Zealand in 1888, began as a private venture dreamed up by a pair of cricket entrepreneurs. The RFU gave permission for the trip to go ahead despite the usual grumbles about professionalism. One player, J.P. Clowes of Halifax, was found to have accepted expenses and was declared a professional shortly before the party left. Clowes travelled on the tour anyway, but according to the records at least the tour management did not allow him to play in any of the 35 matches to avoid professionalising any of the other players.

The marathon trip – with the first match in April and the last in October – did not include any Tests, but the party did play a number of games (18 or 19, reports differ) in Victoria under Australian Rules. During the New Zealand leg of the trip, the home players were surprised by the tourists' tactic of deliberately heeling the ball out of the scrummages to allow the backs to carry out passing movements. At the time, New Zealanders considered that forwards heeling the ball back in a scrum were placing themselves offside. Quarrels about local referees and law interpretations are nothing new it seems.

The only 'Lions' team to date to have a perfect record were the 1891 team in South Africa. Formed entirely of English and Scots, they won all their games and conceded only one point – from a try, according to the scoring values of the time.

GRUELLING EXPERIENCES

Besides the long sea voyage that was a part of every tour until the modern era, the 1891 team and other early parties also had to contend with arduous internal journeys in the host country. In the earliest days many of the journeys were undertaken in horse-drawn transport. Despite technological advances, travel can still be something of an ordeal. A surprising number of top rugby players seem to be reluctant air passengers, and Lions have often found internal air trips in New Zealand to feature dramatic air turbulence.

Tours in the days of sea travel lasted four months or more from start to finish, with some 20 or even more than 30 matches played. Even though many tourists did receive illicit financial assistance from their clubs, such a long absence was obviously asking a lot of a player. Tour parties were usually less than 30 strong, and with so many matches

Above: *The 1924 British Lions photographed in London just before their departure for South Africa. Plagued by injuries, they lost nine and drew three of their 21 games.*

there were many injuries. Players often had to play out of position, and substitutes frequently needed to be found at short notice. A good example of a punishing early tour was the 1924 visit to South Africa. The 1924 team have the worst playing record of all British Isles tours, with a catalogue of injuries being among the reasons for the poor results. One of the three full-backs was injured before playing a single game, a second played only in the first match and the third could not kick goals for toffee. There was no other reliable kicker with the party, and the team landed only five conversions and three penalties in 21 games. An Irish international who happened to be living in Johannesburg played four matches, and one 'McTavish' played against Border towards the end of the tour when the Lions were otherwise unable to field a full side.

Tours have become shorter in the era of air travel, and it is now possible to call up a replacement within a day or two. But short tours present a different problem when it comes to team-building. Earlier tourists usually had several weeks, including some easy games, to find their strongest selection and build up teamwork. By contrast, the 1989 Lions in Australia had only six games before the First Test.

THE SPECTRE OF THE SOUTHERN HEMISPHERE

Since the first World Cup took place in 1987, there has been considerable talk in British rugby circles about 'falling behind the southern hemisphere' and even optimistically about 'catching up with the southern hemisphere'. It is worth remembering here that since their victories in the first two series in South Africa in the 1890s, the Lions have won a Test series only once in each of South Africa and New Zealand. Visits to Australia have usually proved to be easier,

but that had more to do with the relative weakness of Australian rugby union for many years than with the strength of the Lions. After succeeding in Australia, the same Lions parties usually went on to struggle in New Zealand.

DAZZLING BACK PLAY

Time and again, Lions visits to South Africa and New Zealand have shown up a basic lack of power and drive in British packs. There have been numerous fine individual performances, such as by number eight Alun Pask in 1966 and prop Hugh McLeod in 1959, but these have usually been overshadowed by the fitness, size, strength, technique and above all will to win of the Springbok and All Black teams. With the forwards under the cosh, it has usually been the exciting running and dazzling try-scoring of the backs that has been most remembered – and rightly so, for often it was those qualities that kept the Lions in touch with their foes.

The classic example that 'proves' this is the famous First Test on the 1959 tour to New Zealand. The Lions scored four tries, all by backs, while New Zealand kicked six penalties to win 18-17. The Lions predictably were none too happy with the referee, and the Dunedin crowd were scathing in their criticism of their team's lack of enterprise. This was another tour on which the Lions could have done with better goal-kicking. They scored 113 tries in their 25 games in New Zealand, ample testimony to the quality of their backs, but converted only 60 of them. Another interesting statistic to compare with the modern game is that the 36 penalties the Lions landed was only about a third of the number of tries they scored.

The successful Lions were the 1971 side to New Zealand, the 1974 party to South Africa and the squad that toured Australia in 1989. The success of the 1989 Lions is remembered as being based on a hard-nosed forward effort. The bond forged by the mainly English Test pack during the trip provided the foundation for the English forward power that dominated the Five Nations in the early 1990s.

Left: *Lions scrum-half Gareth Edwards in action in the 1971 Fourth Test. Wayne Cottrell holds on as All Blacks Alex Wyllie and Ian Kirkpatrick (right) and Lion John Taylor close in.*

Above: *Lions Bobby Windsor (left) and Fran Cotton rejoice as lock Gordon Brown scores in the Third Test of the 1974 tour. On the right is Lions skipper Willie-John McBride.*

John Dawes' 1971 side were the first of the modern Lions teams to break the mould and succeed in the southern hemisphere. Coach Carwyn James was the mastermind, but the genius on the field was the great Welsh fly-half Barry John. He had the balanced running skills to ghost past tacklers and score tries, and his tactical kicking in the first Test was so finely judged that it finished the international career of the All Black full-back Fergie McCormick. Overall the forwards more than held their own, and in the backs perhaps only Dawes would not be a contender for an 'all-time-greats' team.

The 1974 Lions were even more successful, only a draw in the final Test (with the usual related refereeing controversy) spoiling their 100 per cent record. Willie-John McBride's pack were magnificent, strangling South African rugby at its traditional heart in the scrummage and dominating every other area of the field. Gareth Edwards at the height of his powers controlled operations behind the forwards, and wing J.J. Williams sped over the hard South African grounds to notch try after try. The infamous '99' call for mass retaliation against perceived foul play by the opposition did the Lions no credit, but it did reflect one fact of life in international rugby – a team that steps back from physical confrontation will lose.

But forward domination is not an infallible route to success – ask the 1977 Lions. They were strong enough up front to reduce the All Blacks to fielding a three-man scrum at times but still lost the Test series. Every British fan will hope that the 1997 Lions can combine forward power with pace and ball-handling skills from front row to full-back.

Below: *The 1989 Lions squad celebrate after their 19-18 victory over Australia in the deciding Third Test. Second from left at the front is Ieuan Evans, who scored the clinching try.*

CHAPTER SIXTEEN

· OTHER INTERNATIONAL ·
· COMPETITIONS ·

ACT Brumbies and Australia scrum-half George Gregan in action during ACT's 35-28 defeat of Wellington Hurricanes in the 1996 Super 12. ACT finished fifth in the table, beating three eventual semi-finalists – Auckland, Natal and Queensland – in the process.

The World Cup and the various competitions and rivalries among the big eight may be the brightest stars in the rugby universe, yet they are far from being the game's only international meetings. A range of other championships at country, province and even club level have brought players from different parts of the world into contact on the field of play.

One of the first international rugby tournaments took place as part of the 1900 Olympic Games in Paris, perhaps at the instigation of Baron Pierre de Courbertin, the founding father of the modern Olympics, who was a rugby enthusiast. Three teams participated, and France won the gold ahead of Germany and Great Britain. Rugby continued as an Olympic sport on and off until 1924. Australia triumphed in 1908 in England, and in Antwerp in 1920 the United States became Olympic rugby champions, going on to defend their title successfully in Paris in 1924.

THE FIRA CHAMPIONSHIP

Expulsion from the Five Nations Championship over the matter of professionalism led France to set up the *Fédération Internationale de Rugby Amateur* (FIRA) in 1934. Other FIRA founder members were Germany, the Netherlands, Italy, Portugal, Romania, Czechoslovakia, Sweden and Catalonia, and the organisation was gradually expanded to include Tunisia, Morocco, Argentina and all European rugby-playing countries outside the home unions. For many years, the members played friendly internationals against one another, until in 1973-74 an official FIRA Championship was created. France of course had long been readmitted to the Five Nations by that point, and it comes as no surprise to learn that they have dominated the competition, even though they have tended to field full-strength international sides only against the likes of Romania. Indeed, only Romania have broken the French hold on the title, with four wins in the 1970s and early 1980s, although the 1989-90 competition was a three-way tie, with the Soviet Union getting in on the act. In recent times, Italy have also been a leading side in the competition.

THE SUPER TOURNAMENTS

In 1986, the South Pacific Championship, or Super 6, got under way. The competition was organised on an invitation basis by the New South Wales RU and pitted NSW and fellow Australian state Queensland against the New Zealand provinces of Auckland, Wellington and Canterbury, with Fiji joining the party for good measure. The New Zealanders took an iron grip on the trophy from the word go, with Canterbury winning in the first year and sharing the second title with Auckland, before the latter went on to claim the next three championships outright.

In 1991, NSW pulled out of the competition, a decision which led in turn to the withdrawal of the sponsors and the cancellation of that year's tournament. When the Super 6

Below: *The US squad that won gold at the 1924 Olympics. Standing fourth from left is Morris Kirksey, who also won silver in the 100 metres and gold in the 4 x 100 metres relay.*

resumed in 1992, Queensland grabbed the title. The number of teams participating was upped to ten for 1993, with three South African provinces joining four from New Zealand and Australia's Queensland and NSW; Western Samoa represented the Pacific islands. The teams were split into two pools of five, and the tournament, now known as the Super 10, was decided by a final featuring the winners of the two groups. The 1993 final saw Auckland take on Transvaal, who demonstrated that South African rugby was on its way back after the wilderness years by winning 20-17.

The following year, Natal replaced fellow South Africans Western Province and succeeded in reaching the final at the first attempt. Their opponents were Queensland, who beat the newcomers 21-10, thanks in large part to fly-half Michael Lynagh. The 1995 Super 10 also saw an Australia *v* South Africa final. Queensland made it through for the second year, on this occasion facing Transvaal at Ellis Park, Johannesburg. Once again, Queensland triumphed, this time 30-16, with Australian Test lock John Eales making an outstanding contribution, both in general play and in the role of goal-kicker.

The move to professionalism meant a revamped southern hemisphere competition for 1996 – the Super 12, which featured five sides from New Zealand, four from South Africa and three from Australia. The New Zealand sides were specially created 'super-provinces'. They played under the traditional names of Auckland, Waikato and so on, but players could be drawn from outside the provinces' regular catchment areas. The Australian Capital Territories (ACT) side was assembled in a similar way. Sadly, there was no place in Super 12 for the Pacific islands – another body blow to the development of rugby in those countries.

Above: *France (in blue) pack down against Romania at Auch during their 1990 FIRA Championship clash. Romania won the game 12-6 to record their first away win against France.*

Instead of splitting into two pools as they had in the Super 10, the teams in Super 12 formed a single league, the top four sides going forward to the semi-final stage. The Queensland Reds (each Super 12 side assumed a nickname for the tournament) met the Natal Sharks in the first semi at Brisbane, while the second match, at Auckland, featured the Auckland Blues and the North Transvaal Blue Bulls. Natal turned the Reds over 43-25; Auckland dismissed the Bulls even more emphatically, 48-11.

The final at Auckland was another high-scoring game. Jonah Lomu got a try early on, and All Black flanker Andrew Blowers got a second for the home side before the Sharks rallied and clawed their way back from 20-3 down to 20-16. But a four-try barrage in the second half snuffed out Natal's resistance, and Auckland ran out winners 45-21.

In terms of entertainment, the first Super 12 was an unqualified success, with enterprising rugby the order of the day. The average try count for a Super 12 match was six. A bonus-points system that rewarded any side that scored more than four tries and encouraged losing teams to stay within seven points of their opponents no doubt had something to do with that.

THE HEINEKEN EUROPEAN CUP

Meanwhile in the northern hemisphere, another new international tournament had reached its conclusion even before the Super 12 got under way. This was the Heineken European Cup, a championship competed for by mainly club sides, although in the case of Ireland it was provincial teams that took part. Sadly, no English or Scottish teams were involved, having been barred by their respective unions, and the 12 participants were drawn from France

Left: *Auckland Blues lock Charles Riechelmann launches himself over the line to score one of his side's six tries in the 1996 Super 12 final.*

(three teams), Wales (three), Ireland (three), Italy (two) and Romania (one team). They were split into four pools of three and thus played only two games before passing to the semi-final stage, or out of the competition.

The tournament got off to an almost invisible start, the first match taking place at the end of October 1995 in the relative backwater of Romania. As the competition progressed, though, its profile and public interest rose, aided by some exciting games, notably Welsh club Cardiff's 14-14 draw against Bègles-Bordeaux of France.

This draw helped Cardiff through to the semi-finals, in which they beat Irish province Leinster 23-14 at Lansdowne Road, Dublin. Meanwhile, Toulouse swept aside Welsh club Swansea 30-3 to book their place in the final. Held at Cardiff Arms Park, the final was a thrilling affair. The French side scored two tries in the first ten minutes for an early lead, but in the end extra time was needed to separate the teams after an Adrian Davies penalty had brought Cardiff level at no-side. Eventually, the boot of international fly-half Christophe Deylaud sealed victory for Toulouse, and the Heineken Cup was on its way to France.

For the 1996-97 competition, the number of entries was boosted to 20, with English clubs and Scottish districts joining the fray. The participants were once again split into four pools, this time of five teams, the top two in each to go forward. Dax, Toulouse, Brive, Leicester, Harlequins, Bath,

Below: *Brive's giant flanker, Gregory Kacala, celebrates victory over Leicester in the 1997 Heineken European Cup final. Kacala, a Polish international, had a storming game.*

▪ BRIVE v LEICESTER ▪

Leicester came to the 1997 European final with a hugely powerful pack, led by Dean Richards and built around the massive authority of Martin Johnson in the second row. However, the Leicester forwards were subdued from the start by Brive, with Gregory Kacala in the back row making telling runs, and the Tigers' Johnson unable to dominate in the line-out.

Brive opened the scoring with an early penalty. This was quickly added to by a try from French full-back Sébastien Viars. Leicester stayed in touch against the run of play until half-time with two John Liley penalties and sneaked in front with a third Liley strike just after the break. But the Brivistes then shot ahead with two tries in ten minutes, Gerald Fabré getting the first and Sébastien Carrat the second. A Christophe Lamaison dropped goal extended the lead, and Carrat got a second spectacular score just before no-side. Lamaison added the conversion to complete a comfortable 28-9 victory.

Cardiff and Llanelli contested the quarter-finals, Cardiff creating a mini-shock by halting the progress of English giants Bath. The Welshmen could not overcome Brive in the semis, however, although Leicester did succeed in putting out the holders, Toulouse, thereby preventing an all-French final. Brive nonetheless proved too strong for the Tigers in the final, and Leicester came unstuck to the tune of 28-9. The Heineken European Cup, now one of the major events of the rugby calendar, headed for France once more.

At the same time as the Heineken Cup was expanded, a European Conference was introduced as a second level of competition. The 1996-97 Conference contained 24 sides, drawn from France, Wales, England, Scotland, Ireland, Italy and Romania. All seven French sides that entered made it to the last eight, and France provided all the semi-finalists. Bourgoin had the honour of completing a French European double for the year, beating Castres 18-9 in the final.

The range of international competitions that have been introduced since rugby's move to professionalism does not end there. A Pacific Rim Series, featuring Canada, the United States, Hong Kong and Japan was put in train in 1996, with Canada the first champions. The Canadians and Americans also contested the Pan-American Championship, along with Argentina and Uruguay. Argentina won that title. In 1995, France, Italy and Romania travelled to Argentina for the first Latin Cup competition. France were the winners of the tournament, which is due to be held every two years. All in all, the mix of old and new competitions at all levels has successfully launched rugby into the new professional era. Provided the players are not run into the ground nor spread too thinly in an attempt to stage too many competitions, the status of world game surely beckons for rugby union.

CHAPTER SEVENTEEN

· SEVENS ·

Fiji's Marika Vunibaka during the 1997 Sevens World Cup in Hong Kong. Vunibaka shone even in an extravagantly talented Fiji side and ended up as the tournament's top try-scorer. His 12-try haul included four in as many minutes against Western Samoa.

Seven-a-side rugby is a Scottish invention. It was the brainchild of a Melrose butcher, Adam 'Ned' Haig, who came up with the idea in 1883. Haig had his new form of rugby incorporated into a fund-raising sports day held that year at Melrose's Greenyards ground. Melrose, with Haig in the side, won the tournament, beating Scottish Borders rivals Gala in the final. The event was adjudged a roaring success – and sevens has never looked back.

Indeed, the Scottish Border clubs took to sevens in a big way, with a number of them quickly following the Melrose example and setting up annual competitions of their own. The basic format of the game was established quite early on. Ties lasted seven minutes each way, with ten minutes per half allocated to the final, and teams fielded a three-man scrum and four backs. By the 1920s, a sevens circuit had been established in the Borders, with Melrose, Gala, Hawick,

Jed-Forest and Langholm holding their events in turn at the end of the season, and Selkirk and Kelso convening theirs in the autumn before the start of the northern hemisphere rugby season proper.

THE MIDDLESEX SEVENS

From its stronghold in Scotland, the 'short game' gradually made its way south, arriving at Twickenham in 1926 in the form of the Middlesex Sevens. This world-famous annual tournament is not without its Scottish connection. A prime mover in establishing the competition was an Edinburgh Academical – Dr J.A. Russell Cargill, after whom the winners' prize, the Russell Cargill Trophy, is named.

The Middlesex Sevens is a club competition and takes place at the end of the English rugby season. Qualifying rounds are held, and the clubs that get through join the previous year's finalists and invited teams at Twickenham the following Saturday for finals day, the ticket money for which is donated to charity. Harlequins have won the tournament more often than any other club, their 13 titles including the first four championships uninterrupted and another purple patch of five successive wins from 1986 to 1990. Second in the all-time winners' list are Richmond, who have the singular claim that one of their nine titles, that of 1951, was won by their second VII.

Another team with an unusual claim are Wigan, who in 1996 became the first rugby league club to be invited to the Middlesex Sevens. Code-crossers Martin Offiah and Va'aiga Tuigamala and their league associates ushered in the new professional era by running the union players off the park to take the trophy at the first attempt. A number of players in that Wigan line-up (and from other English rugby league clubs) played union during the 1996-97 season. Offiah, Tuigamala and Wales number eight Scott Quinnell returned to the game at which they first established reputations, being joined by league stars Gary Connolly, Jason Robinson and New Zealander Henry Paul, among others. It was a reconciliation between the codes that also saw the return to union of such players as Scott Gibbs, Allan Bateman and Jonathan Davies of Wales and Scotland's Alan Tait.

THE HONG KONG SEVENS

Major sevens tournaments were slower in getting going outside the British Isles. Then in 1976, what has become one of the great rugby showpieces got underway in Hong Kong. Right from the outset, the Hong Kong Sevens title has been the preserve of the southern hemisphere countries. The British Barbarians upset the apple cart in 1981, but other than that, Australia, New Zealand and Fiji have pretty much monopolised the show. The tournament can often give glimpses of fast-rising stars. In 1983, a young David Campese was one of the stars of Australia's victory. In 1994, it was New Zealand's Jonah Lomu, and in 1996 his fellow All Black Christian Cullen. Cullen's acceleration and blistering pace brought him 18 tries (an average of three a game) and the Player of the Tournament award.

Besides the obvious flair that the southern hemisphere teams show for sevens, a major obstacle to a victory by any of the Five Nations is that they have been generally unwilling to send top-flight sides south in March when there is still so much rugby to be played at home. Whereas Australia, New Zealand and Fiji sent national sevens teams almost from the start, the European home unions have been represented until the most recent years by invitation sides, such as Public School Wanderers, Irish Wolfhounds and of

course the Barbarians. It is, however, a matter of conjecture how much longer the major southern hemisphere countries will be able to send first-class squads to Hong Kong now that the Super 12 competition has arrived on the scene.

THE WORLD CUP SEVENS

Since 1993, the sevens game has had its own world championship – the Rugby World Cup Sevens. That first tournament took place in Scotland and was a highly entertaining but gruelling affair. To reach the final, a team was required to play ten games over three days, against world-class opposition. That is a lot of sevens at this level and the attrition rate among the players was high. In the end, England met Australia in the final and defeated them 21-17. Outstanding tackling and support play by the Englishmen kept the likes of Campese at bay, while the tremendous pace of skipper Andrew Harriman gave England just enough edge in attack.

Below: *Wigan's forwards for the 1996 Middlesex Sevens. From left, Andy Farrell, Va'aiga Tuigamala (a back drafted into the front-row union for the day) and Scott Quinnell.*

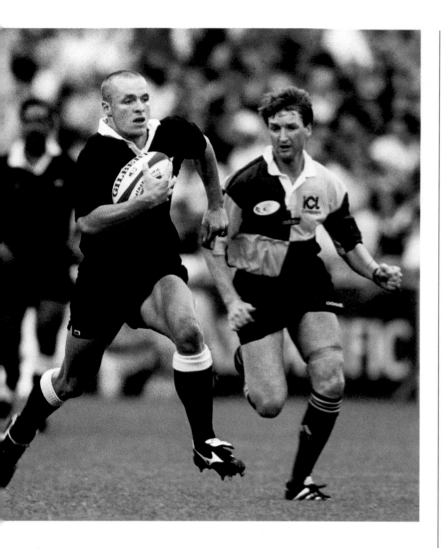

Above: *New Zealand's Christian Cullen turns it on at the 1996 Hong Kong Sevens. Cullen's blazing pace also makes him a handful in the 15-a-side game, in which he plays full-back.*

Like the 15-a-side World Cup, the sevens equivalent comes round every four years. The venue selected for the 1997 event was Hong Kong, and the traditional annual competition held there was incorporated into the world championship to create one super-tournament. On arrival, the 24 qualifiers played a preliminary round on the basis of which they were divided into eight groups of three. Pool games then took place, with the top team in each group going forward into the competition for the Melrose Cup (the World Cup trophy). However, as is the case at the Hong Kong Sevens, and indeed at most sevens tournaments, there was still silverware for the remainder to play for. The second-placed teams moved into the plate competition, and the third-placed teams went off to compete for the bowl.

The standard of rugby on display was astoundingly high, especially from the extravagantly talented and hugely entertaining Fiji, who destroyed everyone they met on the way to the final, rattling up 299 points and conceding only 14 (in fact they had a clean sheet until the semis).

Meanwhile, South Africa were showing that they were no slouches at sevens either, disposing of France and New Zealand in the quarter- and semi-final stages respectively. The final started well for South Africa, too, as they ran in two tries for an early 14-0 lead. There was no denying Fiji, though. Led by Waisale Serevi and spearheaded by Lemeki Koroi and Marika Vunibaka, the tournament's top try-scorer, they fought back to 24-21 at the final whistle and launched their homeland on a two-day public holiday.

Fun and the festival spirit are traditionally at the heart of sevens, although its image was a little tarnished by the dismissal of a Western Samoan in the World Cup semis. Generally though, the players get the chance to show off their running and handling skills, and the crowds get a good day out. The whole affair takes place in a carnival atmosphere, with spectators often cheering on the underdogs or casting a certain, perhaps too successful, team in the role of pantomime villains and booing every move they make. Sevens makes a wonderful complement to the 15-a-side game and with sensitive scheduling the premier tournaments should survive into the professional era.

Below: *Andrew Harriman at speed during the World Cup Sevens in 1993, in which he captained England. Few, if any, players in that competition could live with Harriman for pace.*

CHAPTER EIGHTEEN

· WOMEN'S RUGBY ·

Action from the 1997 British Universities final at Twickenham. St Mark and St John beat Edinburgh (blue and green) 24-20.

The famous English writer Dr Samuel Johnson once said that 'a woman's preaching is like a dog's walking on his hinder legs. It is not done well; but you are surprised to find it done at all.' This remark sums up the attitude of many rugby traditionalists to the development of the women's game. Fortunately this attitude is now becoming increasingly outdated, with any man who watches women's matches being left in no doubt of the growing levels of skill, commitment and enthusiasm that the players bring to the game.

Women's rugby is usually described as a relatively recent phenomenon, but in fact it is not so new. Some of the towns and villages that held free-for-all mass football games in previous centuries also had versions of them reserved for women. At Inverness in Scotland, for example, as well as a men's game, there was traditionally a game in which the married women played the spinsters – the married women usually winning the contest by dint of their superior weight and power.

MODERN TIMES

The modern history of women's rugby dates to the 1970s. It is hard to pin down any particular first matches or oldest clubs, but the game seems to have made its initial mark among colleges and universities in the United States and to have developed almost as quickly in a similar way in England. Colleges remain the backbone of the game in North America – there are currently well over 200 college teams and just 72 outside clubs. In the British Isles there are now about 270 women's set-ups. Many of these are still based in universities, but the majority, and most of the strongest ones, are associated with established men's clubs.

Above: The United States squad celebrate victory in the inaugural women's World Cup, held in Cardiff, Wales, in 1991. The Americans beat England 19-6 in the final.

The top women's teams tend to be attached to famous senior sides, such as Wasps, Richmond, Edinburgh Academicals and Blackrock.

INTERNATIONAL RUGBY

The first recorded women's international match was in 1982, France beating Holland 4-0. The following year, a Women's Rugby Football Union (WRFU) was formed to be the governing body throughout Britain and Ireland. The WRFU fielded a Great Britain side, which played its first international in 1986, losing 14-8 to France at the Richmond ground in London. The Great Britain team played matches up to 1990, but by then national teams from England and Wales had appeared on the scene. They had their first encounter in 1987, won 22-4 by England.

The United States also had their first game in 1987, a comfortable 22-3 win over Canada. The Canadians have been regular opponents ever since but are yet to record their first win in the series. In 1990, the Americans travelled to New Zealand, beating both their hosts and Holland in competition there. The American game also has a well-established domestic structure, with both student and club championships. Bay Area SheHawks have been one of the most successful teams, with three wins in the 1990s. Beantown were the 1996 champions.

In Britain there has been a national cup competition since 1987, when Wasps won in a final held at Twickenham. One of the Wasps try-scorers that day was Sally Treadwell, daughter of a former England men's international. The national league was first contested in 1988, with Richmond

ending up champions. Since those first cup and league competitions, the titles have been shared between those two clubs and Saracens.

The women's game was slower to develop in Scotland than in England and Wales, with a Scottish XV playing its first match, a heavy defeat to Wales, in 1990. Then, in 1992-93, the Scottish women broke away from the WRFU to affiliate to the Scottish Rugby Union. Scotland played its first full international later that season, a 10-0 win over Ireland that was also Ireland's first-ever game. The WRFU dissolved itself in May 1994, with separate unions for England, Ireland and Wales immediately setting up and affiliating to the main men's unions in their respective countries. Each country now also has its own national club competitions, and 1996 saw the first complete series of home union internationals, comfortably won by England. The next ambition is to create a proper Five Nations tournament, which will surely come to fruition.

Raising sponsorship and other revenue continues to be a major problem within the women's game, but it already has the showpiece of a world championship tournament.

Below: A line-out during the World Championship match between England and Russia in 1994, played at Boroughmuir in Scotland. England won 51-0 and went on to lift the trophy.

■ THE 1997 HOME NATIONS ■ ■ TOURNAMENT ■

	P	W	D	L	F	A
England	3	3	0	0	82	17
Scotland	3	2	0	1	41	26
Wales	3	1	0	2	46	37
Ireland	3	0	0	3	8	87

The 1991 World Cup marked a major stage in the game's development. The organisation of the tournament was largely undertaken by the Richmond women's club, who had great difficulty raising all the necessary finance. Even though the tournament generated significant public interest, it ended up with a £7000 loss, which the English RFU agreed to meet. Twelve teams entered, including the Soviet Union, who arrived virtually without funds. New Zealand, France, the United States and England each won their pool matches to reach the semi-finals, with the Americans and England winning close games to go all the way. There was also a plate competition, in which Canada beat Spain in the final.

The main final was quite a game, with the bigger English pack never able to subdue the fitter and quicker Americans. The decisive breaks came early in the second half, when flanker Claire Godwin from Florida State University went over for two tries. The final margin was 19-6, with the solitary English score a penalty try converted by Gill Burns.

THE WORLD CHAMPIONSHIP

The next tournament, properly entitled the World Championship to distinguish it from the men's World Cup, was due to be played in the Netherlands in 1994, but the Dutch organisers pulled out at the start of January that year. Fortunately, the Scottish union stepped in and agreed to take over the job. The tournament duly went ahead in April, games being played at a range of senior Scottish grounds, and the final scheduled for Raeburn Place, where the first-ever men's international had been held in 1871.

There were 16 original entrants, but four dropped out in advance, including the strong New Zealand side, who were unable to attend because of a dispute with the NZRFU. Then to make matters worse, Spain withdrew at the last minute, leaving an uneven number of teams to make up the various pools, a deficiency corrected by the drafting in of a Scottish Students XV. The upheavals had the disappointing effect of making most of the pool games rather one-sided. The surprise package of the tournament were undoubtedly that well-known rugby-playing nation Kazakhstan, who

Above: *A try on the way for England in their 23-3 win over Scotland in 1997's home championship. England scored four tries in the match, two of which came in the closing minutes.*

won the plate competition. In the tournament proper, meanwhile, England and the United States once more made their way with little hindrance to the final.

Again it came down to a contest between the strength of the English pack and the pace and handling skills of the American backs. England routinely opted to scrummage when given penalties, and they gradually took control. They scored two penalty tries from scrums and three more regular tries from driving play to establish a winning lead. The Americans fought back with a couple of late tries of their own, but in the end England triumphed 38-23.

The women's game is growing by leaps and bounds in every rugby nation, with more clubs and players and more sophisticated competitive structures coming into existence. In Australia, for example, 1997 saw the first inter-state championship, while in Hong Kong, New Zealand beat the United States 41-0 in the final of a women's world sevens competition. Several countries are now taking steps to make sure that girls who have been introduced to mini-rugby will have the opportunity to keep playing through their teens to provide an increasing number of skilled recruits to the adult game in due course. Playing standards at the top of the game are certainly rising as levels of experience increase, and everyone is hoping that the next World Championship, to be held in 1998, will be the best yet.

CHAPTER NINETEEN

· GREAT CLUBS AND PLAYERS ·

Above: *Gary Whetton shows off the Ranfurly Shield following Auckland's 50th successive defence in August 1992.*

AGEN

Agen have long been one of France's most famous and successful rugby teams. The club was founded in 1900 and its full name is Sporting Union Agen. Agen first won the French championship in 1930, defeating the 1929 holders Quillan with a dramatic extra-time dropped goal. Since then Agen have made their total of French titles up to eight, with wins in 1945, 1962, 1965, 1966, 1976, 1982 and 1988. Albert Ferrasse, president of the French Rugby Union throughout the 1970s and 1980s, was a player in the 1945 team.

René Benesis, Daniel Dubroca and Pierre Berbizier are among the Agen men who have been prominent in the French team and later as national coaches. Philippe Sella, the world record holder for international caps, played for Agen

throughout his international career. Abdelatif Benazzi is a current star and is generally judged to be France's best forward of the 1990s.

AUCKLAND

Auckland – in their blue-and-white kit – have long been respected as one of the most formidable outfits in New Zealand and world rugby. Auckland rugby began in the 1870s, but the union itself was not actually formed until 1883. The Auckland union was one of the founder members of the New Zealand RFU in 1892.

Almost from the first Auckland had one of the most successful teams in New Zealand and continued to succeed even when parts of Auckland territory split away to form other unions, such as Counties and North Harbour.

Auckland were judged to be the best team in New Zealand in 1902 and so were appointed as the first holders of the Ranfurly Shield. Two years later, they lost it to first challengers Wellington, but they have recaptured it many times since. Auckland's run of 61 successful defences from 1985 to 1993 is easily the longest in Shield history. Auckland have also been the most successful team in the New Zealand National Provincial Championship since it was established in 1976, winning it 11 times in the first 21 years. Auckland have also beaten most top touring teams including the Lions, Australia and South Africa. Playing as the Auckland Blues, they won the first Super 12 tournament in 1996 and had earlier won the first Super 10 in 1993.

Many, many All Blacks have been Auckland men over the years, including three of the finest All Black skippers, Fred Allen, Wilson Whineray and Sean Fitzpatrick.

AUSTRALIAN CAPITAL TERRITORY

The Australian Capital Territory (ACT) Rugby Union has been separate and independent only since 1974, but the strong showing of the ACT Brumbies in the 1996 Super 12 proved, if there was still any doubt, that ACT rugby was truly a force to be reckoned with.

Rugby in what is now the ACT dates back at least to 1878, when there was a match between Queanbeyan and Yass, and various clubs and teams existed between then and World War I. Rugby league became the dominant local winter sport from the 1920s, but union had a revival when the Royal Military College moved back to the ACT in 1937

Left: Australian Capital Territory (ACT) in action against Canterbury Crusaders in the 1996 Super 12 competition.

Below: A scene from the move that led to the try of tries scored by the Baa-Baas against the All Blacks in 1973. The move started under the Barbarians' posts with two outrageous Phil Bennett side-steps and finished with Gareth Edwards crossing near the left-hand corner. Here Baa-Baas centre John Dawes passes to flanker Tom David as All Black scrum-half Sid Going closes in.

after a few years' absence. Local competitions were established, but until 1974 ACT players and clubs came under the NSW Country union for major matches.

Since 'independence' ACT rugby has gone from strength to strength with big wins over Wales and Ireland among the team's notable results. David Campese is the most famous son of the ACT, although later in his career he played mainly for NSW.

BARBARIANS

The Barbarians club was formed in 1890 by a group of London-based players who had just enjoyed an end-of-season tour playing teams in the north of England. The club is one of rugby's oddities and at the same time embodies one of the game's most cherished traditions. The Barbarians have no home ground, little formal organisation, membership is by invitation only and no subscriptions are charged. And even today for matches of virtually Test-match standard Barbarians players appear in uniform shirts and shorts but still wear their own socks in their own club colours.

The traditional annual Barbarians programme includes an Easter tour of South Wales and matches against Leicester at Christmas time and the East Midlands in the spring. But the real highlights for many years have been the Barbarians matches played as the finale to major tours of the British Isles by the great southern hemisphere teams. The first such match was against the Wallabies in 1948 and was played

only because there was a threatened shortfall of funds to cover the tour expenses.

For the international and club matches the Barbarians have almost always stuck to a policy of playing lively attacking rugby, and their games have often turned out to be classics. Heading that list for many is the superb encounter with the All Blacks in 1973, which was led off by that glorious and much-replayed Gareth Edwards try.

One additional reason for the Barbarians' popularity with British fans is that they provide the only occasions when something close to a British Lions XV plays on home soil. The Barbarians' committee have always tried, however, to avoid this typecasting as a shadow Lions team. They have usually chosen at least one uncapped player for their team and in recent years Barbarians selections have included many top stars from outside the British Isles. In earlier years players from the opposing touring party sometimes turned out for the 'Baa-Baas' against their own side, like Wallaby Nick Shehadie in 1958 or All Black Ian Clarke in 1964.

Barbarians teams now exist in New Zealand, Australia, South Africa and France. The demands on players in the professional era are certainly making it more difficult for the original and the new Barbarians to assemble really strong sides for their biggest matches, but fortunately there is as yet no sign that the valuable tradition of Barbarians rugby is seriously endangered in the new era.

BATH

The Bath club was founded in 1865 and is one of the oldest in England. Until the 1980s it had a proud history near, but mostly not quite at, the top of the English game. However, in the 1980s, with players hardened by regular matches with the top Welsh clubs, Bath really became a national force, and were English rugby's strongest club throughout most of that decade and into the 1990s. At the time of writing, there are signs that their dominance may be slipping, but there is no team in world rugby that can afford to take a visit to the Bath Recreation Ground lightly.

Bath won the English club championship six times between 1989 and 1996 and the knockout cup seven times between 1983 and 1996. Throughout these years a host of international players from other countries as well as England have played at the club, and there have been several instances of current Test players being unable to command a regular place in the Bath first XV. The most capped Bath player is the England centre Jeremy Guscott.

W.B. (BILL) BEAUMONT

Lock, born 1952. Fylde, England & British Lions.
34 Tests (+7 for Lions) 1975-82.

Bill Beaumont is one of a select few who have captained their country to a Five Nations Grand Slam. He made his England debut in 1975 but really came to the fore when he was called up as a replacement for the 1977 Lions in New Zealand. He quickly forced his way into the Test team and was at the heart of one of the finest-ever Lions packs.

Beaumont's greatest season was undoubtedly 1979-80. He began it by leading the North of England to a famous 21-9 win over the All Blacks; continued by captaining England to a long-awaited Grand Slam, clinched in spectacular

Above: *Bill Beaumont on duty for Lancashire in the County Championship. Had injury not forced his retirement, he might have become the first player to captain the Lions on two tours.*

fashion in the Scottish match in Edinburgh; next he led Lancashire to the English County Championship; and then carried on as the effective and popular captain of the Lions in South Africa.

Beaumont always described himself as a bit of a donkey and he certainly excelled in every aspect of tight forward play. His scrummaging was powerful and he was strong in ruck and maul. He was also a far better ball-player in the loose than he gave himself credit for and he always took at least his share of line-out ball, usually as a front jumper. Following a series of head injuries in 1982, Beaumont retired rather than risk permanent damage but is still a highly popular commentator on the game.

BÉZIERS

Béziers are one of the most powerful and famous clubs in France. The present club was formed by the amalgamation of a number of other older clubs in the years before and after World War I, but it has been known as Béziers since 1911. Another upheaval at the club came in the 1950s when a breakaway group tried unsuccessfully to convert the local enthusiasts to league.

Béziers won the French club championship in 1961, but the club's real glory spell came from the early 1970s through to the mid-1980s. From 1971 to 1984 they won the championship ten times and were runners-up once more. Prop Armand Vaquerin played in nine winning finals and was also capped 26 times by France. Hooker Alain Paco won 35 caps for France between 1974 and 1980 and is the most-capped player from a club that regularly fielded ten or more international players in their 1974-80 glory days. Béziers' strength throughout those years was based on tough and efficient forwards.

SERGE BLANCO

see page 120

H.E. (NAAS) BOTHA

Fly-half, born 1958. Northern Transvaal,
Rovigo & South Africa. 28 Tests 1980-92.

Naas Botha is South Africa's top points-scorer in international matches with 312 and would undoubtedly have scored many more and made many more appearances, if he had not been playing while South Africa was largely isolated from world rugby. He was just as effective with his goal-kicking in South African domestic matches as he was in internationals, scoring all 24 points for Northern Transvaal when they won the Currie Cup final in 1987, for example.

Botha first starred on the international stage against the 1980 British Lions, when his boot was crucial to South Africa's success in a desperately close series. But he missed a possible series-winning kick for the Springboks in the Third Test during their controversial tour of New Zealand a year later. In the later 1980s he played successfully against both the New Zealand Cavaliers and the World XV recruited by the South Africans to help limit their isolation.

Below: *Naas Botha kicks for touch during the 1992 South Africa v Australia Test at Cape Town. He bowed out of international rugby after the England Test later that year.*

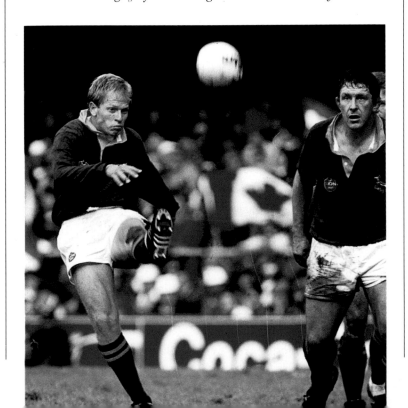

Above: *One of the most exciting and penetrative runners the game has seen. David Campese takes on the Irish in the World Cup quarter-final at Dublin in 1991. Australia won 19-18.*

After South Africa's official return to international competition, Botha was prominent among those helping to integrate South African rugby racially and was an effective and diplomatic leader of the 1992 Springbok tour to Europe.

D.I. (DAVID) CAMPESE

Wing/full-back, born 1962. ACT, NSW &
Australia. 101 Tests 1982-96.

David Campese's 64 tries in Tests put him at the top of the international try-scoring table. His flamboyant skills and his outspoken character off the field meant that he was never far from the rugby headlines. Opposing fans delighted when his unorthodox tactics went badly wrong, as when he gifted a vital try to the 1989 Lions, but he was so good for most of the time that the same fans were always ready to applaud yet another piece of Campo brilliance.

His signature move was his famous 'goose step' stride with which he fooled many opponents, but he could do everything else with style and pace. Although he was best known as a wing, Campese played a good deal of his rugby at full-back and was a powerful tactical kicker. His defence was usually very effective but there were occasional lapses.

Despite his brash image Campese worked very hard at his game and fitness as his more than 14 years of Test rugby testifies. He was also known for the time he was prepared to spend helping younger players develops their skills.

Campese's Wallaby call-up came, when he was still a teenager, for the tour to New Zealand in 1982 and he finally left international rugby in Australia's win over Wales in December 1996. We shall not see his like again.

CANTERBURY

The Canterbury union is the oldest in New Zealand. It was formed in 1879, although rugby was certainly being played in the district earlier in the decade. The game's history in Canterbury may be even longer than that because Christ's College in Christchurch had rules for a game with some rugby-like features in 1862, and there was a football club in the town in 1863. Canterbury provincial colours are traditionally red and black.

Fans of the province often feel that their men are neglected by the All Black selectors, but among the Canterbury stars to have worn the silver fern are Bob Deans, 'scorer' of the try that never was against Wales in 1905, Fergie McCormick, Alex 'Grizz' Wyllie and Tane Norton.

Canterbury have beaten every major overseas touring team at one time or another, but British fans will also remember the brutality used unsuccessfully against John Dawes's Lions in 1971. In New Zealand's domestic competitions, Canterbury have a strong record. They have held the Ranfurly Shield on a number of occasions, with long runs of successful defences in the 1930s, 1950s and 1980s. They have also won the National Provincial Championship twice, in 1977 and 1983.

Playing as the Canterbury Crusaders, the augmented Canterbury team had a grim time in the 1996 Super 12 tournament, coming in last in the preliminary 11-game series. The Christchurch fans will definitely be hoping for better in the future.

CARDIFF

Cardiff are one of the most famous and usually one of the strongest clubs in Wales. The Cardiff club was founded in 1876 by the amalgamation of older, smaller clubs, and Cardiff supporters will tell you that they have been Wales's premier club ever since, although followers of Swansea and Llanelli among others might disagree.

The Cardiff club is generally credited with being the first, in 1884, to employ four players in the threequarters, rather than the previous three, by reducing the number of forwards to eight.

Welsh club rugby came late to formal competitions, but Cardiff have the best record in the unofficial championship with 12 wins from 1898. After the Welsh Cup was introduced in 1971-72, Cardiff took a decade to get their name on the trophy, but then they managed to win it five times in the 1980s. The first half of the 1990s was also a good period for Cardiff with one league and one cup win. They

Below: *Will Carling playing for his club side, Harlequins, against Northampton in the final of the 1991 Pilkington Cup competition. 'Quins won 25-13 after extra time.*

also managed to reach the first Heineken European Cup final in 1996 but lost to Emile N'Tamack's Toulouse in extra time after a classic struggle.

Cardiff have a fine record against touring sides, having beaten all three of the All Blacks, Springboks and Wallabies, which is more than either Scotland or Ireland have achieved. Indeed against Australia, Cardiff have a 100 per cent record from seven meetings to date. The great scrum-half Gareth Edwards is the club's most capped player.

W.D.C. (WILL) CARLING

Centre, born 1965. Harlequins, England & British Lions.
72 Tests (+1 for Lions) 1988-97.

Will Carling is England's longest-serving and most successful captain ever. He was appointed England skipper early in the 1988-89 season after he had played only a handful of internationals and went on to lead the side for 59 Tests, winning 44 of them, until he gave up the job in 1996. After resigning the captaincy, he continued to win a place in the England side.

Carling's leadership was at the heart of England's domination of the Five Nations in the first half of the 1990s. After Scotland had foiled his side in the Grand Slam decider in 1990, Carling and England bounced back to take Grand Slams in the next two seasons and add a third in 1995 plus a further championship, including a Triple Crown, in 1996, making these years England's most successful since the 1920s. Carling led England to the World Cup final in 1991, and kept his own game together well enough to score twice in the semi-final defeat by New Zealand in 1995. His qualities as a strong-running and hard-tackling centre won Carling selection for the 1993 British Lions, but his tour was hampered by injury and he played in only one Test.

Carling has had something of a love-hate relationship with English fans and with England's rugby authorities. He has also suffered from extensive and intrusive reporting of his private life. English rugby, however, owes him a great debt not just for his huge contribution on the field as player and captain but also for his role off the field in raising the game's profile and popularity.

K.W. (KEN) CATCHPOLE

Scrum-half, born 1939. Randwick, NSW & Australia.
27 Tests 1961-68.

Ken Catchpole was one of the finest and quickest passers of a ball ever to play international rugby. He always had his feet and body correctly positioned before he was given the ball so that he was instantly able to send his pass zipping out to his fly-half. He was a very small man for an international player, only 1.4m (5ft 5in) tall but was strong and quick and ready to make breaks and take advantage of any gaps in opposition defences. His fly-half partner in many internationals was Phil Hawthorne, who later became a leading rugby league player.

Catchpole captained Australia in 13 of his Tests, including his debut against Fiji in 1961. His greatest days were probably the Australian wins over the All Blacks in 1964 and the international victories in England and Wales in 1966. His international career ended when he was injured by All Black Colin Meads in 1968. Some commentators condemned Meads for this incident, but Catchpole himself insisted it was a silly accident.

J.T. (JOHANNES) CLAASEN

Lock, born 1930. Western Transvaal & South Africa.
28 Tests 1955-62.

Johan Claasen was a rugged and powerful South African lock who made his Springbok debut against the British Lions in the hard-fought series in 1955. Claasen then went on to be one of the stalwarts of South Africa's 1956 tour to Australia and New

Below: Ken Catchpole prepares to put boot to ball. 'Catchy' was still 11 days short of his 21st birthday when he captained Australia against Fiji in 1961 on his Test debut.

Zealand. Both Tests in Australia were won but the All Blacks came through 3-1 in the series in New Zealand. The forward battle was fierce and uncompromising, with the Second and Third Tests being high on lists of the all-time dirtiest games. Despite all the rough stuff, Claasen finished the tour with the reputation of being the finest lock ever to visit New Zealand.

In 1958, Claasen had the unfortunate distinction of being the first Springbok captain in modern times to lose a home Test series, with one game drawn and one game lost against France. In 1960, however, Claasen helped the Springboks get revenge for 1956 on their All Black visitors.

Claasen remained prominent in the game after he retired from playing. He coached the Springboks on tours to France and Australia in 1968, 1971 and 1974. He was later manager of the Springbok team on the 1981 tour of New Zealand that was heavily disrupted by anti-racist protests. During the tour, Claasen tried hard to project a favourable image for the team in his dealings with the press.

D.H. (DANIEL) CRAVEN

Scrum-half, 1910-93. Stellenbosch University, Western Province & South Africa. 16 Tests 1931-38.

Danie Craven was one of the most influential men in rugby history. He was president of the South African Rugby Board from 1956 until it was reorganised as the non-racist South African Rugby Football Union in 1992, continuing as joint president of the new body until his death. He well deserved his nickname of South Africa's 'Mr Rugby'.

As a player Craven is remembered as a scrum-half and as one of the first and most effective users of the dive-pass technique. But he also holds the distinction of having played Test rugby in four playing positions, the others being fly-half, centre and, astonishingly, number eight. He also appeared at full-back, for a Springbok XV v Queensland. After his playing days were over, Craven became a leading coach, guiding the Springboks for much of the 1950s.

Dr Craven was totally dedicated to what he saw as the good of South African rugby. In his final years, Craven was generally credited with assisting South Africa's return to international competition by his moderate and open-minded attitudes, but it is equally clear that in earlier years he saw little wrong with the racist way in which the South African game was run. South African rugby was also one of the most professionalised in the final sham amateur years and, although Craven denied direct involvement in such matters and in the planning for events like the 1986 New Zealand Cavaliers tour, this did not convince many outside South Africa of his innocence in these areas.

T.G.R. (GERALD) DAVIES

Wing/centre, born 1945. Cambridge Univ, Cardiff, London Welsh, Wales & British Lions. 46 Tests (+5 for Lions) 1966-78.

Gerald Davies was one of the most exciting runners ever seen on a rugby field. Davies began his senior rugby career as a centre and was good enough in that position to play 11 times for his country and once for the 1968 Lions in South Africa. By the time of the 1971 Lions tour to New Zealand he was a wing and on that trip he proved that he was one of the best ever.

Davies had ample pace to outstrip defences for long-range scores and a stunning side-step to leave would-be tacklers clutching at air no matter how congested his path to the try-line. He could side-step off either foot and do it seemingly without slowing down even slightly. One of his finest matches was for the 1971 Lions against Hawke's Bay, in which he scored four superb tries. When he retired he was Wales's most capped threequarter and the joint holder of the Welsh try-scoring record with 20 (plus three in Lions Tests).

F.C.H. (FRIK) DU PREEZ

Lock/flanker, born 1935. Northern Transvaal & South Africa. 38 Tests 1960-71.

Frederick 'Frik' du Preez was one of the powerhouses of South African rugby in the 1960s. He was a powerfully effective tight forward, a tough competitor and fine line-out

Below: *Gerald Davies in the colours of London Welsh. Seven London Welsh players were selected for the 1971 Lions tour of New Zealand. Five, including Davies, played in all four Tests.*

jumper, but he could also contribute substantially in the loose with telling runs and the occasional spectacular try. The South African selectors were not always sure where to pick him – he made 31 appearances as lock and seven as a flanker – but they were usually sure they wanted him in the team. He holds the record for Springbok Test appearances with Jan Ellis, another great flanker of the 1960s and 1970s.

Du Preez had great battles with Colin Meads and Willie-John McBride at various times in his career. He scored a famous try against the Lions in the first Test in 1968 and was at the heart of the Springbok success in the hard-fought 1970 home series win over the All Blacks.

J.A. (JOHN) EALES

Lock, born 1970. Brothers, Queensland & Australia.
41 Tests 1991-

John Eales made his debut for Australia in their home match against Wales in 1991, which they won by the record score of 63-6. Eales has hardly looked back since. Later that season he was one of the stars in the Bledisloe Cup series against the All Blacks and he confirmed an already huge reputation in the World Cup a few months later. Eales won many vital line-out balls for his team – he had one of his most effective games in the final – but he also drove hard in the loose and made many important tackles.

Like all modern second-rows, Eales is a very tall man (2.01m – 6ft 7in), but he also has excellent ball skills to accompany his size. He is even a top-class goal-kicker as well. In the 1996 Super 12 he did most of the Queensland kicking and was actually the competition's top scorer.

Eales missed the whole 1993 season because of injury but on his recovery he was soon back in the Australian Test side. He was appointed captain for the first Tri-Nations series in 1996, in which Australia, with a rebuilt team, won only one match. He then led the team rather more successfully in their tour of Europe. Eales is now one of the truly great forwards in world rugby

G.O. (GARETH) EDWARDS

Scrum-half, born 1947. Cardiff, Wales & British Lions.
53 Tests (+10 for Lions) 1967-78.

If there can be such a thing as the greatest-ever rugby player when the different playing positions demand so many different qualities, then Gareth Edwards may possibly be that man. His 53 internationals for Wales were continuous. He was never dropped and never had to miss a game for his country because of injury. He was first-choice scrum-half on

Above: *Frik du Preez rises above the rest to claim a line-out ball, as South Africa beat the Combined Services 14-6 during the Springboks' 1969 tour of the British Isles.*

Below: *John Eales (No 5) in action against Scotland A on Australia's 1996-97 tour of Europe. An all-round athlete and footballer, Eales is the epitome of the modern rugby forwrd.*

three British Lions tours, including the great 1971 and 1974 teams. His total of 20 tries for Wales was the record (shared with Gerald Davies) for some time and still remains an astonishing total for a scrum-half.

Edwards, it seemed, could do everything. At the very start of his career – he was picked for Wales when he was still a teenager – some people thought that his passing was a little weak and that he did not always choose wisely when to kick. By his later years he had a long and fast pass (though only off one hand) that gave his fly-halves an enormous amount of room, and his tactical kicking was masterful. And he could score from anywhere on the pitch, being just as likely to sprint in from long range as he was to make a close-quarter burst and use his great strength to force his way over the line. And of course it was Edwards who scored that wonderful try in the first minutes of the 1973 Barbarians v All Blacks match, appearing on the wing to finish off a move that had started under the Barbarians posts and seemed to involve virtually every player in the Barbarians side.

Edwards struck up a great partnership with Barry John, his fly-half and team-mate with Cardiff, Wales and the 1971 Lions, and an equally effective pairing with Phil Bennett with Wales and the 1974 Lions team. It is no coincidence that his time in the Welsh team was one of great success for his country, not matched by Wales teams before his arrival or since his retirement.

Above: *Gareth Edwards goes over for his final try for Wales, in the 1978 Five Nations clash with Scotland. Was Edwards the greatest rugby player of them all?*

M.G. (MARK) ELLA

Fly-half, born 1959. Randwick, NSW & Australia.
25 Tests 1980-84.

Mark Ella and his two almost as extravagantly talented brothers first came to the notice of the rugby world outside their native Australia when they toured Britain and Europe with the brilliant and unbeaten Australian Schools team in 1977-78. By 1979 Mark Ella had won a place in the Wallaby party to tour Argentina, although he did not make his Test debut until the 1980 series against the All Blacks.

Ella captained Australia in 1982 and 1983 with modest success and was replaced as skipper by Andrew Slack for the 1984 tour to Britain. On this tour, helped by his new scrum-half partner Nick Farr-Jones, Ella was again one of the stars as the team completed a Grand Slam in the internationals. Ella also completed a personal grand slam of a try in each game, the first player of any nationality to score in all four Tests on a British tour. Despite this achievement Ella did not see eye to eye with the then Wallaby coach Alan Jones and retired from top-level Australian rugby after the tour when he was only 25 years old.

Above: *Wallabies Mark Ella (left), skipper Andy Slack (right) and David Campese celebrate after beating Scotland in 1984 and achieving the Grand Slam against the home countries.*

Ella had an uncanny ability to take the ball flat from his forwards and immediately threaten to cross the gain line either through his own running or through the openings created by his beautiful passing and reading of the game.

Mark's twin brother **Glen** (G.J. Ella) was also a fine full-back or centre, winning four Australian caps. Younger brother **Gary** (G.A. Ella, born 1960) won six caps as a centre. The three often played together at Randwick, helping the club win five consecutive Sydney championships by their dazzling running and handling moves. All three never appeared together in a Test match, however.

ERIC EVANS

Hooker, 1921-91. Sale & England.
30 Tests 1948-58.

Eric Evans completed his long and eventful international career with two seasons as undefeated England captain in 1957 and 1958. The 1958 season included a victory over the Wallabies but was not quite perfect because of draws with Scotland and Wales. The real glory season was 1957 when he led his men to a superb Five Nations Grand Slam with only eight points conceded in the four games.

Early in his rugby career Evans suffered from the inconsistencies of the English selection process. Although most of his rugby was played at hooker, Evans was first picked as a prop for one game against Australia in 1948 and then did not play for England again until selected for a single match, against Wales, in the 1950 championship. He was then in and out of the team for several years until he played, as captain, in all the England internationals in 1956. He captained the side in 13 matches in all, retiring after the 1958 season when he was 37 years old.

I.C. (IEUAN) EVANS

Wing, born 1964. Llanelli, Wales & British Lions.
71 Tests (+6 for Lions) 1987-

Ieuan Evans is Wales's most-capped player and top try-scorer in internationals, with 71 appearances and 33 tries (to the end of the 1996-97 season). Evans also had 28 games from 1991-95 as Welsh captain, the longest run by any Welsh skipper. With better luck he might easily have added to all these records, but several serious shoulder and ankle injuries kept him out of the game at various times.

Evans has genuine pace and the strength and elusiveness to set up attacks from a long way out. He also has an eye for a fleeting gap in the tightest of defences. Evans is a great opportunist, too, ever ready to pounce on opponents' mistakes, as Rory Underwood and David Campese, among others, both know to their cost. His conversion into a try of Campese's defensive error in 1989 is Evans's only score in his six Lions Test appearances, but it was a vital one, helping the Lions clinch the series against Australia.

Below: *Ieuan Evans runs around the Scottish defence to score Wales's fourth try in their 34-19 win at Murrayfield in 1997.*

S.B.T. (SEAN) FITZPATRICK
Hooker, born 1963. Auckland & New Zealand.
83 Tests 1986-

Sean Fitzpatrick is the world's most-capped forward and the most-capped All Black ever. He made his All Black debut in 1986, and from his third appearance late that year he played 63 consecutive Tests, a world record, until he was rested for the 1995 World Cup match against Japan. Since then, he has reeled off a further 18 consecutive matches (to the start of the 1997 season).

Fitzpatrick is a powerful yet mobile hooker who does more than his fair share of the hard work in the tight and pops up in some unusual positions to score important tries, too. He is an especially accurate line-out thrower and always makes sure that referees have the benefit of his input into their decisions. But more important than all that is the will to win that he embodies and has helped impart to the All Black team that he has led for so long. The defeat in the 1995 World Cup final was a major disappointment, but Fitzpatrick bounced back to lead New Zealand to a win in the first Tri-Nations tournament in 1996. Even better, he then went on to become the first All Black skipper to win a Test series in South Africa.

Sean's father **Brian** (B.B.J. Fitzpatrick, born 1931) was an All Black centre with three Test appearances during the 1953-54 tour to the British Isles and France.

Above: *Sean Fitzpatrick (right) complains to referee Brian Stirling after the Le Roux biting incident in the Second Test between New Zealand and South Africa at Auckland in 1994.*

G. J. (GRANT) FOX
Fly-half, born 1962. Auckland & New Zealand.
46 Tests 1985-93.

Grant Fox was one of the most effective fly-halves ever to play for New Zealand and is New Zealand's record points-scorer in internationals. His eventual total was 645 points in his 46 Tests. In addition he holds a variety of points-scoring records in New Zealand provincial rugby.

Fox made his full All Black debut against Argentina in 1985 but then chose to tour South Africa with the rebel New Zealand Cavaliers the following year. He therefore had to wait until the opening game of the 1987 World Cup, against Italy, to make his second All Black appearance. Fox played in all six of New Zealand's matches on the way to winning that tournament and was the top scorer for the competition with 126 points.

Fox was never a great distributor of the ball nor a really threatening runner. He did not even have the massive range of some of the great goal-kickers either, but no one has ever matched his consistent accuracy from slightly shorter distances and his ability to retain his form under the greatest pressure. He was certainly a match-winner. His era in the

Right: *Grant Fox kicks for goal during New Zealand's 30-13 win in the Third Test against the 1993 Lions at Eden Park, Auckland. Besides being New Zealand's top points-scorer, Fox is also their most-capped first five-eighth.*

All Black and Auckland teams were times of great success for both, and his deadly kicking was one of the main reasons why this was so.

GALA

Gala are traditionally one of the strongest clubs in Scottish Border rugby and since their foundation in 1875 they have had a great rivalry with their near neighbours Hawick. Gala would have to concede that their rivals have come out on top more often, however. Their closest encounter was in the national championship in 1976-77. The two were exactly tied after the regular league programme, even when points difference was taken into account, but Hawick had the better of the play-off game. Despite this disappointment Gala did win the league title twice in the early 1980s but fell on harder times when they were relegated from the first division in 1996.

The club's most-capped player is Peter Brown, the Scotland number eight and lock of the late 1960s and early 1970s, who had one of the most unusual goal-kicking styles ever seen in top-class rugby.

J.A. (JOHN) GALLAGHER

see page 105

C.M.H. (MIKE) GIBSON

Centre/fly-half, born 1942. Cambridge Univ, North of Ireland FC, Ireland & British Lions. 69 Tests (+12 for Lions) 1964-79.

Mike Gibson had a long and distinguished career with Ireland and the British Lions. He and Willie-John McBride are the only players ever to travel on five Lions tours. Gibson played in every Test on three of these tours (1966, 1968 and 1971) and was one of the heroes of the series-winning side in New Zealand in 1971.

Gibson first came to rugby prominence with Cambridge University, winning three Blues from 1963 to 1965. He won his first Irish cap against England in 1964 at fly-half and held that position in the side until 1969 when he moved into midfield as a centre. He played 40 of his internationals as a centre, and in the twilight of his career Ireland made further use of Gibson's great experience and reading of the game by giving him four matches on the

wing. He finished his international career with two games against Australia during Ireland's tour down under in 1979. He is the most-capped Irish player ever.

Gibson was never a spectacular player but was always one of the great thinkers of the game who selected the right tactical option and had the quickness and commitment to exploit it. He was not a big man physically, but good judges in every rugby country reckoned that he was one of the true giants of the game.

Above: *Ireland's Mike Gibson lines up a shot at goal. An occasional goal-kicker at international level, Gibson scored 65 of his 115 Test points from place kicks.*

HARLEQUINS

Harlequins are one of the oldest and most famous clubs in the English game. They were among the founder members of the RFU in 1871 and actually date back to 1866. The club's London ground, named the Stoop Memorial Ground after a leading England back and club member of the early 1900s, is very close to the England headquarters at Twickenham in southwest London, and some Harlequins matches have been played at the national ground over the years. Wavell Wakefield, England Grand Slam captain in the 1920s, was a Harlequins stalwart.

For many years Harlequins had a well-deserved reputation for social exclusivity, which limited their recruitment of players. They have gradually lost that in recent years and have been leaders in adjusting fully to the professional era. They now wish to be known as NEC Harlequins and have recruited a slew of top players from other countries and from rugby league. Unfortunately they have also decided to follow the confusing practice of having their players wear squad numbers that bear no relation to their playing positions.

Harlequins appeared twice in English cup finals in the early 1990s, but at the time of writing they had not yet managed to shake off the inconsistency that has dogged their league campaigns to date. Will Carling, Jason Leonard and Peter Winterbottom are among the leading English cap-winners who have played for the club.

A.G. (GAVIN) HASTINGS

Full-back, born 1962. Cambridge Univ, Watsonians, Scotland & British Lions. 61 Tests (+6 for Lions) 1986-95.

Gavin Hastings made his first appearance for Scotland in 1986 and from then until his retirement after the 1995 World Cup was regarded as one of the strongest-running and hardest-tackling full-backs in world rugby. He was also a kicker of prodigious goals. He sometimes missed short, easy penalties, as in the 1991 World Cup semi-final, but he more than made up for this with the many vital long-range efforts that he sent sailing over. His total of 667 points in 61 games for Scotland plus 66 in internationals with the Lions places Hastings second in the all-time points-scoring table – and bearing in mind that there were times when he was not Scotland's first-choice goal-kicker, he might have had more.

Hastings was a member of Scotland's Five Nations Grand Slam team in 1990. Later in his career he was captain of Scotland and of the British Lions in New Zealand in 1993, and was much praised for his leadership on and off the field. He brought his international career to a close with record points-scoring performances in the 1995 World Cup.

Gavin's brother **Scott** (born 1964) holds the record number of Scotland caps. He made his Scotland debut, in the centre, on the same day as Gavin and by the end of the 1996-97 season he had played 65 times for his country. He is best known as a powerful tackler and was chosen for Lions tours in 1989 and 1993, playing in two Tests.

HAWICK

The Hawick club is the oldest of the senior clubs in the Scottish Borders, and since its foundation in 1873 it has been one of the strongest in the Borders district and in Scotland as a whole. Hawick are also known as the 'Greens' from the club colours.

Hawick have a unique competitive history, with the quadruple distinction of having won the unofficial Scottish championship in its first proper year in 1895-96, the Border League in its opening season in 1901-02, the official Scottish league championship in its inaugural season in 1973-74 and the Scottish cup in its first year in 1996. In the official league, Hawick were totally dominant in the early years, winning ten of the first 14 titles.

Hawick men near the top of the Scottish cap-winners' list include Colin Deans, Jim Renwick and Alan Tomes, but perhaps the most famous rugby personality connected with

Above: *Gavin Hastings tears towards the French line to score a dramatic try for Scotland in 1995. Having levelled the scores, Hastings himself converted to give Scotland victory, 23-21.*

Right: *Andy Irvine prepares to hoist one. Irvine, of Heriots and Scotland, was one of the most exciting of full-backs, often joining the line at pace or counter-attacking from his own half.*

the club is the BBC commentator Bill McLaren, a player with Hawick in the 1940s who was forced to give up the game by illness when on the verge of breaking into the Scottish team.

HERIOTS

Heriots Former Pupils, to give the club its full title, have long been one of the most prestigious and powerful clubs in Scotland. For many years before the advent of official leagues, the annual fixture between Heriots (from Edinburgh) and Hawick (the traditional powerhouse of the other main hotbed of Scottish rugby, the Borders) was the most highly regarded domestic game in Scotland. Heriots have not been able to maintain consistent form since formal leagues began in 1973-74, however, only recording a single league title since then, in 1979.

Heriots have had numerous players who have had notable careers with Scotland, but perhaps by coincidence the most famous ones have mostly been full-backs. Dan Drysdale in the 1920s, Ken Scotland in the 1950s and 1960s and then Andy Irvine in the 1970s and 1980s all had long runs in the international side, and five others from the club have also represented their country in this position.

A.R. (ANDY) IRVINE

Full-back, born 1951. Heriots, Scotland & British Lions.
51 Tests (+9 for Lions) 1972-82.

Andy Irvine was one of the players who transformed the full-back position from being one mainly concerned with the defensive duties of tackling, fielding high balls and thumping them back into touch into one that emphasised vibrant attacking running. Indeed Irvine's tackling and catching were sometimes erratic, but his counter-attacking in broken-field situations has rarely been matched.

Irvine made his debut for Scotland against the All Blacks in 1972 and in his 11-season career he scored the then world record total of 301 international points, including ten tries for Scotland and one for the Lions. Irvine went on three Lions tours (1974, 1977 and 1980), playing on the wing for the Lions in two Tests in 1974 and his remaining Lions Tests as a full-back. Perhaps his greatest game was against France in the Five Nations in 1980. Scotland were ten points behind with only about 12 minutes left on the clock when Irvine inspired and led a great comeback, scoring two tries and landing several kicks for Scotland to win 22-14.

M.N. (MICHAEL) JONES

Flanker, born 1965. Auckland & New Zealand.
51 Tests 1986- (including one Test for Western Samoa).

Even in New Zealand's long list of great back-row players Michael Jones's special talents stand out. Jones was born in New Zealand of Samoan parentage and, although he played for Auckland from 1985, he made his international debut in the Western Samoan team in 1986. He played only one game before being called into the All Black squad for the 1987 World Cup. He scored in his first match, the tournament

James, mastermind also of the success of the 1971 Lions in New Zealand. James had earlier been a player with the club but won only two Welsh caps because his career coincided with that of the great Cliff Morgan. However, many other Llanelli men have had long and effective spells in the Welsh national side. The club's and Wales's leading cap-winner and try-scorer is Ieuan Evans.

Llanelli have an especially proud record in the Welsh Cup, which they won nine times in its first 25 seasons, a far better record than any of their leading rivals. They were also Welsh (league) champions in 1993.

J.T. (JONAH) LOMU

see page 114

M.P. (MICHAEL) LYNAGH

Fly-half, born 1963. Queensland, Saracens & Australia.
72 Tests 1984-95.

Michael Lynagh is the highest points-scorer in international rugby history with 911 points for his country. He made his

debut for Australia against Fiji in 1984 and then played as a centre in the four internationals of Australia's tour to the UK later that year. He has played seven Tests in the centre, one as a replacement full-back and the rest at fly-half.

Most of Lynagh's Test points came via his trusty right boot. But he was far more than just a kicking machine. His handling and distribution were equally top class and he scored many important tries, such as the match-saving effort in the 1991 World Cup quarter-final against Ireland.

Lynagh had a long and effective Test partnership with scrum-half Nick Farr-Jones, and when Farr-Jones retired Lynagh took over the captaincy of Australia from him. Lynagh led the team in the 1995 World Cup but retired from international rugby after Australia lost to England in the quarter-finals. He has continued to play at club level, however, and in 1996 joined the English club Saracens.

WILLIE-JOHN MCBRIDE

Lock, born 1940. Ballymena, Ireland & British Lions.
63 Tests (+17 for Lions) 1962-75.

From almost the start of his international career Willie-John McBride had the respect of the biggest, toughest and most competitive of his team-mates and opponents. He developed a dominating will to win, which he showed best as pack leader of the 1971 Lions and captain of the most successful Lions team ever, the great 1974 side in South Africa.

Sometimes McBride's determination never to back down from physical confrontation went too far, but it undoubtedly helped give those Lions teams a resilience that their predecessors had never possessed. When he met a like-minded opponent the collision could be truly fearsome. His first encounter with Colin Meads was fierce and uncompromising on both sides, but the mutual respect it generated lasted for the rest of their careers.

McBride holds the record number of Lions caps and is one of only two men to have gone on five Lions tours. The other five-time Lion, Mike Gibson, is the only man with more Irish caps. In addition to his leadership and his great power in every phase of forward play, McBride was specially skilled in ensuring that the ball he won as a front jumper in the line-out was clean and tidy.

C.E. (COLIN) MEADS

Lock, born 1936. King Country & New Zealand.
55 Tests 1957-71.

Colin Meads is one of the legends of New Zealand rugby. One New Zealand writer summed him up as playing with 'a

Above: World record points-scorer in Tests Michael Lynagh swings his deadly right boot for Saracens against London rivals Wasps in the 1996-97 Courage League.

Above: *Skipper Willie-John McBride (right) and fellow British Lion Roger Uttley in line-out action against Northern Transvaal during the 1974 Lions tour of South Africa.*

total dislike of the opposition' and Fergie McCormick, a colleague in many All Black teams and no softie himself, said Meads was 'a terrible man with the silver fern on'. His commitment to the All Black cause was certainly absolute and every picture of him shows the same stern,

uncompromising features with powerful shoulders slightly leaning forward ready to drive into the next opponent or hit the next ruck. Sometimes Meads's commitment overstepped the mark, and he was sent off in a match against Scotland in 1967, although for a comparatively minor offence compared with some of those he got away with.

After he retired from playing, Meads remained active as a coach and selector. He coached the rebel New Zealand Cavaliers in their tour of South Africa in 1986. The New Zealand authorities' condemnation of this tour was generally half-hearted, but Meads did lose his position as a national selector for a time. By 1995 he was back in favour, however, and was one of the managers of the All Blacks in the World Cup that year.

Meads, also known as 'Pinetree' or 'Piney', first came to the All Blacks as a flanker or number eight but he played most of his international rugby as a lock. His 48 caps as a lock and 55 total appearances stood for some years as New Zealand records. His total of 15 seasons as a full All Black has yet to be beaten.

Colin's brother **Stan** (S.T. Meads, born 1938) also played lock for New Zealand 15 times between 1961 and 1966, usually packing down alongside Colin.

Below: *Colin Meads breaks from a maul during the All Blacks' 33-3 victory over the North of England in 1967. Meads was playing his 90th match in an All Black shirt.*

MELROSE

The Melrose club was founded in 1877 in highly unusual circumstances. The Melrose men were originally part of a combined club with Gala, but one night a Melrose raiding party pinched the posts from the club's ground in Galashiels and set them up in the Greenyards in Melrose. Two separate and successful clubs have existed ever since.

Melrose is best known in the rugby world as a whole as the location where sevens were invented in 1883. Even with a free set of goal-posts the Melrose club finances needed topping up, and the local butcher, Ned Haig, conceived the idea of a sevens tournament as part of a fund-raising Melrose sports day. The home side won the first title, and Haig was in the team. Sevens has spread worldwide since then, of course, but the Melrose competition remains highly prestigious with all Scotland's top sides competing, as well as leading invitation teams from other countries.

Melrose have also been notable competitors in the 15-a-side game and have been Scotland's top club side in the 1990s with six league titles (to 1997). Half-back partnerships have been a feature of Melrose history. The club's current pairing of Craig Chalmers and Bryan Redpath have played an important part in recent success and have also appeared regularly for Scotland. In the 1960s David Chisholm and Alec Hastie had 13 games together for Scotland. Chalmers is the club's most-capped player.

LUCIEN MIAS

Lock, born 1930. Mazamet, Carcasonne & France.
29 Tests, 1951-59.

Lucien Mias was an inspirational figure in French rugby. Before his time France had often had many fine individual players and had recorded numerous impressive victories. Other countries, however, knew that France had never won a Five Nations championship outright and had never beaten any of the top southern hemisphere sides – that is before Mias fought his way into the team.

Mias himself was a powerful, driving forward who played mainly at lock. However, his real skill was as an organiser, pack leader and captain. He was once memorably described as a 'bulldozer with a brain'. Mias was selected fairly regularly for France in the early 1950s following his debut against Scotland in 1951 and played in France's first win over New Zealand, 3-0 in Paris in 1954.

Mias dropped out of top-class rugby then for a while to follow his medical studies but was back in the side in 1958 when France rounded off the Five Nations with their first-ever win in Wales. France then went on a tour of South

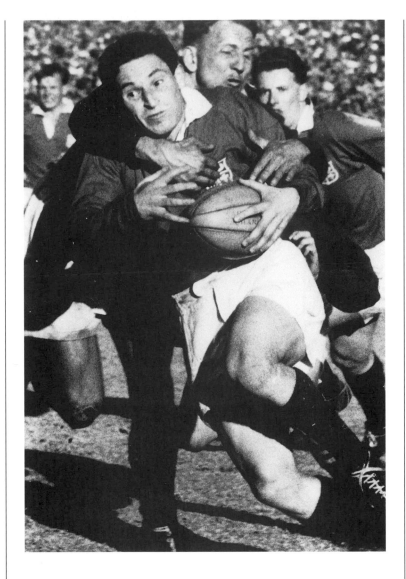

Above: *British Lions fly-half Cliff Morgan is tackled by Theuns Briers near the Springboks' try-line in the First Test of the 1955 tour of South Africa. The Lions won the game 23-22.*

Africa, and Mias took over as captain when the original skipper, Michel Celaya, was injured. France drew the First Test and won the Second Test to claim a series victory over the Springboks on their home ground, the first visitors to South Africa to do so since the 1890s. The reason why was the organisation and will to win that Mias created.

The team came home and Mias led them to France's first ever outright win in the Five Nations the next season. Mias retired then, with a good job done, and no one has ever thought France were a soft touch since.

C.I. (CLIFF) MORGAN

Fly-half, born 1930. Cardiff, Wales & British Lions.
29 Tests (+4 for Lions) 1951-58.

Many Welsh rugby fans believe that Cliff Morgan was the finest of the selection of great players who have come out of the famous Welsh outside-half factory. Morgan had a superb all-round game, but his contemporaries remember his pace off the mark and elusive running, whether making deadly breaks or setting up his outside backs for decisive attacks.

Morgan made his Wales debut against Ireland in 1951 and took a little while to settle into the team and display his best form. But the next season was much better. Morgan provided much of the inspiration that helped Wales to a Triple Crown, although he missed the Grand Slam match against France (which Wales won) at the end of the season.

Morgan could also compete successfully against the great southern hemisphere teams. He was on the winning side for both Cardiff and Wales against the 1953-54 All Blacks and was one of the stars of the 1955 Lions in South Africa. Those Lions shared the Test series, and Morgan actually captained the side in the win in the Third Test. Morgan also captained Wales successfully to the Five Nations championship in 1956. After he retired, Morgan remained well known in rugby as a television commentator and executive.

G.N.K. (GRAHAM) MOURIE

Flanker, born 1952. Wellington, Taranaki & New Zealand. 21 Tests 1977-82.

Graham Mourie was one of the finest captains ever to lead the All Blacks – a very special distinction indeed when one considers the great men who have held that job over the years. When Mourie forced his way into the full All Black side for the final two matches in the 1977 home series with the Lions he had already been marked down as a future All Black skipper. In fact those were the only two games of his Test career in which he did not captain the side.

Aside from his special leadership qualities, Mourie was a fast and tireless open-side flanker. He was not an especially big man, but his support play and tackling were immense and he scrapped for the bits and pieces of possession with the best of them. He was also prepared to stand up for his principles off the field, as when he refused to play against the Springboks during their 1981 tour to New Zealand. His All Black teams did not lose many games, but perhaps the pinnacle of his career was as captain of the 1978 Grand Slam tour of Britain and Ireland.

MUNSTER

Munster is one of Ireland's four traditional provinces, and its team have always embodied the fire and fury of Irish rugby at its best. Many Munster clubs have a long pedigree, with Shannon and Garryowen both being founded in 1884, and the Munster Provincial Cup was first played for in 1886.

Below: *Welsh scrum-half Terry Holmes just gets the ball away as All Black flanker and captain Graham Mourie moves in. New Zealand won this 1980 contest at Cardiff 23-3.*

Above: *Wing James Small, Natal's most-capped Springbok, descends on French full-back Jean-Luc Sadourny in the Second Test of South Africa's 1996-97 visit to France.*

Munster have fought (sometimes literally) some notable battles with major touring teams over the years. They were the first Irish province to beat a top international side when they won 11-8 against the Wallabies in 1967, but there is no doubt that Munster rugby's finest day was in October 1978. The All Blacks came to Limerick and went away on the wrong end of a 12-0 result. To keep an All Black team off the score sheet is a very rare feat, even more so when it is a team that remains undefeated on the rest of its tour and wins a Grand Slam in the internationals. Fly-half Tony Ward, one of Munster's many famous Irish internationals, kicked a conversion and two dropped goals, but the whole team played and tackled heroically.

Cork Constitution are one of Munster's most famous clubs, but in many ways the heart of Munster rugby is in

Limerick. The town has a population of only about 70,000 people but supports four clubs in the first division of the All-Ireland League. Constitution won the league in its first year in 1991, but for the next five years Limerick clubs made it their own, with Garryowen, Young Munster and Shannon all getting their names on the trophy. In Munster's own trophy, the Provincial Cup, Garryowen have most wins.

Tom Kiernan, Ireland and Lions captain in the 1960s, is the most-capped Munster representative.

NATAL

The Natal rugby union was founded in 1890. Standards in the province were modest for some time, and no Natal player represented South Africa until 1921. For many years after that, Natal rugby was strong but not quite strong enough to achieve domestic honours. Natal did, however, beat the Wallabies on several occasions, the first in 1953, but have yet to beat the Lions or the All Blacks. The closest game with the All Blacks was a 6-6 draw in 1960.

Natal had to wait until 1990 for a first Currie Cup win, but with repeat successes in 1992, 1995 and 1996 and the runners-up spots in the 1994 Super 10 and 1996 Super 12 there is no doubt that they are now one of the world's top provincial teams. Perhaps even better, the successes of these years have been based on fast and lively 15-man rugby, which has been exciting to watch as well as being effective.

Natal have had many representatives in Springbok teams. One Natal and Springbok star of the 1930s had the splendid name of Ebbo Bastard, but more famous in those days was Philip Nel, who captained the 1937 Springboks to a series win in New Zealand. Classy full-back André Joubert and controversial wing James Small, both of whom played in the World Cup winning team of 1995, are among the current favourites.

GEORGE NEPIA

Full-back, 1905-86. Hawke's Bay, East Coast & New Zealand. 9 Tests 1924-30.

George Nepia played in only two full Test series as an All Black, with one additional game against Australia, but is still regarded as one of the all-time greats and certainly has legendary status in the New Zealand game.

Nepia was selected as a 19-year-old for the 1924-25 All Black tour of the British Isles and France. That tour finished with a 100 per cent record, and Nepia amazingly played in every match, including games en route in Australia and Canada. Nepia was an exciting and effective runner from full-back, but on that tour he was instructed to concentrate on his defensive duties of tackling, catching and kicking, all of which he did superbly.

Nepia was a Maori, and because the New Zealand authorities in those days were willing to condone South African racism he was 'ineligible' for the 1928 All Black tour to South Africa. He played effectively against the Lions in 1930 but surprisingly missed selection for the 1935 tour to Britain. Nepia then went to rugby league, playing successfully in England and later at home in New Zealand. He was reinstated as an amateur after World War II and played on for a time before becoming a respected referee.

NEW SOUTH WALES

Soldiers of the Sydney garrison were the first reported football players in Australia in 1829, and a game that can definitely be called rugby was being played in and around Sydney in the 1860s. Local players and clubs formed the Southern Rugby Union in 1874, and this body was renamed the New South Wales (NSW) RFU in 1892.

Rugby union in New South Wales has found it hard to compete with rugby league ever since the split began in 1907, and it has only been through the introduction of some levels of legitimate payment for players since the late 1980s, and now full professionalism, that the steady drain of union stars into league has been halted.

New South Wales made the first overseas tour in the history of rugby, sending a team to New Zealand in 1882, and also played their first match against Queensland in the same season. There have been over 250 NSW *v* Queensland matches since that first encounter, with NSW winning more than twice as many of the games as their northern rivals. In the 1980s and 1990s, however, Queensland have had the upper hand.

One of the reasons for NSW's lead overall is that no rugby was played in Queensland for most of the 1920s and it then took a long period for the game there to recover its

Below: *The All Black 'Invincibles', who toured the British Isles and France in 1924-25, winning all 30 of their games. George Nepia is seated at the right-hand end of the centre row.*

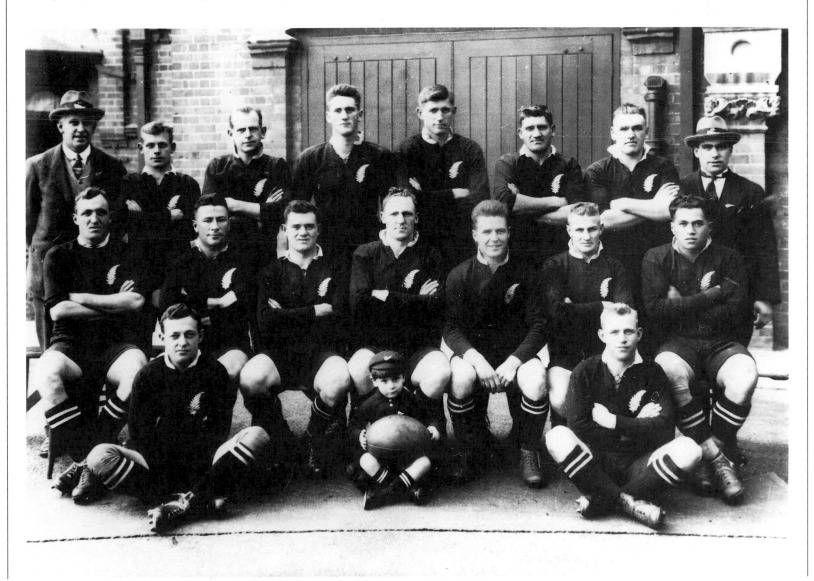

strength. However, while the Queensland game was in recess, the New South Wales team played on effectively as the Australian national side (with occasional Victorians and native Queenslanders making up the numbers). Also known as the 'Waratahs', NSW played the All Blacks home and away a number of times in those years and met the Springboks in Australia in 1920. But most famous was their tour to the British Isles and France in 1927-28. Players who played for these NSW teams are now regarded as full internationals by the Australian RFU.

The Waratah name has been revived as part of the official title for the NSW team in the Super 12.

NORTHERN TRANSVAAL

Rugby in what is now the Northern Transvaal province dates back to the 1870s, when games were played in the Pretoria area. A Transvaal rugby union was formed in 1889 and originally this body represented the game in the north as well. A separate Northern Transvaal union was formed in 1937.

One early stalwart of rugby in the Northern Transvaal area was Loftus Versfeld, after whom the great stadium in Pretoria is named. Loftus Versfeld stadium was opened in 1938, although the ground there had already been in use for 30 years, and ever since has been the home of the Blue Bulls, as the Northern Transvaal side are known.

Northern Transvaal fielded its first Springboks almost immediately the union was formed. Danie Craven (who had recently moved to the province) was the Springbok captain against the Lions in 1938, and several other Northern Transvaal players also featured in that series. Naas Botha, the superb goal-kicker of the 1980s, is perhaps the most famous recent Northern Transvaal star.

'Northerns' notched up their first Currie Cup win in 1946, and since the cup became an annual competition in 1968, they have won it 12 times (to 1996), the best record of any of the provinces. They reached the semi-finals in the first Super 12 competition in 1996. Northerns have also beaten all the major touring teams – the All Blacks, the Wallabies, the Lions and France – on various occasions and are renowned for the tough 'welcome' they give to touring sides.

OTAGO

The Otago rugby union, founded in 1881, is the third-oldest in New Zealand. Rugby in the area dates back to at least 1872, when the first clubs were formed in and around Dunedin, although these sides seem to have played a rather eclectic type of game, with elements of soccer and Australian Rules mixed in. The Dunedin clubs played a genuine rugby match against a touring Auckland side in 1875, however.

Otago played its first match against overseas opposition, a touring New South Wales team, in 1882, and Otago players were included in the New Zealand party that made the return visit in 1884. Otago, however, declined to join the New Zealand Rugby Union when that body was formed in 1892 because of concerns that it would be controlled from Wellington. They did finally sign up in 1895, though.

Otago have also provided several highly important innovators in the techniques of the game. The 2-3-2 scrummage formation, which was long a New Zealand speciality, is believed to have originated in Otago. The five-eighths positions were certainly invented by an Otago man, Jimmy Duncan, who captained New Zealand in their first international in Australia in 1903. Later Vic Cavanagh coached the Otago side to great success for some years after World War II and based his teaching around fast and aggressive rucking to an extent unknown before.

Otago's best period in Ranfurly Shield competition was in that Cavanagh era, but the last time since then that Otago held the Shield was in 1957. Otago have won the National Provincial Championship only once, in 1991. Charlie Saxton, captain of the Kiwis after World War II, Kevin Skinner, hard man in the front row in the 1950s, and Mike Brewer, flanker and skipper in the early 1990s, are among the province's most famous All Blacks.

ROBERT PAPAREMBORDE

Prop, born 1948. Pau & France. 55 Tests 1975-83.

Robert Paparemborde was a hugely powerful tight-head prop, often described as the man around whom the French built their tough and effective teams of the late 1970s and early 1980s. Paparemborde got his first two caps on tour in South Africa in 1975, as tough a baptism of fire as any prop could have, and he also scored a try in each match. For the next eight seasons Paparemborde was a fixture in the French team, including the Grand Slam winning sides of 1977 and 1981.

Paparemborde was a ferociously effective scrummager, combining great strength and superb technique. He could also contribute in other areas around the field, and his eight tries in internationals is a very creditable total for a prop. His 55 caps is the record for a French front-row forward.

J.F. (FRANÇOIS) PIENAAR

Flanker, born 1967. Transvaal, Saracens & South Africa.
29 Tests 1993-

François Pienaar was the brilliantly effective leader of the South African team in their great triumph in the 1995 World

Cup. Even more important, during the cup and in the run up to it, he was a superb ambassador for the new South Africa and a major influence in developing the changed values of the post-apartheid era.

Pienaar is a strong and mobile flanker, effective both in the tackle and as a ball-carrier. He has had considerable success as skipper of the Transvaal side, with Currie Cup wins in 1993 and 1994 and strong performances in the Super 10 tournament. He made his Springbok debut in 1993 against France. He was captain that day and has led the side in all his Tests, making a record 29 appearances as South African captain. Apart from that World Cup success his record in Springbok colours has been mixed, however, with the Springboks being notably outclassed in their 1996 games against New Zealand in both the Tri-Nations and the All Black tour of South Africa.

Partly because of that, but also because of internal South African rugby politics, Pienaar was left out of the Springbok squad for the tour to Argentina and France in late 1996. Gary Teichmann, also a back-row forward, took over

the South African captaincy. At the end of the year Pienaar accepted terms from the English club Saracens, and at the time of writing it seems unlikely that he will now add to his international honours.

HUGO PORTA

Fly-half, born 1951. Banco Nacion & Argentina.
49 Tests (+8 for 'South America') 1971-90.

Hugo Porta may have been the world's finest fly-half during the 1970s and early 1980s. For most of his career he was the star of Argentinian rugby, the man the team looked to for the inspirational performance that was needed to help them compete with the traditional rugby-playing powers. And when they looked to Porta they were seldom disappointed.

Below: *François Pienaar turns on the power against Welsh club Swansea during South Africa's 1994 short tour of Britain, during which they played and beat both Wales (20-12) at Cardiff and Scotland (34-10) at Murrayfield.*

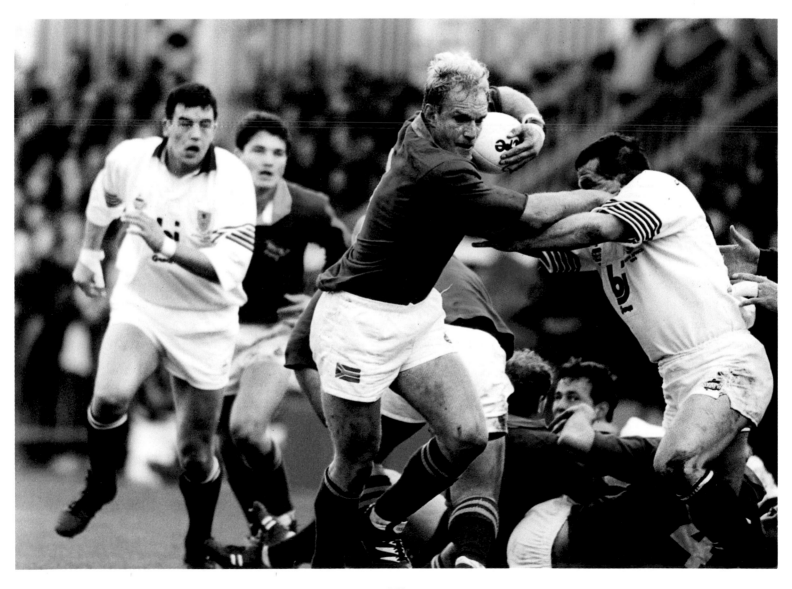

Above: *Argentina's prolific scorer Hugo Porta twice dropped three goals in internationals. Only South Africa's Naas Botha and Jean-Patrick Lescarboura of France have matched this feat.*

Although Porta only began playing fly-half regularly as a 19-year-old (he had previously been a scrum-half), he had all the natural skills for his new position. He was a brilliant tactical kicker off either foot and a deadly converter of penalties or dropped-goal opportunities. Although in later years he curbed his appetite for open play, he was an exciting runner and well able to set his back line moving effectively. He scored 564 points in his international appearances, which was the world record at the time.

For much of his career, Porta captained Argentina and he led his men to many notable successes, including wins over Australia in Buenos Aires and draws with the All Blacks and France. Perhaps his greatest day came when playing for South America (a mainly Argentinian line-up) in South Africa in 1982. Porta scored all 21 points as his men recorded a shock 21-12 win over the Springboks in the Second Test.

QUEENSLAND

Rugby in Queensland was up and running in the 1870s, and the first inter-state match against New South Wales took place in 1882. The local governing body was formed in 1883 as the Northern Union and took the name Queensland Rugby Football Union in 1892.

The Queensland game was strong in its earliest years, and the state won the match against NSW regularly in the 1890s. Queensland also sent a team to New Zealand in 1896 for their first overseas tour, an event that would not be repeated for 67 years. A match against the All Blacks in Brisbane in 1897 was the first in Australia in which the players wore numbers.

In the years before World War I Queensland rugby union lost many players to league and lost more ground by deciding to close down during the war while league played on. Queensland rugby union did not restart for some years after the war ended and the Queensland RFU itself was not reformed until 1929. Individual Queenslanders soon won places in the Australian national side in respectable numbers, but the state team recorded only an occasional win against NSW from the time of the revival until the 1970s. Since then, however, Queensland rugby has gone from strength to strength, recording wins over the All Blacks and the Lions among others, getting the upper hand in their games against NSW, and winning the Super 10 twice, in 1994 and 1995. Andrew Slack, Australian captain in the 1984 Grand Slam tour and the first World Cup, is the player with most appearances for Queensland (133).

Because of their traditional colours, Queensland have long been known as the 'Maroons', but the Queensland team in the Super 12 is known as the Queensland Reds. They came out top in the initial stages of the 1996 competition but lost in the semi-final.

JEAN-PIERRE RIVES

Flanker, born 1952. Toulouse, Racing Club & France.
59 Tests 1975-84.

It was never hard to spot Jean-Pierre Rives on the rugby field during his playing days – his long, blond hair made sure of that. But even if his looks had been unremarkable he would still have been easy to find for he was always right in the middle of the action. Rives was one of the most mobile and effective open-side flankers ever to play the game and he always did more than his share of the hard work, too. He was a superb tackler and the number of times he finished a game with a bloodied wound about his head or face is one token of proof of how often and how fearlessly he put his body on the line to win possession for his team.

Rives made a winning international debut for France against England at Twickenham in 1975 and from then until his retirement in 1984 his position in the French side was never in doubt, unless he was injured. Indeed, he is France's most-capped flanker. He played with the huge Jean-Pierre

Above: *Philippe Sella beats Neil Jenkins to score France's fifth try in their 36-3 defeat of Wales in Paris in 1991. Fast, strong and elusive, Sella scored 30 tries in his 111 internationals.*

Bastiat and Jean-Claude Skrela in the formidable back row that helped France to a Grand Slam in 1977.

Rives took over as French captain in the 1978-79 season. In 1979 he led France in a shared Test series in New Zealand and in 1981 he delighted in a second Grand Slam in the Five Nations. Rives led his men to the verge of another Grand Slam in 1984, only to be foiled in the last match at Murrayfield. No doubt disappointed by the failure of personal and team discipline that helped cause this unexpected defeat, he then retired.

PHILIPPE SELLA

Centre, born 1962. Agen, Saracens & France. 111 Tests 1982-95.

Philippe Sella's 111 internationals for France is the overall world record for Test appearances. Any man who can hold a place in a top international side for 13 seasons must be something special, and many good judges would say that Sella was quite simply the world's best centre for much of the

1980s and early 1990s. When he first came into the French side (against Romania in 1982) he was chosen on the wing. Six of his early French caps were in that position (plus one later as full-back), but he soon made the centre role his own.

Sella was one of the great all-round players. He was an effective runner and handler; his defence was committed and aggressive; and he was a fine try-scorer. In 1986 he became one of a handful of players to score in all four matches of a Five Nations series.

Sella played almost all his club rugby with Agen in his native France, helping them to reach the final of the French championship four times and to win it on two of those occasions (1982 & 1988). After he retired from international rugby, he left France to join Saracens in London to play out his final seasons in the new professional game.

J.F. (FERGUS) SLATTERY

Flanker, born 1949. Ireland & British Lions.
61 Tests (+4 for Lions) 1970-84.

Fergus Slattery was one of the stalwarts of Irish rugby throughout the 1970s and soldiered on into the 1980s as one of the stars of the 'Dad's Army' forward pack that were a

Above: Fergus Slattery flattens Alan McLellan, as the Lions defeat Canterbury in 1971. Slattery played 13 games on tour and was selected for the Third Test but fell ill and withdrew.

real force in the Five Nations tournament. Slattery holds more caps than any flanker from any country and he is joint record holder (with England's Peter Winterbottom) when Lions games are taken into account. From start to finish of his career he was a typical Irish forward, constantly harrying opposition backs and competing wholeheartedly for every loose ball and scrap of possession.

Slattery made his international debut against South Africa at Lansdowne Road, Dublin, during the Springboks' troubled tour of Britain and Ireland in 1970. He was selected for two Lions trips – to New Zealand in 1971, when he did not play in any Tests, and to South Africa in 1974, when he played in all four. The latter Lions only had their 100 per cent record spoiled by a draw in the final Test. In the closing moments of that match Slattery's great support work took him over the line to score what he and his team-mates have always maintained was a perfectly good try, only for the referee to decide that he had not grounded the ball. Slattery

was a highly popular player with fans, team-mates and opponents and captained Ireland 17 times.

I.S. (IAN) SMITH
Wing, 1903-72. Oxford Univ, Scotland & British Lions.
32 Tests (+2 for Lions) 1924-33.

Ian Smith was one of the most prolific try-scorers ever to play international rugby. His total of 24 tries in internationals stood as the world record for over 50 years until finally beaten by David Campese. But even Campese never had a spell to match Smith's performance in Scotland's matches with France and Wales in 1925. Smith scored four tries in each of these games, helping Scotland to a rare Grand Slam in the Five Nations.

At that time Smith was a student at Oxford University, as were the other three Scotland threequarters that season (including an Australian, A.C. 'Johnnie' Wallace, captain of the 1927-28 Waratahs, and George Aitken, All Black skipper in 1921). Smith began his international career with a hat-trick of tries on his debut against Wales and finished as captain of Scotland's 1933 Triple Crown side.

Above: *Although he was born (of Scottish parents) in Melbourne, Australia, Ian Smith was brought up in Scotland and played his international rugby for Scotland and the British Lions.*

D.M.B. (DAVID) SOLE

Prop, born 1962. Bath, Edinburgh Academicals, Scotland & British Lions. 44 Tests (+3 for Lions) 1986-92.

David Sole is one of only three men who have had the honour to lead Scotland to a Grand Slam in the Five Nations tournament. Even better for Scots fans, the final match of that 1990 series saw Scotland beat an England team who were going for their own Grand Slam and were strong favourites to win it. Sole's leadership was one of the factors that turned the game in Scotland's favour.

Sole was a powerful and effective loose-head prop. He was not especially big for an international front-row forward, but his scrummaging was always strong and technically very sound. He also made many effective driving runs as a ball-carrier and tackled, rucked and mauled with the best of them. He played in all three Tests with the 1989 Lions in Australia, contributing to the forward effort that was at the heart of that team's success. Sole led Scotland to the semi-final of the 1991 World Cup and finally retired in 1992 after 25 matches as captain, a Scottish record.

SWANSEA

The Swansea club, like many of Wales's senior clubs, dates back to the 1870s, having been founded in 1873, and many major matches have been played at the club's St Helen's ground, including Wales's first home international in 1883. Billy Bancroft, an elusive runner at full-back, was a Swansea favourite and Welsh star in the 1890s, a decade of great success for Welsh rugby.

Below: *Scotland's captain David Sole (in white) takes on Western Samoa's Stephen Bachop at Murrayfield in the quarter-finals of the 1991 World Cup. Scotland won 28-6.*

Swansea have always been well supported and one of the strongest of the Welsh clubs. In the modern, formally competitive era they have won the league title twice since its inception in 1991 and the cup twice also (to 1996). Swansea supporters will also tell you that, unlike the Welsh national team, their side have registered victories over all three of the Wallabies, Springboks and All Blacks. Most famous of these was the 11-3 win over the 1935 All Blacks. Among the Swansea heroes that day were the two half-backs, Haydn Tanner and his cousin Willie Davies, who were both still schoolboys.

Davies went north and did well as a rugby league player in due course, but Tanner went straight into the Welsh team and was eventually regarded as one of the finest-ever Welsh scrum-halves. Robert Jones, another scrum-half, is the most-capped Swansea player, with 54 appearances between 1986 and 1995.

HAYDN TANNER

Scrum-half, born 1917. Swansea, Cardiff, Wales & British Lions. 25 Tests (+1 for Lions) 1935-49.

Haydn Tanner was one of the finest scrum-halves of his generation, and many of those who saw him play maintained that he was one of the all-time greats. Tanner's

Above: *Toulouse won the inaugural Heineken European Cup competition, beating Cardiff 21-18 in the final. Here Stephane Ougier races away to set up Toulouse's first try of that match.*

career was interrupted by World War II, but he played 14 seasons as an international in all. He could easily have totalled 50 or 60 caps in other circumstances. Although he never scored a try for Wales, Tanner was known as an effective runner and attacker. His greatest skill, however, was in giving good quality possession to his stand-off, a far from easy job with an old-fashioned leather ball and the different offside rules in those days.

Because of injury, Tanner played in only one Test on the Lions tour to South Africa in 1938. He never played in New Zealand, but he played against the All Blacks twice in his native Wales and was on the winning side both times. He was still a schoolboy when he was called into the Swansea side to play the 1935-36 All Blacks, and his performance in the famous 11-3 win earned Tanner selection for Wales against the New Zealanders. Wales won that game 13-12.

TOULOUSE

The Toulouse club was founded in 1899 under the name Stade Olympien des Etudiants and in this guise actually finished runners-up in the French championship in 1903. They merged with another club in 1906 and changed their name to the modern form, Stade Toulousain, in 1909. In the years before and after World War I, Toulouse were the strongest club in France, winning the championship five times in the 1920s. Adolphe Jauréguy and M-F. Lubin-Lubrère, a one-eyed veteran of the war, were among the stalwarts of Toulouse and the French national side in those years.

In more recent times, Jean-Claude Skrela and Pierre Villepreux, France's coaches in 1996-97, were among the stars for Toulouse and France. They saw little championship success with the club, however, which had to wait until the mid-1980s for a second consistent run of titles. Toulouse won the French championship six times between 1985 and 1996 and have now won the championship 13 times (to 1996), more than any other club. Toulouse were also the first winners of the new European club championship in 1996.

TRANSVAAL

The Transvaal rugby union was founded in 1889 and was soon making its mark on rugby in South Africa. The Transvaal union originally included what is now Northern Transvaal, which did not become a separate union until 1937. Transvaal did not win the Currie Cup until 1922, but Transvaal players featured in the first South African Test teams, which played the British Isles in 1891, and Transvaal themselves beat the British Isles team twice in 1903.

The first Springbok touring party in 1905-06 had seven players from Transvaal, including three members of the famous Morkel family (the other seven related Morkels who have been Springboks played their representative rugby for Western Province). More recently, François Pienaar, World Cup winning captain in 1995, was a Transvaal man, as were six more of his side in the final.

Transvaal's headquarters is at the famous Ellis Park, venue for that 1995 final, and Transvaal beat the 1928 All Blacks in the first big match played on the ground. However, in the 1980s the costs of extensive rebuilding work there brought the Transvaal union many financial problems.

Transvaal have won the Currie Cup only seven times in all (to 1996) and had a rather lowly showing in the inaugural Super 12 in 1996. However, these statistics do not really reflect Transvaal's continuing status right at the top of South African rugby.

ULSTER

Rugby in Ulster is thought to have begun around 1868 as a winter sport for members of the North of Ireland Cricket Club. Queen's University club was formed the next year,

and the two clubs had a match the year after that, in 1870. Ulster did not join the Irish Rugby Union when it was formed in 1874, seemingly because they were not properly invited to the meeting, and instead formed the Northern Football Union of Ireland in 1875. The two unions agreed immediately to include players from both organisations in the first Ireland team, picked the same year, and Ireland has played as a single country in rugby union ever since. The unions formally united late in 1879.

Dungannon, Ballymena and Instonians are the top clubs in the province in the modern game, but Queen's University have the greatest number of wins in the Ulster Senior Cup, which was first played for in 1885.

Until the 1950s, many Irish internationals were played in Belfast and major touring teams still regularly face Ulster. Ulster beat the 1984 Grand Slam Wallabies and have had two tough draws against the All Blacks. In the Irish provincial championship Ulster's best period was from the late 1980s, when they won nine consecutive titles.

Willie-John McBride and Mike Gibson are the most-capped Ulstermen, and several more Ireland and Lions captains have also been from the Ulster province.

RORY UNDERWOOD

Wing, born 1963. Leicester, Royal Air Force, England & British Lions. 85 Tests (+6 for Lions) 1984-96.

Rory Underwood is England's most-capped player ever and his country's top try-scorer with 49. Rory has won most of his caps as a left wing, but his most successful England match was against Fiji in 1989, when he notched up five tries playing on the right.

Rory seldom looked like one of the great try-scorers and was sometimes criticised for seeming lapses of concentration, but for all that he was one of the truly great finishers. He could use his great pace to score from far out, as he did when running in his superb match-winner in the Second Test for the 1993 Lions, but he was if anything even more brilliant in using his balance, strength and determination to force his way over and through tackles into the tiniest gap at the corner.

Rory's younger brother **Tony** (born 1969) is also an England wing and had won 25 caps to the end of the 1996-97 season. He made his debut in 1992 against Canada and from then until Rory dropped out of the international reckoning, the Underwoods were regularly paired on the England wings. Tony was the main individual victim of Jonah Lomu's great performance in the 1995 World Cup semi-final and missed much of the following season through injury. He

CHAPTER TWENTY

· STATISTICS ·

Facts and figures correct to 10 May 1997

AUSTRALIA

CLUB COMPETITIONS

The two most prestigious club competitions are the Sydney Premiership (established 1900) and the Brisbane Premiership (established 1887). Winners since 1980 have been:

Sydney
1980 Randwick
1981 Randwick
1982 Randwick
1983 Manly
1984 Randwick
1985 Parramatta
1986 Parramatta
1987 Randwick/
  Northern Suburbs*
1988 Randwick/Port Hacking*
1989 Randwick
1990 Randwick
1991 Randwick

1992 Randwick
1993 Gordon
1994 Randwick
1995 Gordon
1996 Randwick

Brisbane
1980 Brothers
1981 Brothers
1982 Brothers
1983 Brothers
1984 Brothers
1985 Wests
1986 Souths

1987 Brothers
1988 University
1989 University
1990 University
1991 Souths
1992 Souths
1993 Souths
1994 Souths
1995 Souths
1996 Greater Public Schools

* two rival competitions existed in these years

INTER-STATE MATCHES

The major rivalry is between Queensland and New South Wales. They have played each other 264 times (to 1996) since their first game in 1882 – four matches a year, two in each state, was the custom for many years. NSW have won 175, Queensland 78, with 11 draws. The longest winning sequence is 12 games by NSW 1959-63.

Other states have rarely proved a match for the big two, but Victoria did record an occasional win over NSW in the early days, and the 1996 and 1997 Super 12s have shown that the ACT Brumbies are now a force to be reckoned with.

AUSTRALIA INTERNATIONAL RECORDS

v British Isles	P 17	W 3	D 0	L 14	v South Africa	P 35	W 11	D 0	L 24	v Japan	P 3	W 3	D 0	L 0
v England	P 19	W 12	D 0	L 7	v Wales	P 19	W 11	D 0	L 8	v Romania	P 1	W 1	D 0	L 0
v France	P 25	W 10	D 2	L 13						v Tonga	P 3	W 2	D 0	L 1
v Ireland	P 17	W 11	D 0	L 6	v Argentina	P 11	W 7	D 1	L 3	v South Korea	P 1	W 1	D 0	L 0
v New Zealand	P 102	W 27	D 5	L 70	v Canada	P 5	W 5	D 0	L 0	v USA	P 5	W 5	D 0	L 0
v Scotland	P 15	W 8	D 0	L 7	v Fiji	P 15	W 12	D 1	L 2	v Western Samoa	P 2	W 2	D 0	L 0
					v Italy	P 6	W 6	D 0	L 0					

AUSTRALIA INTERNATIONAL TOURS

While Queensland rugby was in recess in the 1920s the NSW Waratahs continued to play against international opposition. For results of these games see tours to British Isles, France and New Zealand below (marked *). See the New Zealand section for All Black tours to Australia in this period.

Australia/NSW also played 16 games v New Zealand Maoris 1922-58 which are regarded as Tests by the ARFU. Australia/NSW have 8 wins and 2 draws from these matches. These games are not listed as Tests in the tours sections.

	All matches				Tests			
	P	W	D	L	P	W	D	L
to British Isles								
1908-09 to England								
& Wales	31	25	1	5	2	1	0	1
1927-28*	28	22	2	4	4	2	0	2
1947-48	30	25	0	5	4	3	0	1
1957-58	30	14	3	13	4	0	0	4
1966-67	30	15	2	13	4	2	0	2
1968 to Ireland &								
Scotland	5	2	0	3	2	0	0	2
1973 to England								
& Wales	8	2	1	5	2	0	0	2
1975-76	25	18	1	6	4	1	0	3
1981-82	23	16	1	6	4	1	0	3
1984	18	13	1	4	4	4	0	0
1988 to England								
& Scotland	13	9	0	4	2	1	0	1
plus matches								
in Italy	2	2	0	0	1	1	0	0

1992 to Ireland								
& Wales	13	10	0	3	2	2	0	0
1996 to Scotland,								
Ireland & Wales	9	9	0	0	3	3	0	0
plus matches								
in Italy	2	2	0	0	1	1	0	0
to France								
1927-28*	3	2	0	1	1	0	0	1
1947-48	5	4	0	1	1	0	0	1
1957-58	4	2	0	2	1	0	0	1
1966-67	4	2	1	1	1	0	0	1
1971	8	4	0	4	2	1	0	1
1976	9	3	0	6	2	0	0	2
plus matches								
in USA	1	1	0	0	1	1	0	0
and Italy	1	1	0	0	–	–	–	–
1983	9	4	2	3	2	0	1	1
plus matches								
in Italy	2	2	0	0	1	1	0	0
1989	8	3	0	5	2	1	0	1
plus matches								
in Canada	2	2	0	0	–	–	–	–
1993	8	6	0	2	2	1	0	1
to New Zealand								
1905	7	3	0	4	1	0	0	1
1913	9	4	0	5	3	1	0	2
1921*	10	9	0	1	1	1	0	0
1923*	10	2	0	8	3	0	0	3
1925*	11	9	0	2	1	0	0	1
1928*	10	5	0	5	3	1	0	2
1931	10	3	1	6	1	0	0	1
1936	10	3	0	7	2	0	0	2

1946	12	5	0	7	2	0	0	2
1949	12	11	0	1	2	2	0	0
1952	10	8	0	2	2	1	0	1
1955	13	10	0	3	3	1	0	2
1958	13	6	1	6	3	1	0	2
1962	13	6	1	6	3	0	1	2
1964	8	4	0	4	3	1	0	2
1967◊	1	0	0	1	1	0	0	1
1972	13	5	1	7	3	0	0	3
1978	13	8	0	5	3	1	0	2
1982	14	10	0	4	3	1	0	2
1985◊	1	0	0	1	1	0	0	1
1986	14	11	1	2	3	2	0	1
1989◊	1	0	0	1	1	0	0	1
1990	12	7	0	5	3	1	0	2
1991‡	1	0	0	1	1	0	0	1
1993◊	1	0	0	1	1	0	0	1
1995‡	1	0	0	1	1	0	0	1
1996	see Tri-Nations, page 182							

◊ one-off matches for Bledisloe Cup
‡ plus Test in Australia making up a Bledisloe Cup series

to South Africa								
1933	23	12	1	10	5	2	0	3
1953	27	16	1	10	4	1	0	3
1961	6	3	1	2	2	0	0	2
1963	24	15	1	8	4	2	0	2
1969	26	15	0	11	4	0	0	4
1992	4	4	0	0	1	1	0	0
1996	see Tri-Nations, page 182							

TOP CAP-WINNERS

Player	State	Caps	Years
1. David Campese	ACT/NSW	101	1982-96
2. Michael Lynagh	Queensland	72	1984-95
3. Nick Farr-Jones	NSW	63	1984-93
4. Simon Poidevin	NSW	59	1980-91
5. Phil Kearns	NSW	49	1989-95
6= Tim Gavin	NSW	47	1988-
6= Tim Horan	Queensland	47	1989-
6= Ewen McKenzie	NSW	47	1990-
9. Peter Johnson	NSW	42	1959-72
10= Tony Miller	NSW	41	1952-67
10= Tom Lawton	Queensland	41	1983-89
10= Tony Daly	NSW	41	1989-95
10= Jason Little	Queensland	41	1989-
10= John Eales	Queensland	41	1991-

TOP CAP-WINNERS BY POSITION

Position	Player	State	Caps	Years
Full-back	Roger Gould	Queensland	25	1980-87
Wing	David Campese		85 (+16 as full-back)	
Centre	Tim Horan		45 (+2 as wing)	
Fly-half	Michael Lynagh		64 (+7 as centre, 1 as full-back)	
Scrum-half	Nick Farr-Jones		62 (+1 as rep wing)	
Prop	Ewen McKenzie		47	
Hooker	Phil Kearns		49	
Lock	John Eales		41	
Flanker	Simon Poidevin		59	
Number 8	Tim Gavin		44 (+3 as lock)	

BEST WINS

Most points and biggest margin

v Western Samoa 73-3 1994 Sydney

Most points in a win

v British Isles	30-12	1989	Sydney
v England	40-15	1991	Sydney
v France	48-31	1990	Brisbane
v Ireland	42-17	1992	Dublin
v New Zealand	30-16	1978	Auckland
v Scotland	37-12	1984	Edinburgh
also	37-13	1992	Brisbane
v South Africa	28-20	1993	Brisbane
v Wales	63-6	1991	Brisbane

Biggest winning margins (as above except)

v France	24-3	1993	Paris
v New Zealand	26-10	1980	Sydney
v South Africa	26-3	1993	Cape Town

WORST DEFEAT (Highest opposition score and biggest margin)

v New Zealand 46-6 1996 Wellington

MOST POINTS IN INTERNATIONALS

911 Michael Lynagh

MOST TRIES IN INTERNATIONALS

64 David Campese

MOST INTERNATIONALS AS CAPTAIN

36 Nick Farr-Jones, 1988-92

NATIONAL CHAMPIONS

(competition established 1976)

1976	Bay of Plenty
1977	Canterbury
1978	Wellington
1979	Counties
1980	Manawatu
1981	Wellington
1982	Auckland
1983	Canterbury
1984	Auckland
1985	Auckland
1986	Wellington
1987	Auckland
1988	Auckland
1989	Auckland
1990	Auckland
1991	Otago
1992	Waikato
1993	Auckland
1994	Auckland
1995	Auckland
1996	Auckland

RANFURLY SHIELD

New Zealand's original inter-provincial championship was first competed for in 1904. It takes the form of a challenge match with the holders playing, usually at home, against various competitors in turn. Auckland were nominated as the holders in 1902 but did not defend the Shield in 1903 because all their matches that season were away from home. They were first challenged, and beaten, by Wellington in 1904. The listing gives holders and the years in which they gained the title. Thus in 1972 Auckland beat the holders North Auckland but lost later in the same season to Canterbury, who in turn gave up the title in 1973.

1904	Wellington
1906	Auckland
1913	Taranaki
1914	Wellington
1920	Southland
1921	Wellington
1922	Hawke's Bay
1927	Wairarapa
1927	Manawhenua
1927	Canterbury
1928	Wairarapa
1929	Southland
1930	Wellington
1931	Canterbury
1934	Hawke's Bay
1934	Auckland
1935	Canterbury
1935	Otago
1937	Southland
1938	Otago
1938	Southland
1947	Otago
1950	Canterbury
1950	Wairarapa
1950	South Canterbury
1950	North Auckland
1951	Waikato
1952	Auckland
1952	Waikato
1953	Wellington
1953	Canterbury
1956	Wellington
1957	Otago
1957	Taranaki
1959	Southland
1959	Auckland
1960	North Auckland
1960	Auckland
1963	Wellington
1963	Taranaki
1965	Auckland
1966	Waikato
1966	Hawke's Bay
1969	Canterbury
1971	Auckland
1971	North Auckland
1972	Auckland
1972	Canterbury
1973	Marlborough
1974	South Canterbury
1974	Wellington
1974	Auckland
1976	Manawatu
1978	North Auckland
1979	Auckland
1980	Waikato
1981	Wellington
1982	Canterbury
1985	Auckland
1993	Waikato
1994	Canterbury
1995	Auckland
1996	Taranaki
1996	Waikato
1996	Auckland

Longest tenure

Auckland 1985-93, 61 successful defences.

Shortest tenure

Several teams have given up the Shield to the first challenger.

NEW ZEALAND INTERNATIONAL RECORDS

v Australia*	P 102	W 70	D 5	L 27	v South Africa	P 47	W 22	D 3	L 22	
v British Isles	P 35	W 26	D 3	L 6	v Wales	P 16	W 13	D 0	L 3	
v England	P 18	W 14	D 0	L 4						
v France	P 32	W 24	D 0	L 8	v Argentina	P 1	W 1	D 0	L 0	
v Ireland	P 13	W 12	D 1	L 0	v Canada	P 2	W 2	D 0	L 0	
v Scotland	P 20	W 18	D 2	L 0	v Fiji	P 1	W 1	D 0	L 0	
					v Italy	P 3	W 3	D 0	L 0	

v Japan	P 1	W 1	D 0	L 0
v Romania	P 1	W 1	D 0	L 0
v USA	P 2	W 2	D 0	L 0
v Western Samoa	P 2	W 2	D 0	L 0

* does not include games v New South Wales 1920-28

NEW ZEALAND INTERNATIONAL TOURS

	All matches				Tests			
	P	W	D	L	P	W	D	L
to Australia								
1884	8	8	0	0	–	–	–	–
1893	10	9	0	1	–	–	–	–
1897	10	9	0	1	–	–	–	–
1903	10	10	0	0	1	1	0	0
1907	7	5	1	1	3	2	1	0
1910	7	6	0	1	3	2	0	1
1914	10	10	0	0	3	3	0	0
1920*	7	7	0	0	3	3	0	0
1922*	5	3	0	2	3	1	0	2
1924*	4	3	0	1	3	2	0	1
1925*	6	5	0	1	3	3	0	0
1926*	6	5	0	1	3	2	0	1
1929	10	6	1	3	3	0	0	3
1932	10	9	0	1	3	2	0	1
1934	8	6	1	1	2	0	1	1
1938	9	9	0	0	3	3	0	0
1947	9	8	0	1	2	2	0	0
1951	12	12	0	0	3	3	0	0
1957	14	14	0	0	2	2	0	0
1960†	5	5	0	0	–	–	–	–
1962	10	9	0	1	2	2	0	0
1968	11	11	0	0	2	2	0	0
1970†	2	2	0	0	–	–	–	–
1974	12	11	1	0	3	2	1	0
1979◊	1	0	0	1	1	0	0	1
1980	13	9	1	3	3	1	0	2
1983◊	1	1	0	0	1	1	0	0
1984	14	13	0	1	3	2	0	1
1987◊	1	1	0	0	1	1	0	0
1988	13	12	1	0	3	2	1	0
1991‡	1	1	0	0	1	1	0	0
1992	11	8	0	3	3	1	0	2
1994◊	1	0	0	1	1	0	0	1
1995‡	1	1	0	0	1	1	0	0
1996	see Tri-Nations, page 182							

* 'Tests' were matches against NSW
† matches played en route to South Africa
◊ one-off matches for Bledisloe Cup
‡ plus Test in NZ making up Bledisloe Cup series

	All matches				Tests			
	P	W	D	L	P	W	D	L
to British Isles								
1905-06	32	31	0	1	4	3	0	1
1924-25	28	28	0	0	3	3	0	0
1935-36	28	24	1	3	4	2	0	2
1953-54	29	25	2	2	4	3	0	1
1963-64	30	28	1	1	4	3	1	0
1967	11	10	1	0	3	3	0	0
1972-73	26	20	2	4	4	3	1	0
1974 mainly to Ireland	8	7	1	0	1	1	0	0
1978	18	17	0	1	4	4	0	0
1979 to England & Scotland	11	10	0	1	2	2	0	0
plus match in Italy	1	1	0	0	–	–	–	–
1980 to Wales	5	5	0	0	1	1	0	0
plus matches in Canada & USA	2	2	0	0	–	–	–	–
1983 to England & Scotland	8	5	1	2	2	0	1	1

	All matches				Tests			
	P	W	D	L	P	W	D	L
1989 to Wales & Ireland	13	13	0	0	2	2	0	0
plus match in Canada	1	1	0	0	–	–	–	–
1993 to Scotland & England	13	12	0	1	2	1	0	1
to France								
1906	1	1	0	0	1	1	0	0
1924-25	2	2	0	0	1	1	0	0
1953-54	2	0	0	2	1	0	0	1
1963-64	4	4	0	0	1	1	0	0
1967	4	4	0	0	1	1	0	0
1972-73	4	3	0	1	1	0	0	1
1977	9	8	0	1	2	1	0	1
1981	10	8	1	1	2	2	0	0
plus matches in Romania	2	2	0	0	1	1	0	0
1986	8	7	0	1	2	1	0	1
1990	8	6	0	2	2	2	0	0
1995	6	5	0	1	2	1	0	1
plus matches in Italy	2	2	0	0	1	1	0	0
to South Africa								
1928	22	16	1	5	4	2	0	2
1949	24	14	3	7	4	0	0	4
1960	26	20	2	4	4	1	1	2
1970	24	21	0	3	4	1	0	3
1976	24	18	0	6	4	1	0	3
1992	5	5	0	0	1	1	0	0
1996	7	5	1	1	3	2	0	1

see also Tri-Nations, page 182

TOP CAP-WINNERS

	Player	Province	Caps	Years
1.	Sean Fitzpatrick	Auckland	83	1986-
2.	John Kirwan	Auckland	63	1984-94
3=	Gary Whetton	Auckland	58	1981-91
3=	Ian Jones	North Auckland/North Harbour	58	1990-
5.	Colin Meads	King Country	55	1957-71
6.	Michael Jones	Auckland	50*	1987-
7.	Richard Loe	Waikato/Canterbury	49	1987-95
8.	Zinzan Brooke	Auckland	47	1987-
9=	Steve McDowell	Auckland/Bay of Plenty	46	1985-92
9=	Grant Fox	Auckland	46	1985-93

* plus one for Western Samoa in 1986

TOP CAP-WINNERS BY POSITION

Full-back	Don Clarke	Waikato	31	1956-64
Wing	John Kirwan		63	
Centre*	Walter Little	North Harbour	40 (+4 as fly-half)	1990-
Fly-half	Grant Fox		46	
Scrum-half	Graeme Bachop	Canterbury	31	1989-95
Prop	Richard Loe		48 (+1 as temp rep)	
Hooker	Sean Fitzpatrick		83	
Lock	Ian Jones		58	
	Gary Whetton		58	
Flanker	Michael Jones		48 (+2 as No 8)	
Number 8	Zinzan Brooke		41 (+6 as flanker)	

* includes 2nd five-eighth

BEST WINS
Most points and biggest margin

v Japan	145-17	1995	World Cup

Most points in a win

v Australia	43-6	1996	Wellington
v British Isles	38-6	1983	Auckland
v England	45-29	1995	World Cup
v France	38-8	1906	Paris
v Ireland	59-6	1992	Wellington
v Scotland	62-31	1996	Dunedin
v South Africa	33-26	1996	Pretoria
v Wales	54-9	1988	Auckland

Biggest winning margins (as above except)

v England	42-15	1985	Wellington
v Scotland	51-15	1993	Edinburgh
v South Africa	20-3	1965	Auckland
v Wales	52-3	1988	Auckland

WORST DEFEATS
Highest opposition score

v South Africa	32-22	1996	Johannesburg

Biggest margin

v South Africa	17-0	1928	Durban

MOST POINTS IN INTERNATIONALS
645 Grant Fox

MOST TRIES IN INTERNATIONALS
35 John Kirwan

MOST INTERNATIONALS AS CAPTAIN
43 Sean Fitzpatrick, 1992-

CURRIE CUP

The Currie Cup has been contested annually only since 1968. Before that it was usually played for every other year, except in wartime and when there was an incoming All Black or Lions tour. The cup itself was presented to Griqualand West by the British touring team in 1891, but the first South African provincial competition had already been held, as noted below. Winners have been as follows (with results of finals since 1968):

1889 Western Province
1892 Western Province
1894 Western Province
1895 Western Province
1897 Western Province
1898 Western Province
1899 Griqualand West
1904 Western Province
1906 Western Province
1908 Western Province
1911 Griqualand West
1914 Western Province
1920 Western Province
1922 Transvaal
1925 Western Province
1927 Western Province
1929 Western Province
1932 Western Province & Border
1936 Western Province
1939 Transvaal
1946 Northern Transvaal
1947 Western Province
1950 Transvaal

1952 Transvaal
1954 Western Province
1956 Northern Transvaal
1959 Western Province
1964 Western Province
1966 Western Province
1968 Northern Transvaal 16, Transvaal 3
1969 Northern Transvaal 28, Western Province 13
1970 Griqualand West 11, Northern Transvaal 9
1971 Transvaal 14, Northern Transvaal 13
1972 Transvaal 25, Eastern Transvaal 19
1973 Northern Transvaal 30, Orange Free State 22
1974 Northern Transvaal 17, Transvaal 15
1975 Northern Transvaal 12, Orange Free State 6
1976 Orange Free State 33, Western Province 16
1977 Northern Transvaal 27, Orange Free State 12
1978 Northern Transvaal 13, Orange Free State 6
1979 Northern Transvaal 15, Western Province 15
1980 Northern Transvaal 39, Western Province 9
1981 Northern Transvaal 23, Orange Free State 6
1982 Western Province 24, Northern Transvaal 3
1983 Western Province 9, Northern Transvaal 3
1984 Western Province 19, Natal 9
1985 Western Province 22, Northern Transvaal 15
1986 Western Province 22, Transvaal 9
1987 Northern Transvaal 24, Transvaal 18
1988 Northern Transvaal 19, Western Province 18
1989 Western Province 16, Northern Transvaal 16
1990 Natal 18, Northern Transvaal 12
1991 Northern Transvaal 27, Transvaal 15
1992 Natal 14, Transvaal 13
1993 Transvaal 21, Natal 15
1994 Transvaal 56, Orange Free State 33
1995 Natal 25, Western Province 17
1996 Natal 33, Transvaal 15

LION CUP

Results of finals:

1983 Orange Free State 24, Transvaal 12
1984 Western Province 30, Orange Free State 22
1985 Northern Transvaal 12, Orange Free State 10
1986 Transvaal 22, Orange Free State 18
1987 Transvaal 24, Northern Transvaal 18
1988 Western Province 24, Northern Transvaal 12
1989 Western Province 21, Northern Transvaal 16
1990 Northern Transvaal 25, Western Province 12
1991 Northern Transvaal 62, Natal 6
1992 Transvaal 17, Orange Free State 12
1993 Transvaal 20, Natal 11
1994 Transvaal 29, Western Province 20
No longer contested

NATIONAL CLUB CHAMPIONSHIP

1975 Stellenbosch University
1976 Pretoria University
1977 Stellenbosch University
1978 Stellenbosch University
1979 Stellenbosch University
1980 Villagers
1981 Stellenbosch University
1982 Stellenbosch University
1983 Pretoria Harlequins
1984 Stellenbosch University
1985 Despatch
1986 Shimlas
1987 Defence (Cape Town)
1988 Despatch
1989 Roodeport
1990 Pretoria University
1991 Old Greys
1992 Rand Afrikaans University
1993 Parow NTK
1994 Crusaders
1995 Pretoria Police
1996 Pretoria Police

SOUTH AFRICA INTERNATIONAL RECORDS

v Australia	P 35	W 24	D 0	L 11
v British Isles	P 40	W 20	D 6	L 14
v England	P 13	W 8	D 1	L 4
v France	P 26	W 16	D 5	L 5
v Ireland	P 10	W 8	D 1	L 1
v New Zealand†	P 47	W 22	D 3	L 22
v Scotland	P 9	W 6	D 0	L 3
v Wales	P 10	W 9	D 1	L 0
v Argentina*	P 14	W 13	D 0	L 1
v Canada	P 1	W 1	D 0	L 0
v Fiji	P 1	W 1	D 0	L 0
v Italy	P 1	W 1	D 0	L 0
v Romania	P 1	W 1	D 0	L 0
v USA	P 1	W 1	D 0	L 0
v Western Samoa	P 2	W 2	D 0	L 0

† does not include 1986 matches against New Zealand Cavaliers (SA 3 wins, NZ 1 win)
* includes matches against 'South America'

SOUTH AFRICA INTERNATIONAL TOURS

	All matches				Tests			
	P	W	D	L	P	W	D	L
to Australia								
1921*	5	5	0	0	–	–	–	–
1937	11	10	0	1	2	2	0	0
1956	6	6	0	0	2	2	0	0
1965	6	3	0	3	2	0	0	2
1971	13	13	0	0	3	3	0	0
1993	12	9	0	3	3	1	0	2
1996	*see Tri-Nations, page 182*							

* three of these matches were against New South Wales and are regarded as Tests by the Australian RU

	All matches				Tests			
to British Isles								
1906-7	28	25	1	2	4	2	1	1
1912-13	26	23	0	3	4	4	0	0
1931-32	26	23	2	1	4	4	0	0
1951-52	27	26	0	1	4	4	0	0
1960-61	30	28	1	1	4	4	0	0
1965 to Ireland & Scotland	5	0	1	4	2	0	0	2
1969-70	24	15	4	5	4	0	2	2
1992 to England	4	3	0	1	1	0	0	1
1994 to Scotland & Wales	13	11	0	2	2	2	0	0
1995 to England & Italy	2	2	0	0	2	2	0	0
1996 to Wales	1	1	0	0	1	1	0	0

	All matches				Tests			
to France								
1907	1	1	0	0	–	–	–	–
1912-13	1	1	0	0	1	1	0	0
1951-52	4	4	0	0	1	1	0	0
1960-61	4	3	1	0	1	0	1	0
1968	6	5	0	1	2	2	0	0
1974	9	8	0	1	2	2	0	0
1992	9	5	0	4	2	1	0	1
1996	5	3	0	2	2	2	0	0
plus matches in Argentina	4	4	0	0	2	2	0	0

	All matches				Tests			
to New Zealand								
1921	19	15	2	2	3	1	1	1
1937	17	16	0	1	3	2	0	1
1956	23	16	1	6	4	1	0	3
1965	24	19	0	5	4	1	0	3
1981	14	11	1	2	3	1	0	2
1994	14	10	1	3	3	0	1	2
1996	*see Tri-Nations, page 182*							

SOUTH AFRICA

TOP CAP-WINNERS

Player	Province	Caps	Years
1= Frik du Preez	N Transvaal	38	1961-71
1= Jan Ellis	South-West Africa	38	1965-76
3= Hannes (J.F.K.) Marais	W Province	35	1963-74
3= James Small	Natal	35	1992-
5= John Gainsford	W Province	33	1960-67
5= Jan Engelbrecht	W Province	33	1960-69
7. André Joubert	Natal	30	1989-
8= François (J.F.) Pienaar	Transvaal	29	1993-96
8= Mark Andrews	Natal	29	1994-
10= Johan (J.T.) Claasen	W Province	28	1955-62
10= Naas (H.E.) Botha	N Transvaal	28	1980-92
10= Joost van der Westhuizen	N Transvaal	28	1993-

TOP CAP-WINNERS BY POSITION

Position	Player	Province	Caps	Years
Full-back	André Joubert		30	
Wing	James Small		33 (+2 as full-back)	
	Jan Engelbrecht		33	
Centre	John Gainsford		33	
Fly-half	Naas Botha		28	
Scrum-half	Joost van der Westhuizen		28	
Prop	Hannes Marais		35	
Hooker	Abie (G.F.) Malan	W Province	18	1958-65
Lock	Frik du Preez		31 (+7 as flanker)	
Flanker	Jan Ellis		38	
Number 8	Doug Hopwood	W Province	22	1960-65

BEST WINS
Most points and biggest margin

v Western Samoa 60-8 1995 Johannesburg

Most points in a win

v Australia	30-11	1969	Johannesburg
v British Isles	34-14	1969	Bloemfontein
v England	35-9	1984	Johannesburg
v France	38-5	1913	Bordeaux
also	38-25	1975	Bloemfontein
v Ireland	38-0	1912	Dublin
v New Zealand	32-22	1996	Johannesburg
v Scotland	44-0	1951	Edinburgh
v Wales	40-11	1995	Johannesburg

Biggest winning margins (as above except)

v Australia	28-3	1961	Johannesburg
v New Zealand	17-0	1928	Durban

WORST DEFEATS
Highest opposition score

v England	33-16	1992	London
v New Zealand	33-26	1996	Pretoria

Biggest margin

v Australia 26-3 1992 Cape Town

MOST POINTS IN INTERNATIONALS
312 Naas Botha

MOST TRIES IN INTERNATIONALS
19 Danie Gerber, Eastern Province/Western Province, 24 Tests, 1980-92

MOST INTERNATIONALS AS CAPTAIN
29 François Pienaar, 1993-96

SUPERS/TRI-NATIONS

TRI-NATIONS SERIES 1996

New Zealand 43, Australia 6	6 July, Wellington
Australia 21, South Africa 16	13 July, Sydney
New Zealand 15, South Africa 11	20 July, Christchurch
Australia 25, New Zealand 32	27 July, Brisbane
South Africa 25, Australia 19	3 August, Bloemfontein
South Africa 18, New Zealand 29	10 August, Cape Town

FINAL TABLE

	P	W	D	L	F	A	Pts
New Zealand	4	4	0	0	119	60	17
South Africa	4	1	0	3	70	84	6
Australia	4	1	0	3	71	116	6

SUPER 6/SOUTH PACIFIC CHAMPIONSHIP

1986 Canterbury
1987 Auckland & Canterbury (joint champions)
1988 Auckland
1989 Auckland
1990 Auckland
1991 not held
1992 Queensland

SUPER 10 FINALS

1993 Transvaal 20, Auckland 17
1994 Queensland 21, Natal 10
1995 Queensland 30, Transvaal 16

SUPER 12 COMPETITION 1996

	P	W	D	L	F	A	Pts
Queensland Reds	11	9	0	2	320	247	41
Auckland Blues	11	8	0	3	408	350	41
Northern Transvaal	11	6	0	5	389	277	38
Natal Sharks	11	6	0	5	389	277	33
ACT Brumbies	11	7	0	4	306	273	32
Waikato Chiefs	11	6	0	5	291	269	28
NSW Waratahs	11	5	0	6	332	391	28
Wellington Hurricanes	11	3	0	8	233	299	17
Transvaal	11	3	0	8	233	299	16
Western Province	11	3	1	7	251	353	15
Canterbury Crusaders	11	2	1	8	234	378	13

Semi-finals: Queensland 25, Natal 43 (in Brisbane)
Auckland 48, Northern Transvaal 11 (in Auckland)

Final: Auckland 45, Natal 21 (in Auckland)

COURAGE LEAGUE CHAMPIONS

1988 Leicester
1989 Bath
1990 Wasps
1991 Bath
1992 Bath
1993 Bath
1994 Bath
1995 Leicester
1996 Bath
1997 Wasps

Official merit tables were organised in 1985-86 and 1986-87, won by Gloucester and Bath respectively.

COUNTY CHAMPIONSHIP

Before the establishment of the club leagues and knockout cup, the principal English domestic competition was the County Championship. This continues, but leading players gradually dropped out and have been excluded entirely since 1994. Multiple winners (to 1997) include: Gloucestershire 16 titles, Lancashire 16, Yorkshire 12, Warwickshire 10, Middlesex 8.

RFU KNOCKOUT CUP
Results of finals:

1972 Gloucester 17, Moseley 6
1973 Coventry 27, Bristol 15
1974 Coventry 26, London Scottish 6
1975 Bedford 28, Rosslyn Park 12
1976 Gosforth 23, Rosslyn Park 14
1977 Gosforth 27, Waterloo 11
1978 Gloucester 6, Leicester 3
1979 Leicester 15, Moseley 12
1980 Leicester 21, London Irish 9
1981 Leicester 22, Gosforth 15
1982 Gloucester 12, Moseley 12†
1983 Bristol 28, Leicester 22
1984 Bath 10, Bristol 9
1985 Bath 24, London Welsh 15
1986 Bath 25, Northampton 13*
1992 Bath 15, Harlequins 12*
1993 Leicester 23, Harlequins 16
1994 Bath 21, Leicester 9
1995 Bath 36, Wasps 16
1996 Bath 16, Leicester 15
1997 Leicester 9, Sale 3
* after extra time
† after extra time; trophy shared

ENGLAND INTERNATIONAL RECORD

v Australia	P 19	W 7	D 0	L 12
v France	P 74	W 40	D 7	L 27
v Ireland	P 110	W 64	D 8	L 38
v New Zealand	P 18	W 4	D 0	L 14
v Scotland	P 114	W 58	D 17	L 39
v South Africa	P 13	W 4	D 1	L 8
v Wales	P 103	W 43	D 12	L 48
v Argentina	P 7	W 5	D 1	L 1
v Canada	P 2	W 2	D 0	L 0
v Fiji	P 3	W 3	D 0	L 0
v Italy	P 3	W 3	D 0	L 0
v Japan	P 1	W 1	D 0	L 0
v Romania	P 3	W 3	D 0	L 0
v USA	P 2	W 2	D 0	L 0
v Western Samoa	P 2	W 2	D 0	L 0

ENGLAND INTERNATIONAL TOURS

	All matches				Tests			
	P	W	D	L	P	W	D	L
to Australia								
1963	1	0	0	1	1	0	0	1
1975	8	4	0	4	2	0	0	2
1988	8	5	0	3	2	0	0	2
plus match in Fiji	1	0	0	1	1	0	0	1
to New Zealand								
1963	4	1	0	3	2	0	0	2
1973	4	1	0	3	1	1	0	0
plus match in Fiji	1	1	0	0	–	–	–	–
1985	7	4	0	3	2	0	0	2
1991	7	3	0	4	1	0	0	1
plus match in Fiji	1	1	0	0	1	1	0	0
to South Africa								
1972	7	6	1	0	1	1	0	0
1984	7	4	1	2	2	0	0	2
1994	8	3	0	5	2	1	0	1

TOP CAP-WINNERS

	Player	Principal club(s)	Caps (Lions)	Seasons
1.	Rory Underwood	Leicester	85 (6)	1984-96
2.	Will Carling	Harlequins	72 (1)	1988-97
3.	Rob Andrew	Wasps	71 (5)	1985-97
4.	Brian Moore	Nottingham/Harlequins	64 (5)	1987-95
5=	Peter Winterbottom	Headingley/Harlequins	58 (7)	1982-93
5=	Wade Dooley	Preston Grasshoppers/Fylde	58 (2)	1985-95
7.	Jason Leonard	Saracens/Harlequins	55 (2)	1990-
8.	Dean Richards	Leicester	48 (6)	1986-96
9.	Jeremy Guscott	Bath	48 (5)	1989-
10.	Tony Neary	Broughton Park	43 (1)	1971-80

TOP CAP-WINNERS BY POSITION

Full-back	Jonathan Webb	Bristol/Bath	33	1987-93
Wing	Rory Underwood		85	
Centre	Will Carling		72	
Fly-half	Rob Andrew		70 (+1 as full-back)	
Scrum-half	Richard Hill	Bath	29	1984-91
Prop	Jason Leonard		55	
Hooker	Brian Moore		64	
Lock	Wade Dooley		58	
Flanker	Peter Winterbottom		58	
Number 8	Dean Richards		47 (+1 as temp rep)	

BEST WINS
Most points

v Japan	60-7	1987	World Cup
v Canada	60-19	1994	London

Biggest margin

v Romania	58-3	1989	Bucharest

Most points in a win (against big 8 nations)

v Australia	28-19	1988	London
v France	41-13	1907	London
v Ireland	46-6	1997	Dublin
v New Zealand	16-10	1973	Auckland
v Scotland	41-13	1997	London
v South Africa	33-16	1992	London
v Wales	34-6	1990	London
also	34-13	1997	Cardiff

Biggest winning margins (as above except)

v Australia	23-6	1976	London
also	20-3	1973	London
v France	37-0	1911	London
v New Zealand	13-0	1936	London
v South Africa	as above but also		
	32-15	1994	Pretoria

WORST DEFEATS
Highest opposition score

v New Zealand	45-29	1995	World Cup

Biggest margin

v New Zealand	42-15	1985	Wellington
v Scotland	33-6	1986	Edinburgh

MOST POINTS IN INTERNATIONALS
385 Rob Andrew (+11 for Lions)

MOST TRIES IN INTERNATIONALS
48 Rory Underwood (+1 for Lions)

MOST INTERNATIONALS AS CAPTAIN
59 Will Carling 1988-96

FRANCE

FRENCH CLUB CHAMPIONSHIP
Winners have been:

SU Agen: 1930, 45, 62, 65, 66, 76, 82, 88
Bayonne: 1913, 34, 43
Bègles: 1969, 91
Béziers: 1961, 71, 72, 74, 75, 77, 78, 80, 81, 83, 84
Biarritz: 1935, 39
Bordeaux (Stade Bordelais): 1899, 1904, 05, 06, 07, 09, 11
Carmaux: 1951
Castres Olympique:1949, 50, 93
Grenoble: 1954
FC Lourdes: 1948, 52, 53, 56, 57, 58, 60, 68
Lyon: 1910, 32, 33
Montauban: 1967
Narbonne: 1936, 79
Paris Olympique: 1896

Pau: 1928, 46
USA Perpignan: 1914, 21, 25, 38, 44, 55
Quillan: 1929
Racing Club de France: 1892, 1900, 02, 59, 90,
Stade Français: 1893, 94, 95, 97, 98, 1901, 03, 08
Tarbes: 1920, 73
Toulon: 1931, 87
Toulouse (Stade Toulousain): 1912, 22, 23, 24, 26, 27, 47, 85, 86, 89, 94, 95, 96
Vienne: 1937
La Voulte: 1970

Multiple winners:
Toulouse 13, Béziers 11, Agen 8, Lourdes 8, Stade Français 8, Bordeaux 7

Recent results in the final have been:
1980 Béziers 10, Toulouse 6

1981 Béziers 22, Bagnères 13
1982 Agen 18, Bayonne 9
1983 Béziers 14, Nice 6
1984 Béziers 21, Agen 21*
1985 Toulouse 36, Toulon 22†
1986 Toulouse 16, Agen 6
1987 Toulon 15, Racing Club de France 12
1988 Agen 9, Tarbes 3
1989 Toulouse 18, Toulon 12
1990 Racing Club de France 22, Agen 12
1991 Bègles 19, Toulouse 10
1992 Toulon 19, Biarritz 14
1993 Castres 14, Grenoble 11
1994 Toulouse 22, Montferrand 16
1995 Toulouse 31, Castres 16
1996 Toulouse 20, Brive 13

* Béziers win on penalties
† after extra time

FRANCE INTERNATIONAL RECORDS
v Australia	P 25	W 13	D 2	L 10
v British Isles	P 1	W 0	D 0	L 1
v England	P 74	W 27	D 7	L 40
v Ireland	P 71	W 41	D 5	L 25
v New Zealand	P 32	W 8	D 0	L 24
v Scotland	P 69	W 34	D 3	L 32
v South Africa	P 25	W 5	D 5	L 15
v Wales	P 72	W 31	D 3	L 38
v Argentina	P 29	W 24	D 1	L 4
v Canada	P 3	W 2	D 0	L 1
v Czechoslovakia	P 2	W 2	D 0	L 0
v Fiji	P 3	W 3	D 0	L 0
v Germany	P 15	W 13	D 0	L 2
v Italy	P 19	W 18	D 0	L 1
v Ivory Coast	P 1	W 1	D 0	L 0
v Japan	P 1	W 1	D 0	L 0
v Romania	P 43	W 33	D 2	L 8
v Tonga	P 1	W 1	D 0	L 0
v USA	P 5	W 4	D 0	L 1
v Zimbabwe	P 1	W 1	D 0	L 0

FRANCE INTERNATIONAL TOURS

	All matches				Tests			
	P	W	D	L	P	W	D	L
to Australia								
1961	2	2	0	0	1	1	0	0
1968	2	1	0	1	1	0	0	1
1972	9	8	1	0	2	1	1	0
1981	9	6	0	3	2	0	0	2
1986	3	1	1	1	1	0	0	1
1990	8	4	0	4	3	1	0	2
to New Zealand								
1961	13	6	0	7	3	0	0	3
1968	12	8	0	4	3	0	0	3
1979	9	6	0	3	2	1	0	1
1984	8	6	0	2	2	0	0	2
1986	2	1	0	1	1	0	0	1
1989	8	4	0	4	2	0	0	2
1994	8	6	0	2	2	2	0	0

to South Africa								
1958	10	5	2	3	2	1	1	0
1964	6	5	0	1	1	1	0	0
1967	13	8	1	4	4	1	1	2
1971	9	7	1	1	2	0	1	1
1975	11	6	1	4	2	0	0	2
1980	4	3	0	1	1	0	0	1
1993	8	4	2	2	2	1	1	0

LATIN CUP
(first played 1995 in Argentina)

France 34, Italy 22
Argentina 51, Romania 16
France 52, Romania 8
Argentina 26, Italy 6
Italy 40, Romania 3
Argentina 12, France 47

Winners: France; *Runners-up:* Argentina

TOP CAP-WINNERS
	Player	Principal club(s)	Caps	Seasons
1.	Philippe Sella	Agen	111	1982-95
2.	Serge Blanco	Biarritz	93	1980-91
3.	Roland Bertranne	Bagnères	69	1971-81
4=	Michel Crauste	Racing Club/Lourdes	63	1957-66
4=	Benoit Dauga	Mont-de-Marsan	63	1964-72
4=	Philippe Saint-André	Montferrand	63	1990-
7=	Jean Condom	Biarritz	61	1982-90
7=	Olivier Roumat	Dax	61	1989-
9.	Jean-Pierre Rives	Toulouse/Racing Club	59	1975-84
10=	Laurent Rodriguez	Montferrand/Dax	56	1981-90
10=	Pierre Berbizier	Agen	56	1981-91
10=	Franck Mesnel	Racing Club	56	1986-95

TOP CAP-WINNERS BY POSITION
Full-back	Serge Blanco		81 (+12 as wing)	
Wing	Philippe Saint-André		61 (+2 as centre)	
Centre	Philippe Sella		104 (+6 as wing, 1 as full-back)	
Fly-half	Jean-Pierre Romeu	Montferrand	33 (+1 as full-back)	1972-77
Scrum-half	Pierre Berbizier		56	
Prop	Robert Paparemborde	Pau	55	1975-83
Hooker	Philippe Dintrans	Tarbes	50	1979-90
Lock	Jean Condom		61	
Flanker	Jean-Pierre Rives		59	
Number 8	Guy Basquet	Agen	33	1945-52

BEST WINS
Most points and biggest margin
v Zimbabwe	70-12	1987	World Cup

Most points in a win
v Australia	34-6	1976	Paris
v England	37-12	1972	Paris
v Ireland	45-10	1996	Paris
v New Zealand	24-19	1979	Auckland
v Scotland	47-20	1997	Paris
v South Africa	29-16	1992	Paris
v Wales	36-3	1991	Paris

Biggest winning margin (as above except)
v New Zealand	22-8	1994	Christchurch

WORST DEFEAT (Highest opposition score and biggest margin)
v Wales	14-49	1910

MOST POINTS IN INTERNATIONALS
367 Thierry Lacroix, Dax/Harlequins, 38 caps, 1989-

MOST TRIES IN INTERNATIONALS
38 Serge Blanco

MOST INTERNATIONALS AS CAPTAIN
34 Jean-Pierre Rives, 1978-84

CUP COMPETITIONS

Before the establishment of the All-Ireland leagues, the most important club competitions were the Senior Cups of each province. These have been contested since 1882 in Leinster, 1885 in Ulster, 1886 in Munster, 1896 in Connacht. Most frequent winners (to 1997) are as follows:

Connacht:	University College Galway
Leinster:	Lansdowne
Munster:	Garryowen
Ulster:	Queen's University

IRELAND INTERNATIONAL RECORDS

v Australia	P 17	W 6	D 0	L 11
v England	P 110	W 38	D 8	L 64
v France	P 71	W 25	D 5	L 41
v New Zealand	P 13	W 0	D 1	L 12
v Scotland	P 109	W 45	D 5	L 58
	(one match abandoned)			
v South Africa	P 10	W 1	D 1	L 8
v Wales	P 101	W 37	D 6	L 58
v Argentina	P 1	W 1	D 0	L 0
v Canada	P 1	W 1	D 0	L 0
v Fiji	P 1	W 1	D 0	L 0
v Italy	P 3	W 1	D 0	L 2
v Japan	P 2	W 2	D 0	L 0
v Namibia	P 2	W 0	D 0	L 2
v Romania	P 2	W 2	D 0	L 0
v Tonga	P 1	W 1	D 0	L 0
v USA	P 2	W 2	D 0	L 0
v Western Samoa	P 2	W 1	D 0	L 1
v Zimbabwe	P 1	W 1	D 0	L 0

BEST WINS

Most points and biggest margin

v Romania	60-0	1986	Dublin

Most points in a win

v Australia	27-12	1979	Brisbane
v England	26-21	1974	London
v France	25-5	1911	Cork
also	25-6	1975	Dublin
v Scotland	26-8	1953	Edinburgh
v South Africa	9-6	1965	Dublin
v Wales	30-17	1996	Dublin

Ireland drew 10-10 with New Zealand in Dublin in 1973 but have never beaten them.

Biggest winning margins (as above except)

v England	22-0	1947	Dublin
v France	24-0	1913	Cork
v Scotland	21-0	1950	Dublin
v Wales	19-3	1925	Belfast

WORST DEFEAT (Highest opposition score and biggest margin)

v New Zealand	59-6	1992	Wellington

MOST POINTS IN INTERNATIONALS

308 Michael Kiernan, Dolphin/Lansdowne, 43 Tests (+3 for Lions, no points), 1982-91

MOST TRIES IN INTERNATIONALS

17 Brendan Mullin (no tries for Lions)

MOST INTERNATIONALS AS CAPTAIN

24 Tom Kiernan, 1963-73

INTER-PROVINCIAL CHAMPIONSHIP

The All-Ireland Provincial Championship was first played in 1946-47. Winners have been:

1946-47 Ulster	1960-61 Leinster	1978-79 Munster
1947-48 Munster	1961-62 Leinster	1979-80 Leinster
1948-49 Leinster	1962-63 Munster	1980-81 Leinster
1949-50 Leinster	1963-64 Leinster	1981-82 Leinster
1950-51 Ulster	1964-65 Leinster	1982-83 Leinster/Munster/ Ulster
1951-52 Ulster	1965-66 Munster	
1952-53 Munster	1966-67 Munster/Ulster	1983-84 Leinster
1953-54 Ulster	1967-68 Ulster	1984-85 Ulster
1954-55 Leinster/Munster	1968-69 Munster	1985-86 Ulster
1955-56 Connacht/Ulster	1969-70 Ulster	1986-87 Ulster
1956-57 Connacht/Leinster/ Ulster	1970-71 Ulster	1987-88 Ulster
	1971-72 Leinster	1988-89 Ulster
1957-58 Munster	1972-73 Leinster/Munster/ Ulster	1989-90 Ulster
1958-59 Leinster		1990-91 Ulster
1959-60 Munster	1973-74 Munster	1991-92 Ulster
	1974-75 Ulster	1992-93 Ulster
	1975-76 Leinster/Munster/ Ulster	1993-94 Leinster
		1994-95 Munster
	1976-77 Ulster	1995-96 Leinster
	1977-78 Leinster/Munster/ Ulster	1996-97 Munster

IRELAND INTERNATIONAL TOURS

	All matches				Tests			
	P	W	D	L	P	W	D	L
to Australia								
1967	6	4	0	2	1	1	0	0
1979	8	7	0	1	2	2	0	0
1994	8	2	0	6	2	0	0	2
to New Zealand								
1976	7	4	0	3	1	0	0	1
plus match in Fiji	1	1	0	0	–	–	–	–
1992	8	3	0	5	2	0	0	2
to South Africa								
1961	4	3	0	1	1	0	0	1
1981	7	3	0	4	2	0	0	2

ALL-IRELAND CLUB CHAMPIONSHIPS
(first played 1990-91)

1991 Cork Constitution
1992 Garryowen
1993 Young Munster
1994 Garryowen
1995 Shannon
1996 Shannon
1997 Shannon

TOP CAP-WINNERS

	Player	Principal club(s)	Caps (Lions)	Seasons
1.	Mike (C.M.H.)Gibson	Camb Univ/NIFC	69 (12)	1964-79
2.	Willie-John McBride	Ballymena	63 (17)	1962-75
3.	Fergus Slattery	UC Dublin/Blackrock Coll	61 (4)	1970-84
4.	Phil Orr	Old Wesley	58 (1)	1976-87
5.	Brendan Mullin	Blackrock Coll/Lon Irish	55 (1)	1984-95
6.	Tom Kiernan	Cork Constitution	54 (5)	1960-73
7.	Donal Lenihan	Cork Constitution	52*	1981-92
8.	Moss Keane	Lansdowne	51 (1)	1974-84
9.	Jack Kyle	Queens Univ/NIFC	46 (6)	1947-58
10.	Ken Kennedy	Queens Univ/Lon Irish	45 (4)	1965-75

* toured with the Lions in 1983 & 1989 but was not capped

BY POSITION

Full-back	Tom Kiernan		54	
Wing	Keith Crossan	Instonians	41	1982-92
Centre	Brendan Mullin*		55	
Fly-half	Jack Kyle*		46	
Scrum-half	Michael Bradley	Dolphin	40	1984-95
Prop	Phil Orr		58	
Hooker	Ken Kennedy		45	
Lock	Willie-John McBride		63	
Flanker	Fergus Slattery		61	
Number 8	Willie Duggan	Blackrock Coll	39† (+2 as flanker)	1975-84

* Mike Gibson won 40 caps as a centre and 25 as fly-half
† Willie Duggan won 4 Lions caps, all at Number 8

SCOTLAND

CLUB CHAMPIONSHIPS

An unofficial Scottish championship table was widely published from the 1890s and has been compiled for each year since regular fixtures began. The first 'champions' were Edinburgh Academicals in 1865-66; the last Boroughmuir in 1972-73. Edinburgh Academicals have the most 'titles' – 22 including shared wins – but of these, 17 came before the end of the nineteenth century. Other multiple winners include Watsonians 14, Glasgow Academicals 13, Hawick 11 and West of Scotland 10.

BORDER LEAGUE

A Border League was created in 1901-02, Kelso and Selkirk joining the original five clubs in 1912 The annual home and away fixtures are still maintained even though some clubs are now widely separated in the formal league structure. Hawick have most wins (43 to 1997) followed by Melrose 14, Jed-Forest 10, Gala 6, Kelso 5, Selkirk 3, and Langholm 1.

CLUB LEAGUE WINNERS

(competition first played 1973-74)
1974 Hawick
1975 Hawick
1976 Hawick
1977 Hawick
1978 Hawick
1979 Heriots FP
1980 Gala
1981 Gala
1982 Hawick
1983 Gala
1984 Hawick
1985 Hawick
1986 Hawick
1987 Hawick
1988 Kelso
1989 Kelso
1990 Melrose
1991 Boroughmuir
1992 Melrose
1993 Melrose
1994 Melrose
1995 Stirling County
1996 Melrose
1997 Melrose

CUP FINALS

(first played 1996)
1996 Hawick 17, Watsonians 15
1997 Melrose 31, Boroughmuir 23

SCOTLAND INTERNATIONAL RECORDS

v Australia	P 15	W 7	D 0	L 8
v England	P 114	W 39	D 17	L 58
v France	P 69	W 32	D 3	L 34
v Ireland	P 109	W 58	D 5	L 45
(one match abandoned)				
v New Zealand	P 20	L 18	D 2	W 0
v South Africa	P 9	W 3	D 0	L 6
v Wales	P 101	W 44	D 2	L 55
v Argentina	P 3	W 2	D 0	L 1
v Canada	P 1	W 1	D 0	L 0
v Fiji	P 1	W 1	D 0	L 0
v Italy	P 1	W 1	D 0	L 0
v Ivory Coast	P 1	W 1	D 0	L 0
v Japan	P 1	W 1	D 0	L 0
v Romania	P 7	W 5	D 0	L 2
v Tonga	P 1	W 1	D 0	L 0
v Western Samoa	P 2	W 1	D 1	L 0
v Zimbabwe	P 2	W 2	D 0	L 0

SCOTLAND INTERNATIONAL TOURS

	All matches				Tests			
	P	W	D	L	P	W	D	L
to Australia								
1970	6	3	0	3	1	0	0	1
1982	9	6	0	3	2	1	0	1
1992	8	2	2	4	2	0	0	2
to New Zealand								
1975	7	4	0	3	1	0	0	1
1981	8	5	0	3	2	0	0	2
1990	8	5	1	2	2	0	0	2
1996	8	4	0	4	2	0	0	2
to South Africa								
1960	3	2	0	1	1	0	0	1

BEST WINS

Most points and biggest margin

v Ivory Coast	89-0	1995	World Cup

Most points in a win

v Australia	24-15	1981	Edinburgh
v England	33-6	1986	Edinburgh
v France	31-3	1912	Edinburgh
v Ireland	38-10	1997	Edinburgh
v South Africa	8-5	1965	Edinburgh
v Wales	35-10	1924	Edinburgh

Scotland have drawn with New Zealand but never beaten them. The highest Scotland score against the All Blacks is 31 points in a 62-31 defeat in Dunedin in 1996.

Biggest winning margins (as above except)

v South Africa	6-0	1906	Glasgow

WORST DEFEATS

Highest opposition score

v New Zealand	62-31	1996	Dunedin

Biggest margin

v South Africa	44-0	1951	Edinburgh

MOST POINTS IN INTERNATIONALS

601 Gavin Hastings (+66 for Lions)

MOST TRIES IN INTERNATIONALS

24 Ian Smith, Oxford Univ, 32 Tests (+2 for Lions, no tries), 1924-33

MOST INTERNATIONALS AS CAPTAIN

25 David Sole, Edinburgh Academicals, 1989-92 (44 caps +3 for Lions, 1986-92)

TOP CAP-WINNERS

	Player	Principal club(s)	Caps (Lions)	Seasons
1.	Scott Hastings	Watsonians	65 (2)	1986-97
2.	Gavin Hastings	Watsonians	61 (6)	1986-95
3=	Jim Renwick	Hawick	52	1972-84
3=	Colin Deans	Hawick	52*	1978-87
3=	Craig Chalmers	Melrose	52 (1)	1989-
6.	Andy Irvine	Heriots FP	51 (9)	1972-82
7.	Sandy (A.B.) Carmichael	West of Scotland	50†	1967-78
8.	Alan Tomes	Hawick	48‡	1976-87
9.	Roy Laidlaw	Jed-Forest	47 (4)	1980-88
10=	Tony Stanger	Hawick	45	1989-
10=	Doddie (G.W.) Weir	Melrose/Newcastle	45	1990-

* Colin Deans toured with the 1983 Lions but was not capped
† Sandy Carmichael toured with the 1971 and 1974 Lions but was not capped
‡ Alan Tomes toured with the 1980 Lions but was not capped

TOP CAP-WINNERS BY POSITION

Full-back	Gavin Hastings		61	
Wing	Tony Stanger		42 (+3 as centre)	
Centre	Scott Hastings		63 (+2 as wing)	
Fly-half	Craig Chalmers		51 (+1 as wing)	
Scrum-half	Roy Laidlaw		47	
Prop	Sandy Carmichael		50	
Hooker	Colin Deans		52	
Lock	Alan Tomes		48	
Flanker	John Jeffrey	Kelso	40*	1984-91
Number 8	Derek White	Gala	29† (+12 as flanker/lock)	1982-92

* John Jeffrey toured with the 1989 Lions but was not capped
† Derek White won one Lions cap as a flanker

CUP FINALS
(first played 1971-72)
1972 Neath 15, Llanelli 9
1973 Llanelli 30, Cardiff 7
1974 Llanelli 12, Aberavon 10
1975 Llanelli 15, Aberavon 6
1976 Llanelli 15, Swansea 4
1977 Newport 16, Cardiff 15
1978 Swansea 13, Newport 9
1979 Bridgend 18, Pontypridd 12
1980 Bridgend 15, Swansea 9
1981 Cardiff 14, Bridgend 6
1982 Cardiff 12, Bridgend 12*
1983 Pontypool 18, Swansea 6
1984 Cardiff 24, Neath 19
1985 Llanelli 15, Cardiff 14
1986 Cardiff 28, Newport 21
1987 Cardiff 16, Swansea 15†
1988 Llanelli 28, Neath 13
1989 Neath 14, Llanelli 13
1990 Neath 16 Bridgend 10
1991 Llanelli 24, Pontypool 9

1992 Llanelli 16, Swansea 7
1993 Llanelli 21, Neath 18
1994 Cardiff 15, Llanelli 8
1995 Swansea 17, Pontypridd 12
1996 Pontypridd 29, Neath 22
1997 Cardiff 33, Swansea 26
* Cardiff win on try count
† after extra time

UNOFFICAL CLUB CHAMPIONS
(since 1946-47)
1947 Neath
1948 Cardiff
1949 Cardiff
1950 Maesteg
1951 Newport
1952 Ebbw Vale
1953 Cardiff
1954 Ebbw Vale
1955 Cardiff
1956 Newport
1957 Ebbw Vale

1958 Cardiff
1959 Pontypool
1960 Ebbw Vale
1961 Aberavon
1962 Newport
1963 Pontypridd
1964 Bridgend
1965 Newbridge
1966 Bridgend
1967 Neath
1968 Llanelli
1969 Newport
1970 Bridgend
1971 Bridgend
1972 London Welsh
1973 Pontypool
1974 Llanelli
1975 Pontypool
1976 Pontypridd
1977 Llanelli
1978 Pontypridd
1979 Pontypridd

1980 Swansea
1981 Bridgend
1982 Cardiff
1983 Swansea
1984 Pontypool
1985 Pontypool
1986 Pontypool
1987 Neath
1988 Pontypool
1989 Neath
1990 Neath
Replaced by official leagues

LEAGUE CHAMPIONS
(competition first played 1990-91)
1991 Neath
1992 Swansea
1993 Llanelli
1994 Swansea
1995 Cardiff
1996 Neath
1997 Pontypridd

WALES INTERNATIONAL RECORDS

v Australia	P19	W 8	D 0	L 11
v England	P 103	W 48	D 12	L 43
v France	P 72	W 38	D 3	L 31
v Ireland	P 101	W 58	D 6	L 37
v New Zealand	P 16	W 3	D 0	L 13
v Scotland	P 101	W 55	D 2	L 44
v South Africa	P 10	W 0	D 1	L 9
v Argentina	P 1	W 1	D 0	L 0
v Canada	P 3	W 2	D 0	L 1
v Fiji	P 4	W 4	D 0	L 0
v Italy	P 3	W 3	D 0	L 0
v Japan	P 2	W 2	D 0	L 0
v Namibia	P 3	W 3	D 0	L 0
v Portugal	P 1	W 1	D 0	L 0
v Romania	P 3	W 1	D 0	L 2
v Spain	P 1	W 1	D 0	L 0
v Tonga	P 3	W 3	D 0	L 0
v USA	P 2	W 2	D 0	L 0
v Western Samoa	P 4	W 2	D 0	L 2
v Zimbabwe	P 2	W 2	D 0	L 0

WALES INTERNATIONAL TOURS

	All matches				Tests			
	P	W	D	L	P	W	D	L
to Australia								
1969	1	1	0	0	1	1	0	0
1978	9	5	0	4	2	0	0	2
1991	6	3	0	3	1	0	0	1
1996	8	3	0	5	2	0	0	2
to New Zealand								
1969	5	2	1	2	2	0	0	2
1988	8	2	1	5	2	0	0	2
to South Africa								
1964	4	2	0	2	1	0	0	1
1995	2	0	0	2	1	0	0	1

BEST WINS
Most points and biggest margin

v Portugal	102-11	1994	Lisbon

(World Cup qualifier)

Most points in a win

v Australia	28-3	1975	Cardiff
v England	34-21	1967	Cardiff
v France	49-14	1910	Swansea
v Ireland	34-9	1976	Dublin
v New Zealand	13-8	1953	Cardiff
v Scotland	35-12	1972	Cardiff

Wales have never beaten South Africa. Their best result is 6-6 in Cardiff in 1970.

Biggest winning margins (as above except)

v England	25-0	1905	Cardiff
v France	47-5	1909	Paris
v Ireland	29-0	1907	Cardiff
v Scotland	*as above and also*		
	29-6	1994	Cardiff

WORST DEFEAT (Highest opposition score and biggest margin)

v Australia	63-3	1991	Brisbane

MOST POINTS IN INTERNATIONALS
534 Neil Jenkins

MOST TRIES IN INTERNATIONALS
32 Ieuan Evans (+1 for Lions)

MOST INTERNATIONALS AS CAPTAIN
28 Ieuan Evans, 1991-95

TOP CAP-WINNERS

Player	Principal club(s)	Caps (Lions)	Seasons
1. Ieuan (I.C.) Evans	Llanelli	71 (6)	1987-
2. Gareth (G.O.) Llewellyn	Neath	57	1989-
3. J.P.R. Williams	London Welsh/Bridgend	55 (8)	1969-81
4. Robert (R.N.) Jones	Swansea	54 (3)	1986-95
5. Gareth Edwards	Cardiff	53 (10)	1967-78
6. Neil Jenkins	Pontypridd	50	1991-
7. Phil Davies	Llanelli	46	1985-95
8. Ken (K.J.) Jones	Newport	44 (3)	1947-57
9. Mike Hall	Bridgend/Cardiff	42 (1)	1988-95
10= Graham Price	Pontypool	41 (12)	1975-83
10= Emyr (E.W.) Lewis	Llanelli/Cardiff	41	1991-96

TOP CAP-WINNERS BY POSITION

Full-back	J.P.R. Williams		54 (+1 as flanker)	
Wing	Ieuan Evans		71	
Centre	Mike Hall		32 (+10 as wing)	
Fly-half	Neil Jenkins		35 (+15 as full-back/centre)	
Scrum-half	Gareth Edwards		53	
	Robert Jones		53 (+1 as rep wing)	
Prop	Graham Price		41	
Hooker	Bryn Meredith	Newport	34 (+8 for Lions)	1954-62
Lock	Gareth Llewellyn		56 (+1 as flanker)	
Flanker	Dai (W.D.) Morris	Neath	32 (+ 2 as No 8)	1967-74
Number 8	Mervyn (T.M.) Davies	Swansea/L Welsh	38 (+8 for Lions)	1969-76

FIVE NATIONS

The first home international championship was played by the four British Isles countries in 1882-83. This and all other seasons are listed below under the date for the second half of the season. Matches were not played in 1915-19 and 1940-46 because of the world wars. The championships of 1883, 85, 88, 89, 97, 98 and 1914 were not completed for various reasons, as more recently was the 1972 championship when Scotland and Wales refused to travel to Dublin because of Ireland's terrorist problems.

England are listed as champions for 1914, since they recorded a Grand Slam even though Scotland and France did not fulfill their fixture. In 1883 England achieved a Triple Crown and are similarly listed as champions even though Wales and Ireland did not play their game.

France joined the championship in 1910 but were expelled after the 1931 season because of 'professionalism'. An incomplete programme of Victory Internationals was played in 1946, and all five nations resumed the tournament in 1947. Up to 1993, championships could be shared, but since then points difference has been used to separate teams with the same record of wins, draws and losses.

CHAMPIONSHIP WINNERS
England: 1883, 84, 86*, 90*, 92, 1910, 12*, 13, 14, 20*, 21, 23, 24, 28, 30, 32*, 34, 37, 39*, 47*, 53, 54*, 57, 58, 60*, 63, 73†, 80, 91, 92, 95, 96
France: 1954*, 55*, 59, 60*, 61, 62, 67, 68, 70*, 73†, 77, 81, 83*, 86*, 87, 88*, 89, 93, 97
Ireland: 1894, 96, 99, 1906*, 12*, 26*, 27*, 32*, 35, 39*, 48, 49, 51, 73†, 74, 82, 83*, 85
Scotland: 1886*, 87, 90*, 91, 95, 1901, 03, 04, 07, 20*, 25, 26*, 27*, 29, 33, 38, 64*, 73†, 84, 86*, 90
Wales: 1893, 1900, 02, 05, 06*, 08, 09, 11, 20*, 22, 31, 32*, 36, 39*, 47*, 50, 52, 54*, 55*, 56, 64*, 65, 66, 69, 70*, 71, 73†, 75, 76, 78, 79, 88*, 94
* shared title; † five-way tie

SUMMARY
England 32 wins (10 shared), including 20 Triple Crowns (5 in seasons in which France did not play), 11 of which were also Grand Slams. Grand Slams: 1913, 14, 21, 23, 24, 28, 57, 80, 91, 92, 95. Triple Crowns: 1883, 84, 92, 1934, 37, 54, 60, 96, 97.
France 19 wins (8 shared); five Grand Slams 1968, 77, 81, 87, 97.
Ireland 18 wins (8 shared), including one Grand Slam in 1948 and additional Triple Crowns in 1894, 99, 1949, 82, 85.
Scotland 21 wins (8 shared), including 10 Triple Crowns (7 in seasons in which France did not play); the other three were also Grand Slams. Grand Slams: 1925, 84, 90. Triple Crowns: 1891, 95, 1901, 03, 07, 33, 38.
Wales 33 wins (11 shared), including 17 Triple Crowns (6 of them in seasons in which France did not play), 6 of which were also Grand Slams. Grand Slams: 1911, 50, 52, 71, 76, 78. Triple Crowns: 1893, 1900, 02, 05, 08, 09, 65, 69, 77, 79, 88. Wales also played and beat France in 1908 and 1909, so some record books count these as Grand Slam seasons also, even though France did not play all the other nations.

BRITISH LIONS

BRITISH LIONS TOUR RECORDS

	All Matches				Tests			
	P	W	D	L	P	W	D	L
1888 in Aus	*16	14	2	0	–	–	–	–
in NZ	19	13	4	2	–	–	–	–
1891 SA	20	20	0	0	3	3	0	0
1896 SA	21	19	1	1	4	3	0	1
1899 Aus	21	18	0	3	4	3	0	1
1903 SA	22	11	3	8	3	0	2	1
1904 in Aus	14	14	0	0	3	3	0	0
in NZ	5	2	1	2	1	0	0	1
1908 in Aus	9	7	0	2	–	–	–	–
in NZ	17	9	1	7	3	1	1	1
1910 SA	24	13	3	8	3	1	0	2
1924 SA	21	9	3	9	4	0	1	3
1930 in Aus	7	5	0	2	1	0	0	1
in NZ	21	15	0	6	4	1	0	3
1938 SA	23	17	0	7	3	1	0	2
1950 in Aus	6	5	0	1	2	2	0	0
in NZ	23	17	1	5	4	0	1	3
1955 SA	25	19	1	5	4	2	0	2
1959 in Aus	6	5	0	1	2	2	0	0
in NZ	25	20	0	5	4	1	0	3
in Canada	2	2	0	0	–	–	–	–
1962 SA	25	16	4	5	4	0	1	3
1966 in Aus	8	7	1	0	2	2	0	0
in NZ	25	15	2	8	4	0	0	4
in Canada	2	1	0	1	1	1	0	0
1968 SA	20	15	1	4	4	0	1	3
1971 in Aus	2	1	0	1	–	–	–	–
in NZ	24	22	1	1	4	2	1	1
1974 SA	22	21	1	0	4	3	1	0
1977 in NZ	25	21	0	4	4	1	0	3
in Fiji	1	0	0	1	1	0	0	1
1980 SA	18	15	0	3	4	1	0	3
1983 NZ	18	12	0	6	4	0	0	4
1989 Aus	12	11	0	1	3	2	0	1
1993 NZ	13	7	0	6	3	1	0	2

* plus 18 or 19 matches played in Victoria under 'Australian' rules

There were no Tests during the first 'Lions' tour in 1888.
The Lions also played an unofficial match against Ceylon (now Sri Lanka) on the way home in 1950, winning 44-6. The 1955 and 1962 teams each played one match against East Africa; both were won. Each Lions tour to South Africa from 1910 to 1974 included matches against Rhodesia (modern Zimbabwe), then regarded in rugby terms as a province of South Africa, the Lions winning all nine games. All these matches are included in the main tour statistics.
The Lions have played twice in Britain: in 1977, beating a Barbarians side 23-14 and in 1986, losing 13-32 to a World XV. A semi-official British Isles XV beat France 29-27 in Paris in 1989.

EURO CUP

HEINEKEN EUROPEAN CUP

1995-96 Competition

Semi-finals
Leinster 14, Cardiff 23
Toulouse 30, Swansea 3

Final
Cardiff 18, Toulouse 21 (in Cardiff)
(after extra time, 18-18 after 80 minutes)

1996-97 Competition

Quarter-finals
Brive 35, Llanelli 14
Cardiff 22, Bath 19
Leicester 23, Harlequins 13
Dax 18, Toulouse 26

Semi-finals
Leicester 37, Toulouse 11
Brive 26, Cardiff 13

Final
Brive 28, Leicester 9 (in Cardiff)

WORLD CUP 1987 TOURNAMENT

Pool 1
	P	W	D	L	F	A
Australia	3	3	0	0	108	41
England	3	2	0	1	100	32
USA	3	1	0	2	39	99
Japan	3	0	0	3	48	123

Pool 2
	P	W	D	L	F	A
Wales	3	3	0	0	82	31
Ireland	3	2	0	1	84	41
Canada	3	1	0	2	65	90
Tonga	3	0	0	3	29	98

Pool 3
	P	W	D	L	F	A
New Zealand	3	3	0	0	190	34
Fiji	3	1	0	2	56	101
Argentina	3	1	0	2	49	90
Italy	3	1	0	2	40	110

Pool 4
	P	W	D	L	F	A
France	3	2	1	0	145	44
Scotland	3	2	1	0	135	69
Romania	3	1	0	2	61	130
Zimbabwe	3	0	0	3	53	151

Quarter-finals
New Zealand 30, Scotland 3
France 31, Fiji 16
Australia 33, Ireland 15
Wales 16, England 3

Semi-finals
Australia 24, France 30
New Zealand 49, Wales 6

Third-place match
Wales 22, Australia 21

Final
New Zealand 29, France 9

WORLD CUP 1991 TOURNAMENT

Pool 1
	P	W	D	L	F	A
New Zealand	3	3	0	0	95	39
England	3	2	0	1	85	33
Italy	3	1	0	2	57	76
USA	3	0	0	3	24	113

Pool 2
	P	W	D	L	F	A
Scotland	3	3	0	0	122	36
Ireland	3	2	0	1	102	51
Japan	3	1	0	2	77	87
Zimbabwe	3	0	0	3	31	158

Pool 3
	P	W	D	L	F	A
Australia	3	3	0	0	79	25
W Samoa	3	2	0	1	54	34
Wales	3	1	0	2	32	61
Argentina	3	0	0	3	38	83

Pool 4
	P	W	D	L	F	A
France	3	3	0	0	82	25
Canada	3	2	0	1	45	33
Romania	3	1	0	2	31	64
Fiji	3	0	0	3	27	63

Quarter-finals
England 19, France 10
Scotland 28, Western Samoa 6
Australia 19, Ireland 18
New Zealand 29, Canada 13

Semi-finals
England 9, Scotland 6
Australia 16, New Zealand 6

Third-place match
New Zealand 13, Scotland 6

Final
Australia 12, England 6

WORLD CUP 1995 TOURNAMENT

Pool A
	P	W	D	L	F	A
South Africa	3	3	0	0	68	26
Australia	3	2	0	1	87	41
Canada	3	1	0	2	45	50
Romania	3	0	0	3	14	97

Pool B
	P	W	D	L	F	A
England	3	3	0	0	95	60
W Samoa	3	2	0	1	96	88
Italy	3	1	0	2	69	94
Argentina	3	0	0	3	69	87

Pool C
	P	W	D	L	F	A
New Zealand	3	3	0	0	222	45
Ireland	3	2	0	1	93	94
Wales	3	1	0	2	89	68
Japan	3	0	0	3	55	252

Pool D
	P	W	D	L	F	A
France	3	3	0	0	114	47
Scotland	3	2	0	1	149	27
Tonga	3	1	0	2	44	90
Ivory Coast	3	0	0	3	29	172

Quarter-finals
France 36, Ireland 12
South Africa 42, Western Samoa 14
England 25, Australia 22
New Zealand 48, Scotland 30

Semi-finals
South Africa 19, England 15
New Zealand 45, England 29

Third-place match
France 19, England 9

Final
South Africa 15, New Zealand 12
(after extra time, 9-9 after 80 mins)

WOMEN'S RUGBY

1991 WORLD CUP
The pool winners proceeded to the semi-finals of the cup; the other eight teams entered a plate competition.

Plate final
Canada 18, Spain 4

Cup semi-finals
USA 7, New Zealand 0
England 13, France 0

Final
USA 19, England 6

1994 WORLD CHAMPIONSHIP

Plate final
Kazakhstan 29, Sweden 12

Cup quarter-finals
USA 76, Ireland 0
England 24, Canada 10
France 99, Japan 0
Wales 8, Scotland 0

Semi-finals
USA 56, Wales 15
England 18, France 6

Third-place match
France 27, Wales 0

Final
England 28, USA 23

RUGBY WORLD CUP SEVENS 1993

Semi-finals
England 21, Fiji 7
Australia 21, Ireland 19

Final
England 21, Australia 17

1997 WORLD CUP SEVENS

Quarter-finals
Fiji 56, Korea 0
Western Samoa 21, England 5
New Zealand 38, Australia 12
South Africa 19, France 14

Semi-finals
Fiji 38, Western Samoa 14
South Africa 31, New Zealand 7

Final
Fiji 24, South Africa 21

HONG KONG SEVENS

1976 Cantabrians (NZ)
1977 Fiji
1978 Fiji
1979 Australia
1980 Fiji
1981 Barbarians
1982 Australia
1983 Australia
1984 Fiji
1985 Australia
1986 New Zealand
1987 New Zealand
1988 Australia
1989 New Zealand
1990 Fiji
1991 Fiji
1992 Fiji
1993 Western Samoa
1994 New Zealand
1995 New Zealand
1996 New Zealand
1997 see World Cup Sevens

MIDDLESEX SEVENS
Harlequins won the first tournament in 1926 and are the most frequent winners to date, with 13 titles. Other multiple winners include Richmond 9, London Welsh 8, and London Scottish 7. Recent winners have been:

1988 Harlequins
1989 Harlequins
1990 Harlequins
1991 London Scottish
1992 Western Samoa
1993 Wasps
1994 Bath
1995 Leicester
1996 Wigan

· INDEX ·